Parliaments and Legislatures
Janet M. Box-Steffensmeier and David T. Canon, Series Editors

THE FOLEY INSTITUTE

The Thomas S. Foley Institute
for Public Policy and Public Service

Washington State University
PO Box 644840
Pullman, WA 99164-4840
Phone: 509-335-3477
www.libarts.wsu.edu/foleyinst/

The Foley Institute is pleased to have supported:

Parties, Rules, and the Evolution of Congressional Budgeting

By

Lance T. LeLoup

The Foley Institute supports congressional research, public policy research, and public service. The archives contain the complete papers of former Speaker Thomas S. Foley and are open to scholars.

Parties, Rules, and the Evolution of Congressional Budgeting

Lance T. LeLoup

The Ohio State University Press
Columbus

Copyright © 2005 by The Ohio State University.

All rights reserved.

Library of Congress Cataloging-in-Publication Data

LeLoup, Lance T.
  Parties, rules, and the evolution of congressional budgeting / Lance T.
LeLoup.
      p. cm. — (Parliaments and legislatures)
  Includes bibliographical references and index.
  ISBN 0-8142-1007-4 (cloth : alk. paper) — ISBN 0-8142-5144-7 (pbk. :
alk. paper) — ISBN 0-8142-9086-8 (cd-rom) 1. Budget—United States. 2.
Budget process—United States. I. Title. II. Parliaments and legislatures series.
  HJ2051.L45 2005
  328.73'0778—dc22
                                    2005010666

Cover design by Dan O'Dair.
Type set in Sabon.
Printed by Thomson-Shore, Inc.

The paper used in this publication meets the minimum requirements of the
American National Standard for Information Sciences—Permanence of Paper
for Printed Library Materials. ANSI Z39.48–1992.

9 8 7 6 5 4 3 2 1

In loving memory of Fred "Poppy" Kirk

CONTENTS

List of Illustrations   ix

Preface   xi

CHAPTER 1   Macrobudgeting   1

CHAPTER 2   Budgeting in Congress through 1980   23

CHAPTER 3   Congress and the Reagan Budgets, 1981–1982   54

CHAPTER 4   Legislating Deficit Reduction:
            Gramm-Rudman-Hollings, 1985 and 1987   82

CHAPTER 5   The Budget Summit Agreement, 1990   111

CHAPTER 6   Clinton and the Democratic Deficit
            Reduction Plan, 1993   137

CHAPTER 7   The Balanced Budget Agreement, 1997   158

CHAPTER 8   Bush, Congress, and Tax Cuts, 2001 and 2003   181

CHAPTER 9   Conclusion   201

Notes   223

Index   243

ILLUSTRATIONS

Figures

Figure 2–1   Party support for debit limit extensions in the House,
1953–1990: percentage voting for extension   49

Figure 2–2   Party support for debt limit extensions in the Senate,
1962–1990: percentage voting for extension   50

Figure 7–1   Comparison of deficit reduction agreements, 1990, 1993,
and 1997 (in constant 1997 dollars): deficit reduction over
five years   177

Figure 9–1   Party cohesion in votes on budget resolutions in the
House, 1975–2003   206

Figure 9–2   Party cohesion in votes on budget resolutions in the
Senate, 1975–2003   207

Figure 9–3   Party voting on individual appropriations bills in the
House and Senate, 1975–2003   209

Tables

Table 1–1   Institutional differences between macrobudgeting and
microbudgeting in Congress   7

Table 2–1   Original congressional budget timetable   36

Table 2–2   Votes on first budget resolutions, 1975–1980   41

Table 3–1   Key votes on Reagan's economic plan in the House and
Senate   76

Table 3–2   Votes on budget resolutions, 1981–1985   79

Table 4–1   Revised budget timetable, 1985   94

Table 9–1   Consequences of divided government: number of days past
deadline for passage of budget resolution   216

Table 9–2   Divided government and government shutdowns: appropriation funding gaps, FY 1981–2001   217

Table 9–3   Divided government and omnibus appropriations,
1993–2003   218

PREFACE

The congressional budget process adopted in 1974 has been controversial and often messy. Both insiders and outsiders have derided its instability, its lack of controls, its improvisational nature, its contribution to unorthodox lawmaking, its failure to prevent deficits, and its encouragement of budgetary tricks and gimmicks—"blue smoke and mirrors"—to make it look as if Congress was doing something that it was not. But is that an accurate judgment, taking the longer view of its thirty-year performance? In fact, despite its many failures, the budget process has been an integral part of sweeping changes in Congress as an institution and in Congress's legislative capacity. It has changed not only the way in which Congress budgets but also how major taxing and spending issues are negotiated between executive and legislative branches. The creation of "macrobudgeting" in Congress altered the way budget choices were framed and, with it, the kinds of coalitions that would organize to support or oppose those choices. Congressional budgeting rules have facilitated the increase of partisanship and the changing role of legislative parties and leaders.

Restructuring of the budget process in 1974 was first and foremost a change in rules and congressional institutions. Those budget rules continued to adapt and develop over time and affect other critical congressional institutions such as committees and parties. From the time the budget process was first implemented in 1975, the relationship between budget rules and congressional parties was a fascinating one. At the time, parties in Congress were not receiving much scholarly attention. In the 1980s, budget issues took center stage on the national policy agenda, and burgeoning deficits during an era of divided government restored interest in party control and budgeting. By the 1990s, the role of parties in Congress and the consequences of divided government were increasingly the subject of theory and research.

Scholarship on Congress has also changed in the past thirty years, from predominantly sociological approaches to economic approaches based on instrumental rationality. The "New Institutionalism," both formal and historical variants, has fostered theoretical progress by focusing on legislative institutions and their consequences. Perhaps because of the influence of scholars such as David Mayhew and Richard Fenno, formal and nonformal approaches coexist more easily in congressional studies and allow a certain theoretical and methodological pluralism. In taking a historical institutional approach to congressional budgeting, recent work on rules, parties, and divided government provided important insights.

My interest in this subject began when I was a graduate student at The Ohio State University, during the battles between President Nixon and Congress over the federal budget. Although I have periodically left the subject for long periods of time, my interest in it has never completely waned. The enactment of the Budget and Impoundment Control Act of 1974 provided an opportunity to study institutional changes and policy results. After "soaking and poking" and interviewing Budget Committee members, I published *The Fiscal Congress: Legislative Control of the Budget* in 1980. Such interviews would be increasingly difficult to find. I went back to the Hill at the time of Gramm-Rudman-Hollings to study that fascinating experiment. Since then, I have long envisioned a study of the evolution of congressional budgeting. After various administrative posts and international research and consulting activities, this project finally came to the front burner in 2003. The premise of the book is that macrobudgeting fundamentally changed the way in which congressional budget choices were framed and enacted. Macrobudgeting not only increased the political stakes for the parties but also created a set of rules and procedures that strengthened party leaders, reflected in a steady increase in partisanship. With budgeting increasingly partisan, divided government has taken on increased significance as well.

The approach chosen to explain the evolution of congressional budgeting was to examine in detail landmark budget legislation since 1974, from the Budget Act itself to the recent Bush tax cuts. Each step in the progression allows an assessment of institutional changes, the role of parties, and relations with the president. The concluding chapter assesses congressional budget rules and party leaders and party voting, and it examines the consequences of divided government.

In a project of such long duration, a debt of gratitude is owed to many. I particularly want to thank the Thomas Foley Institute at Washington State and its director, Ed Weber, for supporting this research, and the Everett Dirksen Center for earlier support. I would like to thank those who reviewed all or parts of this manuscript in various phases, including Dennis Ippolito, Ron Peters, Cornell Clayton, Steven Shull, earlier collaborators Carolyn Long, Linda Kowalcky, Barbara Graham, and a number of anonymous reviewers. Thanks to Brian Jones and his colleagues, including Donald Mathews, at the University of Washington's Center for the Study of American Politics for their invitation and comments on the framework for this study. I am grateful for the ideas and suggestions for this project shared by invited visitors to our Congressional Scholars program at Washington State University, including Barbara Sinclair, C. Lawrence Evans, and Sean Kelly. I want to thank my graduate research assistants who contributed so much to this study, including Pat Taylor, Tyler Fitch, Jack McGuire, Eric Gruelke, and James Dukeshirer. I am particularly grateful to Lisa Janowski and Cynthia Avery in the political science department at WSU for their help in preparing the manuscript and countless other acts of kindness. Thanks to Malcolm Littlefield, Maggie Diehl, and the other staff members at The Ohio State University Press for their interest in and strong support of this project. Publishing with The Ohio State University Press for the first time reminds me to thank the faculty at OSU who more than thirty years ago tried to help me become a political scientist, particularly Randall Ripley, John Kessel, Aage Clausen, and Herb Asher. Finally, my most heartfelt thanks go to my adorable wife Pamela Kirk LeLoup who supports and inspires me and makes it all worthwhile.

Lance T. LeLoup
Pullman, Washington
April 2005

CHAPTER 1

Macrobudgeting

Introduction and Overview

The evolution of congressional budgeting since the 1970s has been a significant component in changes in American national politics. From its traditional, fragmented authorization and appropriation process, congressional budgeting added a more centralized process focusing on large, multiyear taxing and spending packages. This has restructured congressional rules and institutions, changed the way Congress legislates, and enhanced congressional capacity to make decisions. It has altered how Congress negotiates with the president. Changes in budget rules and institutions have buttressed the foundations of party leadership in the House and Senate and have reinforced the trend toward greater partisanship in Congress. In doing so, it has elevated the consequences of divided party control of the legislative and executive branches in budgeting. This book examines major budget and deficit legislation enacted over the past thirty years, focusing on legislative rules and institutions, the role of partisanship, and the consequences of divided government.

Throughout most of the twentieth century, Congress made taxing and spending decisions in a piecemeal process through passing individual spending bills and tax bills, rather than producing a comprehensive budget like that of the president. In the face of growing conflicts with President Nixon, in 1974 Congress adopted a sweeping reform of its budget processes, allowing it to set its own broad priorities for taxes, spending, and the size of the deficit or surplus. The institutional creation of "macrobudgeting" in the form of budget resolutions and other comprehensive budget legislation changed the way in which Congress framed budget choices and enacted major budget policy. Now a handful of votes bundle many diverse issues and programs, setting the overall direction of national policy over the subsequent three, five, or even ten years. This was not a "clean" congressional reorganization, however. A new set of rules and procedures was superimposed on the old system,

1

resulting in a hybrid system with certain path dependencies from the earlier process.[1] Nor was it a restructuring that took place all at once. Instead, congressional budgeting evolved through both informal adaptation and formal statutory and rules changes. New rules, institutions, and practices changed the legislative process, relationships between leaders and committees, and the look of budget legislation.

The evolution of congressional budgeting rules and institutions has affected partisanship and the strength of party leaders. While recent scholarship has recognized and provided theoretical explanations for the growth of partisanship in Congress,[2] it has not emphasized the creation of macrobudgeting and budget process changes as a significant explanation of increasing party power. In changing how choices are structured, macrobudgeting has increased the stakes for parties, enhancing opportunities to define and build party reputation and encouraging message politics. Majority party control of budget legislation has become more centralized, and rules for floor consideration more restrictive.

The evolution of congressional budgeting, particularly reconciliation and other omnibus legislation combined with stronger congressional parties and enforcement rules, has had important consequences for the presidency. Despite mixed findings in the literature, this study suggests that party control of the legislative and executive branches has become increasingly significant for both budget outcomes and the nature of congressional-presidential bargaining. Rules changes that strengthen party leaders may also strengthen the hand of a president of the same party. Conversely, under divided control, presidents face a capable opposition, requiring new strategies and increasing reliance on extraordinary means of resolution. Supermajority institutions, the Senate filibuster and presidential veto, have been emphasized in a number of spatial models of the legislative process and gridlock.[3] Changes in budget rules have eliminated the potential of a filibuster but increased the importance of the veto and veto bargaining under divided government.[4] Budget summits, bipartisan commissions, and bargaining outside the normal channels have become more frequent and consequential. Divided government is characterized by longer delays in enacting the budget and increases the possibility of government shutdown.

Major Budget Legislation

For the past three decades, major macrobudgetary legislation was often the dominant focus of the national policy agenda. This study examines the adoption of what are arguably the most important of these:

- In 1974, Congress adopted the Budget and Impoundment Control Act (referred to as the Congressional Budget Act or the Budget Act) which restructured the congressional budget process and changed the nature of congressional choices. The implementation of the Budget Act through 1980 established patterns and precedents that would be consequential.
- President Ronald Reagan made his budget plan the centerpiece of his domestic agenda in his first year. Despite facing a Democratic House of Representatives, Republicans were able to create a cross-partisan majority and enact a sweeping package of tax cuts, defense spending increases, and domestic spending cuts. Subsequently, combined with an economic recession, the United States faced chronic budget deficits through the 1980s.
- In 1985, Congress adopted the Balanced Budget and Emergency Deficit Reduction Act (Gramm-Rudman-Hollings), a controversial plan for mandatory deficit reduction, requiring across-the-board cuts if reduced deficits were not achieved. Although the mandatory approach would be abandoned five years later, the law also made several important changes in budget rules.
- In 1990, President Bush and the Democratic Congress negotiated for months to create a deficit reduction package that included new taxes. In addition to adopting the largest deficit reduction plan ever, Congress again changed the rules of the budget process.
- In 1993, under unified government for the first time in twelve years, President Bill Clinton and congressional Democrats narrowly enacted another contentious deficit reduction package, the most important domestic policy change in 1993. Not a single Republican voted for the budget.
- In 1997, following two years of confrontations and the longest government shutdown in history, Clinton and the Republican Congress did what was once thought impossible by agreeing on a balanced budget plan.
- In 2001 and 2003, President George W. Bush and the Republican Congress passed tax cuts of nearly $2 trillion over ten years, the largest since 1981. But by the middle of the decade, as in the 1980s, the United States faced large budget deficits projected to add up to more than $2.2 trillion by 2010.[5]

All of these enactments occurred in a certain political and economic context that helps explain the choices faced and the decisions made. But in addition, changes in Congress as an institution help explain results. To help develop an explanation for the evolution of congressional budgeting, recent theory and research on rules and institutions, congressional parties, and relations with the presidency are explored in this chapter.

Research Approaches to Congress

Since the late 1970s, congressional scholarship has increasingly focused on instrumental rationality to explain the organization of Congress and legislative decisions. In formal approaches, scholars have developed deductive models focusing on structure-based equilibria.[6] Institutions and rules have received considerable attention in these models but focus on different dimensions. A number of formal theories center on a spatial model of the legislative process, where members of the House and Senate are conceptualized on a left-right continuum based on policy preferences.[7] The main institutional emphasis is on supermajority features of American politics—the presidential veto and Senate filibuster—which provide critical "pivot points" that determine whether policy can change from the status quo or whether gridlock occurs. In these models the role of political parties is minimal. Other formal theories suggest an enhanced role for political parties. David Rohde developed a theory of "conditional party government" based on intraparty unity and interparty conflict.[8] Cox and McCubbins developed a theory of "limited party government" based on the model of the cartel.[9] Formal theories have provided interesting and insightful ways of thinking about Congress, but critics have asserted that empirical testing and validation have been limited.[10]

In nonformal approaches, the "new institutionalism" focuses on understanding a broad array of institutional arrangements and historical changes to explain developments in Congress.[11] This is part of a larger community of scholars emphasizing historical-institutional explanations rather than deductive models based on policy preferences and strategic calculations.[12] The analysis presented in this book follows this institutionalist tradition but finds formal theories helpful in suggesting possible causal relations. In turn, empirical evidence about congressional budgeting can contribute to scholarly debate on congressional decision making. The study presumes the importance of instrumental rationality, manifested in multiple member goals as Richard Fenno and other congressional scholars have suggested.[13]

The remainder of this chapter takes an overview of budget rules and the development of macrobudgeting; it also looks at theories on the role of parties in the legislative process and research on the consequences of divided or unified control of Congress and the presidency.

Macrobudgeting, Rules, and Institutions

The Appropriations Process

From 1920 to the late 1960s, congressional budgeting was dominated by the appropriations process. Fenno's classic analysis of the appropriations process in *The Power of the Purse* (1965) emphasized the strong norms of consensus and bipartisanship.[14] The appropriations process was also characterized as "responsible," allowing reasonable growth in government programs but providing a fiscally responsible brake on rapid expansion of government spending.[15] The norms of fiscal restraint began to weaken in the late 1960s, and conflict between legislative and executive branches escalated over Nixon's impoundment of (refusal to spend) monies legally appropriated by Congress.[16] After a period of instability and growing deficits, the Budget and Impoundment Control Act of 1974 was adopted.[17] As chapter 2 will detail, the Budget Act created a congressional budget, a defined timetable, House and Senate Budget Committees, and the Congressional Budget Office (CBO), and it restricted the ability of the president to impound funds.

The enactment of the Congressional Budget Act in 1974 represented a mix of motives and interests, but a common goal was to increase Congress's overall ability to shape budget totals.[18] Republicans and fiscally conservative Democrats wanted a process that would restrain spending by making members go on the record in voting for a deficit. Liberal Democrats saw the new budget process as an opportunity to debate national priorities and make explicit comparisons and tradeoffs between, for example, health care and defense. Others wanted Congress to play a stronger role in shaping fiscal policy by having more direct votes on overall budget totals. For all of these various goals, a new means for voting on budget totals was created. The new process and institutions did not replace the authorization/appropriation process but rather were superimposed on the old system.

Macrobudgeting

As a result of these overlaid systems, congressional budgeting can be conceptualized as operating at two levels.[19] Macrobudgeting—high-level decisions on total spending, revenues, deficits or surpluses, and relative budget shares, decisions often made from the top down—is the primary focus of this study. Microbudgeting—intermediate-level decisions on agencies, programs, and line items, usually made from the bottom up—remains a critical part of budgeting through agency requests and the authorization and appropriation processes. Microbudgeting and macrobudgeting are related as parts are to the whole. Yet in terms of legislative decision making, an underlying hypothesis of this study is that macrobudgeting and microbudgeting are quite distinct, comprising a different set of legislative issues, dominated by different actors, and usually producing different divisions in roll-call voting.

Macrobudgeting or macrobudgetary legislation generally encompasses the following: (1) the Concurrent Resolution on the Budget (budget resolution), (2) omnibus reconciliation bills which include a range of taxing and spending decisions, (3) continuing resolutions and omnibus appropriations which fund agencies and programs if a regular appropriation has not been passed by the start of the fiscal year, (4) comprehensive tax bills that make major changes in future government revenues, (5) statutes limiting the national debt, and (6) major supplemental appropriations that cut across committee jurisdictions. Occasionally, a significant entitlement reform with severe consequences for spending can be considered macrobudgeting. *Not* included are other common congressional decisions including authorizing bills (annual, multiyear, or permanent) that provide the legal basis for agencies to exist and spend money, and individual appropriation bills that contain line items and detailed agency budgets. Also excluded from macrobudgeting are tax reform bills that restructure the tax code but do not make major changes in government revenues, such as the Tax Reform Act of 1986.

After the implementation of the Budget Act in 1975, macrobudgeting initially remained secondary to the traditional authorization/appropriations process. Budget totals in the final budget resolutions were largely the sum of actions taken earlier by the taxing and spending committees.[20] Beginning in 1980, however, the budget process developed more teeth and became a more significant constraint on the decisions made by authorizing and appropriations committees and subcommittees. In addition, with the growth of entitlements, by 1980 only 40 percent of the total budget was funded by annual appropriations.[21] This did not eliminate the importance of authorizations and appropriations; many important policy decisions are still shaped by executive and legislative branch actors at this level.[22] A number of factors combined to strengthen macrobudgeting in Congress after 1980. The transition was fueled as much by informal adaptation of the rules, such as moving reconciliation to the beginning of the process (1981), as it was by formal rules changes adopted in 1975, 1985, and 1990.

Table 1–1 summarizes some of the key differences between microbudgeting and macrobudgeting in Congress.

Macrobudgeting changed the way budget issues are framed and increased the stakes for political parties. Once a budget resolution or omnibus spending bill is finalized and brought to the floor, members are confronted with an

Table 1–1

Institutional differences between macrobudgeting and microbudgeting in Congress

	Microbudgeting	Macrobudgeting
Institutional Actors	Authorizing and appropriations committees and subcommittees	Budget committees and majority party leaders
Legislation	Individual authorization bills and appropriations bills	Budget resolutions, omnibus reconciliation bills, continuing resolutions, debt limit extensions, comprehensive tax bills, major supplemental appropriations
Institutional Processes	More fragmented, bottom-up, often bipartisan	More centralized, top-down, partisan
Institutional Reforms	Strengthening appropriations and authorizing oversight, sunset laws, biennial budgeting	Budget Act of 1974, Emergency Deficit Control Act of 1985, Budget Enforcement Act of 1990

up or down vote on a comprehensive bill with little chance to amend or obstruct. Dozens of complex issues are reduced to a single choice. These bills are often "must-pass" legislation. Although terms such as *gridlock* and *stalemate* are often used to characterize stalled budget negotiations, final approval of the national budget cannot be deadlocked for years as can other policy areas (welfare reform, prescription drug benefits, etc.). The need for government to have a budget serves as a *forcing mechanism:* Congress and the president must ultimately act to prevent default on debt, to prevent programs from shutting down, and to provide benefits that are guaranteed by law. On those occasions when funding expired and the government was forced to shut down, the political consequences were severe.

Macrobudgeting is not precise. Reducing deficits or shaping entitlement trends is like piloting a slow-moving supertanker. Decisions have long-term consequences that can take many years to reach fruition. Fiscal policy, the manipulation of taxing and spending totals to stabilize the economy, is the bluntest of policy weapons. Despite these limitations, macrobudgeting has increasingly dominated the agenda of national government since the 1970s.

Formal and Informal Changes in Institutions

Changes in budget rules and institutions have occurred through formal statute and rules changes as well as informal adaptation and precedent. The

Budget Act was formally revised a number of times, most notably in 1985, 1987, and 1990. Other changes came through using the so-called elastic clause of the Budget Act which allowed changes to be made concerning "such other matters relating to the budget as may be appropriate to carry out the purposes of this Act."[23] One of the most important changes under the elastic clause was the decision to move reconciliation from the end of the process to the beginning of the process in 1981. This development fundamentally changed the nature of reconciliation from adjusting totals at the finish to shaping the budget at the start.

The most significant statutory overhaul of the Budget Act took place with the enactment of the Balanced Budget and Emergency Deficit Reduction Act of 1985 (better known as Gramm-Rudman-Hollings). It is best remembered for its mandatory deficit reduction procedures and the five-year fixed deficit targets, but it also made many important changes in budget rules. For the Senate, the 1985 act provided budget resolutions with a privileged position, protected against filibusters by limiting floor debate. The Byrd rule, adopted around the same time, imposed germaneness requirements on the Senate. Both of these rules changes imposed unprecedented limitations on the permissive rules of the upper chamber.

The budget process was formally amended again in 1987 and 1990. In 1987, Congress needed to alter the deficit targets enacted two years earlier and to respond to a Supreme Court decision that had rendered Gramm-Rudman-Hollings unconstitutional. In 1990, Congress scrapped the mandatory deficit reduction scheme and passed the Budget Enforcement Act. It imposed appropriations caps, introduced "pay-as-you-go" (PAYGO) rules requiring offsets for tax cuts or spending increases, and established "firewalls" to protect entitlements. Some of these provisions, such as appropriation caps and PAYGO rules, were allowed to expire by 2000.

These changes in rules and procedures and the way budget choices are framed have altered relations between Congress and the presidency and the nature of the legislative process. Throughout the 1980s and 1990s, disputes were often resolved through budget summits involving a small group of legislators and negotiators for the administration. Changes in budget rules contributed to what Barbara Sinclair has described as "unorthodox lawmaking." She notes that between 1987 and 1998, only 21 percent of House measures and 31 percent of Senate measures were not subject to at least one of the following: multiple referral, omnibus legislation, a legislative-executive summit, bypassing committees, post-committee adjustment, or a restrictive rule.[24] Budget rules have also affected committee autonomy and the relationship between majority party leadership, committees, and subcommittees.

Party leaders' influence in budgeting has been enhanced through a variety of means. One is the relationship with members of the House and Senate Budget Committees. Budget committees increasingly resemble the House Rules Committee as a leadership or a "control" committee.[25] In a number of cases, task forces or ad hoc leadership groups write legislation. Budget resolutions, reconciliation bills, and omnibus budget packages are considered on the House and Senate floor under restrictive rules. Budget summits with the White House greatly limit the number of members who have a hand in shaping policy, and they are disproportionately top party leaders. Ratification of these agreements by rank-and-file members signals an acceptance by members of the leaders' ability to represent the interests and reputation of the party. These changes in budget rules and institutions took place along with other organizational developments in Congress.

Additional Congressional Organizational Reforms

The late 1960s and 1970s were periods of significant internal reforms in Congress (primarily the House) focusing on the rules of the majority Democratic Party. Initial analysis of congressional reforms in the 1970s emphasized their decentralizing aspects, consistent with a view of members as individual political entrepreneurs seeking reelection and structuring the institution to foster that goal. Leroy Reiselbach broke down the thrust of the reforms into three broad categories: (1) democratization, weakening the grip of powerful committee chairmen; (2) ethics and openness, providing more transparency in the post-Watergate era; and (3) strengthening the caucus and party leaders.[26]

Democratization was pushed by younger, more liberal Democrats who wanted to break down the hierarchical structures and existing power bases in the House, particularly committee chairmen. Reformers wanted to be able to attain positions of power and influence public policy earlier in their legislative careers. They accomplished this by weakening the seniority system, the practice of awarding committee chairmanships to the member of the majority party who had been on the committee the longest. Although seniority was still practiced in the vast majority of cases, both parties officially declared that criteria other than mere seniority would be used in selecting chairmen. In 1974, Democrats deposed three sitting chairs and replaced them with younger, more liberal, less senior replacements. Perhaps the most striking effect of reform at the time was the devolution of power from full committees to subcommittees.[27] The Ways and Means Committee was forced to create subcommittees, reducing the power of Chairman Wilbur Mills (D-AR) who had abolished subcommittees in the 1950s.

In 1973, the Democratic caucus adopted the "subcommittee bill of rights," which limited the discretion of the chair, allowing subcommittees to select their own chairmen, write their own rules, hire their own staffs, schedule their own sessions, and control their own budgets. The center of legislative action shifted from full committees to subcommittees. In 1970, only 35 percent of all bills were initially heard in subcommittee. By 1980, 80 percent of all initial hearings were held in subcommittee.[28] The consequences for Congress of these reforms were criticized by a number of political scientists. Dodd and Oppenheimer argued that "subcommittee government created a crisis of interest aggregation," weakening the ability of committees to compromise and broker and strengthening the role of interest groups.[29]

The second thrust of reform reflected members' concerns with low public evaluations of Congress in the Watergate era. Members pressed for open meeting (sunshine) requirements, greater financial disclosure, and ethics codes. The Legislative Reorganization Act of 1970 allowed television cameras in committee hearings for the first time, and later in the 1970s CSPAN began broadcasting gavel-to-gavel coverage of the House of Representatives. These changes also affected congressional performance, not always in ways intended by their advocates. Interest groups and the media took advantage of the greater transparency more than the general public. Members had less opportunity to trade votes, to help committee chairs, and to take a public position against the interest of the district in support of a broader national interest.

The third thrust of the reforms, increasing congressional capability by strengthening party leaders, would prove more potent in the long run in conjunction with other changes in the political environment. In 1973, the Democrats established the Policy and Steering Committee, consisting of the three top party leaders and twelve members elected by the caucus by region. In 1975, the caucus transferred the power to make Democratic committee assignments from the Ways and Means Committee to the Policy and Steering Committee.[30] The Speaker was given the right to nominate Democratic members of the Rules Committee, making this committee, with control over the House agenda and rules for debate and amendment, loyal to the leadership. The Speaker was given greater influence in determining the referral of bills to committee, in creating special ad hoc committees, and in setting time limits on consideration. The leadership was expanded, increasing the number of regional whips. To strengthen party control of the most crucial committees, the Democratic caucus established supermajorities (as high as 2 to 1 plus 1), notably on the Rules and Budget Committees. Fewer reforms were adopted in the Senate, but several were significant. The vote needed to invoke cloture during a filibuster was reduced from two-thirds present and voting to three-fifths of the constitutional membership (sixty votes). The majority leader was given more control over bill referrals and scheduling legislation in 1977. The numbers of standing committees and subcommittees were reduced and jurisdictions were clarified. These changes to strengthen party leaders in the 1970s would prove to be important in the post-reform Congresses of the 1980s, 1990s, and 2000s.[31]

Why are congressional rules changed? Recent models of rules changes in the House of Representatives highlight competing explanations: control by the majority party or governed by changes in the ideological balance of power on the House floor. Cox and McCubbins have been at the forefront of the partisan explanation, arguing that the majority is able to "usurp the rule-making power of the House" to create rules and institutions that advantage party members.[32] Eric Schickler has argued for a nonpartisan explanation based primarily on whether the ideological balance of House members' preferences, as measured by the median member, moves toward or away from the majority party.[33] The following section explores partisan and nonpartisan approaches to Congress more closely.

The Role of Parties in Congressional Budgeting

Responsible Parties Model

The role of political parties in American democracy has a long history. The founders, from Madison's warning against the evils of faction in Federalist #10 to Washington's farewell address, agreed that Americans should not break up into political parties. Yet within a few short years (in the 1790s) the first party system in the United States had developed. One of the more enduring perspectives on political parties in the United States is the responsible parties model. Based on an admiration for the Westminster system of disciplined British political parties, Woodrow Wilson was one of the early advocates of responsible parties.[34] One can identify four characteristics of responsible parties.[35] First, parties are specific in terms of policy promises. Second, once in office, parties act on and carry out their policy promises. Third, when out of power, parties act in opposition to, not in concert with, the party in power and develop policy alternatives. Fourth, there must be significant differences between the ideological positions of the parties. A famous articulation of the responsible party doctrine was a report issued by the American Political Science Association in 1950, *Towards a More Responsible Two-Party*

System.[36] Responsible congressional parties would be programmatic parties with strong party discipline on roll-call votes.

This normative view of political parties came under increasing criticism in the 1950s and 1960s as more empirical work revealed that such a model was unrealistic in the American context of separation of powers. A more realistic view of American parties characterized them as broad coalitions under a "big tent."[37]

By the 1970s, because of the emphasis on the reelection motive and the perceived autonomy of members, the role of political parties was minimized. In his landmark 1974 work, *The Electoral Connection,* David Mayhew wrote that "no theoretical treatment of the United States Congress that posits parties as analytic units will go very far."[38] By the mid-1970s, many scholars accepted the view that parties were relatively unimportant in analyzing Congress. Ironically, about same time, the organizational changes discussed above were strengthening party leaders, and partisanship in voting began to increase in Congress.

Electoral Changes and Party Polarization

Much of the increase in partisanship in Congress can be traced to changes in the electorate and constituencies. Since the 1970s, congressional delegations of both parties have become more ideologically homogeneous and more distinct from each other. For a large part of the twentieth century, the Democrats were divided into northern and southern factions, coexisting by keeping civil rights legislation off the agenda. In many cases, the more ideologically conservative southern Democrats voted with Republicans, creating the so-called conservative coalition. At its apex in the 1940s and 1950s, the conservative coalition sometimes appeared on as many as one-third of the votes.[39] The civil rights movement in the 1950s and the 1960s began a process of partisan realignment in the South. A number of conservative Democrats were gradually replaced by Republicans. Redistricting created a number of new black-majority districts that elected more liberal Democratic members. Ideological differences between northern and southern Democrats declined steadily after 1970.[40]

The increase in district partisanship has been reflected in party voting in Congress. Voting studies by Congressional Quarterly show a steady increase in the percentage of time that the average Republican and Democrat votes with his or her own party on a party unity vote (where a majority of Republicans oppose a majority of Democrats).[41] In 1970, the average member voted with the party less than 60 percent of the time, but by 2002, the figure was greater than 85 percent. The proportion of votes that qualify as party unity votes has increased as well. In the House in 1970, less than 30 percent of the votes found a majority of Republicans opposing a majority of Democrats. By the mid-1990s, after the Republican takeover of the House and Senate, as many as 70 percent of votes were party unity votes.

The degree of ideological homogeneity within parties and polarization between parties has been increasingly documented in recent years. The work of Keith Poole and Howard Rosenthal based on analysis of roll-call voting over time has found that some 90 percent of all votes can be aligned on a single liberal-conservative dimension.[42] Looking at the changing distribution of the ideology of members over time, both the Republican and the Democratic caucuses have become more unified since the 1970s, with fewer moderates in both parties.[43] In 1968, a significant number of Democrats fell on the conservative side of the scale, while a number of Republicans fell on the more liberal side. By 1998, these outliers had all but disappeared. Aldrich and Rohde conclude that "the separation of each party from the other is almost the maximum possible."[44] This conclusion is reinforced by other evidence. Although voters remain more moderate in their ideology than candidates or elite groups of core supporters, there is a strong congruence between district ideology and candidate ideology. Using data from surveys of candidates by Project Vote Smart in 1998, Erickson and Wright found consistent and sharp differences in policy preferences among congressional candidates.[45]

Conditional Party Government

Recent scholarship has placed more emphasis on the role of political parties in serving the interests of individual members and in terms of the development of institutions and rules to direct the legislative process.[46] In particular, David Rohde developed the notion of "conditional party government" (CPG) which suggests that strong majority party leadership occurs when the parties are polarized and internally cohesive.[47] His 1991 book on the post-reform House of Representatives argued that too much emphasis had been placed on reforms such as the subcommittee bill of rights that tended to decentralize power in the House and not enough emphasis on the reforms that strengthened party leadership, centralizing power. Rohde built on the earlier work of Cooper and Brady which argued that the degree of partisanship in Congress was a measure of the degree of polarization between the constituency bases of the two parties.[48]

Conditional party government is premised on members having multiple goals, not just reelection. Because policy goals are also important, members may be willing to take some electoral risks to achieve certain policy objectives. Party activists and elites within electoral constituencies tend to be even more polarized than other voters and tend to play a more crucial role in determining candidacies for Congress. As constituencies in the primary electorate for the two parties become more dissimilar, so do the preferences of the representatives that they elect.

This provides the basis for polarized congressional delegations and more powerful party leaders to promote the interests of the party. Rohde goes further with the argument, suggesting that during times of high intraparty cohesion and interparty conflict, more assertive leaders are recruited, and these leaders seek rules strengthening their hand.

> The amount of preference homogeneity with legislative parties is reinforced by the amount of disagreement over preferences (preference conflict) between them. As conflict increases, the negative consequences of a legislative victory by one party increase for its opponents. . . . Members of the majority would have a lot more incentive to empower their leaders to prevent a minority victory. . . . These two considerations—preference homogeneity and preference conflict—together form the "condition" in the theory of conditional party government.[49]

When a party is ideologically diverse, such as the northern and southern wings of the Democratic Party for much of the twentieth century, rank-and-file members will generally oppose ceding significant amounts of power to the leadership. When those differences begin to disappear, the basis for stronger congressional leadership is established.

Majority Party Leadership as Cartel

Much emphasis in congressional scholarship in the 1970s and 1980s was placed on distributive politics where nonpartisan coalitions formed to support legislation that dispensed tangible benefits to congressional districts.[50] Committees were modeled as autonomous units dominated by self-selection to promote reelection goals.[51] That view was increasingly challenged in the 1990s. Party leaders can be conceptualized as agents that coordinate legislative activities and solve collective action problems of members while satisfying their individual goals.[52] One of the strongest statements of this perspective was Cox and McCubbins, *Legislative Leviathan* (1993), based on the economic model of the cartel.

> Our view is that parties in the House—especially the majority party—are a species of "legislative cartel." These cartels usurp the power, theoretically resident in the House, to make rules governing the structure and process of legislation. Possession of this rule-making power leads to two main consequences. First, the legislative process in general—and the committee system in particular—is stacked in favor of majority party interests. Second, because members of the majority party have all the structural advantages, the key players in most legislative deals are members of the majority party, and the majority party's central agreements are facilitated by cartel rules and policed by the cartel's leadership.[53]

Cox and McCubbins challenged the largely accepted view of committee autonomy and independent decision-making power. In particular, they assert (as the title of their book implies) that parties have significant control over committee membership and that the preferences of committee members are not distinctive from those of the majority. As a procedural coalition, the majority party in the House has both active and latent influences, the latter encompassing the notion that the majority party constitutes committees to do its bidding. Their analysis begins by raising doubts about member self-selection, a key element of the committee-dominant perspective. Looking at data on committee assignments, they find evidence that the committee selection process is much more complicated than the mere accommodation of member requests. Examining various group ratings and measures of ideology, they found little evidence that committee members' preferences were unrepresentative of the House.[54]

Cox and McCubbins' model of "limited party government" is based on a view of the party as an organization that solves collective dilemmas of legislators. Individual legislators are still rational actors interested in reelection, but parties play a critical role in their reelection success depending on a party's reputation with the voters. The public record of a party represents issue positions adhered to by substantial majorities of the party, and the reputation depends on citizens' beliefs about those positions.[55] Elected party leaders are induced to internalize the collective interests of the party. Individual members desire the institutional and policy stability that comes from having an established leadership team in place. The party structures are key to preventing the overturning of previous policies that might be caused by shifting majorities. They argue that the impact of party leaders on voting coalitions has been underestimated in the past because of overemphasis on rewards and sanctions from leaders rather than policy alliances created by leaders.

An increasingly important part of maintaining the party reputation is "message" politics and the message agenda: each party emphasizing issues where it is favored by voters and trying to reframe or spin issues where it is disadvantaged.[56] Party positions and the message agenda become particularly important in negotiating highly visible deficit reduction plans and other major budget packages. The traditional appropriations process was characterized by bipartisanship since it allowed members of both parties to deliver tangible benefits to constituents and engage in credit claiming. It appears that the calculus changed with the advent of macrobudgeting. Major budget issues of taxes, deficits, and entitlements are encompassed in reconciliation and omnibus spending bills, with votes on these packages seeming to be of increasing electoral importance for members.

Nonpartisan Alternatives

Despite the evidence of growing partisanship in Congress, several scholars have developed theories of lawmaking that do not include party as a significant factor in determining outcomes. Keith Krehbiel's "pivotal politics" theory is particular relevant since he applies it to the congressional budget process.[57] Rather than party, the median preferences of legislators are the most important determinant of major policy change. The position of the median member of the House and Senate creates a crucial "pivot" point for determining whether changes in the status quo will occur. Divided or unified party control and the size of the majority make little difference in outcomes. In other words, in a spatial model of lawmaking, partisanship may simply be an artifact of preferences—that is, members on the left are Democrats, and members on the right are Republicans. Therefore, budget preferences may correlate perfectly with party. Krehbiel writes:

> If so, then legislators' party identification brings no marginal predictive power. . . . beyond what a purely preference-driven theory, such as the pivotal politics theory, already captures. In other words, voting may be an instance of straightforward, individual preference revelation, independent of collective dilemmas, party persuasion, cajoling, and coercion. . . .[58]

The problem, he argues, is that given current measures, it is impossible to determine whether party is in fact exerting an independent impact on voting despite the high levels of party voting observed. Measures of party unity in voting, he argues, should not be cited as support for the importance of partisanship. A second element of his analysis of congressional budgeting concerns outcomes. He argues that if the party theorists are correct, one should observe *"abrupt and large swings in policy whenever party control changes."*[59] Instead, he observes that policy change is incremental, marginal at best, after a change in both party control of the presidency in 1992 and party control of the Congress in 1994. Finally, Krehbiel casts doubt on another aspect of the partisan theories—that members use party reputation as a "brand name" in their reelection bids.[60]

As he acknowledges, in its quest for simplicity, the pivotal politics theory omits a number of elements of contemporary lawmaking: the role of parties, the multidimensionality of policy (particularly dramatic in macrobudgeting), agenda setting by party leaders, the dynamics of bargaining, and uncertainty concerning the consequences of budget changes on the status quo.[61] Even if measures of party unity cannot disprove the pivotal politics theory, trends in party cohesion and party voting are important to an explanation of congressional budgeting. Also relevant are the role of party leaders in bargaining in order to craft successful budget packages, the stance taken by minority party leaders, the actions of party leaders in enacting budget bills, and the kinds of party messages they attempt to associate with the legislation. Comparisons between voting patterns on macrobudgetary measures, such as budget resolutions and reconciliation bills on one hand and appropriations bills on the other, will also help test the contention that the macro/micro distinction is significant.

Relations with the Presidency, Divided Government, and Budget Gridlock

Have the changes in congressional budget institutions and rules since the 1970s changed the relationship between Congress and the presidency in budgeting? It was the intention of many members of both parties to strengthen Congress vis-à-vis President Nixon and his successors as indicated in the floor debates at the time of the adoption of the Budget Act in 1974. It was passed by nearly unanimous majorities: 401–6 in the House and 75–0 in the Senate.[62] Bipartisanship did not carry over into implementing the budget process and passing a budget, however, as we shall see in subsequent chapters. Reagan, Clinton, and the second Bush all appeared to be helped by congressional budget rules when party majorities in Congress were favorable. Conversely, Reagan, Bush, Clinton, and Bush all served during some period of divided government and confronted a Congress capable of formulating and enacting a budget and negotiating with the president over it. As recent scholarship on congressional parties provides some important perspectives on congressional budgeting, so too does recent research on divided government and gridlock.

Consequences of Divided Government

Concern with the perceived debilitative effects of divided government surged in the 1980s with increasing public rancor between Republican President Reagan and the Democratic House of Representatives. The term *political gridlock* entered the parlance of pundits and scholars. Much of the discontent with divided government was related to the federal budget and the burgeoning deficits. Divided government was blamed both for causing deficits and for the apparent inability of Congress and the presidency to do anything about them. Former Carter White House Counsel Lloyd Cutler asserted that budget deficits tended to be larger under divided government than under unified government: "In modern times high deficits have occurred only with divided government. . . . The correlation between unacceptably high deficits and divided government is much too exact to be a coincidence."[63] He received some support for his hypothesis in a study by McCubbins that linked deficits and divided government in the 1980s.[64] McKenzie and Thorton also concluded that divided government inhibits the ability of government to reduce large budget deficits.[65]

The general debate over the consequences of divided government changed with the publication of David Mayhew's *Divided We Govern* in 1991.[66] Identifying significant legislation through a two-stage process, Mayhew found no meaningful differences in terms of legislative output under divided government versus unified government. Because this finding challenged existing assumptions and conventional wisdom, it stimulated theoretical and empirical work on gridlock and the consequences of divided government. Using a more stringent definition of significant legislation, Kelly found that, in fact, more important legislation is produced under unified government than under divided government.[67] Another way to analyze the effects of divided government is to look at significant legislation that does not pass. Edwards, Barrett, and Peake did just that and found the divided government increases the probability that important legislation fails by 45 percent.[68] Fiorina observed that Mayhew looked only at the supply of legislation by a given Congress, not the demand.[69] In other words, Mayhew had produced a numerator in the form of significant legislation passed, but no denominator in terms of the agenda of potential enactments for a given Congress. Sarah

Binder developed just such a denominator in her analysis of legislative grid-lock.[70] Using editorials in the *New York Times* between 1947 and 1996, she constructed a data set that measured the systematic agenda for a given year. The data allowed her to measure gridlock as a ratio of major enactments as a percentage of the agenda. Her analysis found that there was a statistically significant relationship between divided government and gridlock.

Binder also found that partisan polarization contributes to gridlock and that policy change is less likely as the parties become more ideologically distinct. She also found that the greater the policy distance between House and Senate, the more likely is gridlock to occur. John Coleman added measures of party responsiveness and institutional features of American politics to his study of unified and divided government.[71] By *responsiveness* he means whether unified or divided government is in tune with the public mood for more activism or less activism by government. He suggests that if parties are cohesive and the transaction costs of bargaining are lower within rather than across parties, unified government should produce more significant legislation. Greater intraparty factionalism, on the other hand, should tend to reduce legislative output. Using a range of measures of legislative output employed by previous studies—indicators of public mood and intraparty cohesion—he concludes that unified government is significantly more productive than divided government and is more responsive to the public mood: "Parties do, as party government theorists maintain, generate incentives to cooperation that help transcend some of the policymaking gaps created by the Constitution."[72]

Nonpartisan Explanations of Gridlock

An alternate explanation to partisan theories of gridlock is found again in the spatial models of Krehbiel and of Brady and Volden. Krehbiel argues that the supermajoritarian features of U.S. politics (two-thirds requirement for a veto override, sixty-vote requirement to break a filibuster in the Senate) make deadlock equally likely under divided or unified government.[73] A similar analysis is provided by Brady and Volden in *Revolving Gridlock* (1998).[74] Conceptualizing members of Congress as arrayed on a single dimension of preferences, gridlock occurs when the status quo is closer to the median members' preferences than proposed alternative policies.[75] Given this preference distribution, the major determinant of gridlock is the filibuster and the presidential veto. They assert that the impact of party need not be directly included in the model because its effect is subsumed in members' preferences which change after elections. Gridlock does not depend on whether the median member is a Republican or a Democrat. Based on their theory, strong parties actually expand the gridlock region.[76]

Budget deficits in the 1980s combined with supermajority institutions to create gridlock in several ways, they argue.[77] First, with severe fiscal constraints, the concessions needed to sway the vote of pivotal members were eliminated. Second, packaging major budget decisions increased the difficulty of gaining a supermajority coalition that could move from the gridlock zone. Third, the increasing dominance of budget issues on the agenda helped extend gridlock to other policies as well. Fourth, the complexity of major budget packages themselves contributed to gridlock.

Divided or Unified Government and Budgeting

Whether party-influenced or purely preference-driven, it remains instructive to examine congressional and presidential bargaining positions in milestone budget legislation. If divided or unified party control of Congress and the presidency matters, it could be reflected in the *processes of budgeting and in the content of policy.* In terms of process, Sarah Binder has already found that divided government increases budget delay: it takes an average of forty-one more days to pass a budget resolution under divided government than under unified government.[78] In addition, this study examines whether divided government is also related to omnibus appropriations and whether it increases the probability of government shutdowns. We can also examine whether the use of extraordinary means to resolve budget conflicts, such as interbranch summits and bipartisan commissions, are more common under divided government than unified government. Even though the federal budget, dominated by entitlements, is relatively inflexible, divided versus unified government could be reflected in the content of major budget packages. One would expect the content of deficit reduction packages in terms of share of the reduction coming from tax increases, entitlement reductions, or defense and domestic discretionary spending cuts to be different, depending on what party alignment exists.

To the extent that legislation is protected from filibuster by budget rules, the presidential veto emerges as the key supermajority institution. Cameron found that veto bargaining is not only more likely under divided government but also more likely with highly significant legislation.[79] If this holds in budgeting, a veto or the threat of a veto in major budget packages is more likely to be used under divided government than under unified government. Congressional budget resolutions do not require the signature of the president, but they are binding only on subsequent actions by Congress. Even though members chose the concurrent resolution (as opposed to the joint resolution that does require the signature of the president) as the vehicle for defining the parameters of the congressional budget, they recognized that all implementing legislation would require presidential approval. Reconciliation bills and omnibus taxing and spending packages carrying out the budget resolution can be vetoed by the president.

Summary and Plan of the Book

Congress makes different kinds of taxing and spending decisions, some at the macro-level and others at the micro-level. In the evolution of congressional budgeting, macro-level decisions have become particularly important since the 1970s. At that time, when the Congressional Budget Act was being enacted and implemented, scholarship on Congress and the presidency was significantly different than it is today. This chapter has examined various approaches and theoretical perspectives that relate to congressional budgeting. They suggest several foci that guide the examination of major budget legislation in the following chapters.

The first concerns congressional rules, institutions, and macrobudgeting. The primary hypothesis of this study is that the creation of macrobudgeting in Congress changed how policy choices were framed and enacted, affecting how Congress operates as a policymaker. The findings will suggest that budget rules and institutions have affected the nature of budget choices, the distribution of power, committee autonomy, the legislative process, and relationships with the executive branch. A second focus surrounds the changes in parties and partisanship related to congressional budgeting. The analysis will suggest that parties are important in explaining congressional budgeting and that budget institutions have empowered party leaders and contributed to the overall increase in congressional partisanship. A third focus concerns the relationship between Congress and the president in budgeting and the consequences of divided or unified control of national government. The results will suggest that divided government is important in explaining congressional budgeting outcomes.

The following chapters examine in more detail significant major budget legislation of the past generation. Following the evolution of congressional budgeting chronologically, each chapter examines the economic and political context, changes in budget institutions and rules, partisanship and the role of party leaders, the relationship of the president to congressional budget decision making, and the effects of party control of the legislative and executive branches on budget process and outcomes. The concluding chapter integrates and assesses the earlier chapters and provides some additional data on trends in partisanship and the consequences of divided government over the period.

Specifically, chapter 2 examines budget reform and the budget process through 1980, chapter 3 the Reagan economic and budget plan in 1981, chapter 4 the Balanced Budget and Emergency Deficit Reduction Act of 1985, chapter 5 the budget summit agreement adopted in 1990 during the Bush administration, chapter 6 the 1993 deficit reduction package enacted in the first year of the Clinton administration, chapter 7 the 1997 bipartisan balanced budget agreement, and chapter 8, the 2001–2003 tax cut packages enacted during the administration of George W. Bush. Inevitably, this list is not exhaustive—many important budget issues and conflicts during this period are not included. However, important developments between these particular years will also be discussed. Finally, in chapter 9, some thought is given to what the experience of the past thirty years might reveal about how (and whether) Congress and the president might be likely to deal with the huge budget deficits projected over the next decade.

The main goal of this book is to enable a better understanding of congressional budgeting and its relationship with broader developments in American politics. It is not a study of the budget policy per se, although some details concerning taxes, entitlements, and domestic and defense discretionary spending are essential to understanding the politics. The book is not intended to be normative or partisan in terms of judging the relative merits of presidential, legislative, or party positions or in prescribing what budget choices should have been made. Chapter 2 begins the analysis by examining congressional budgeting through the first part of the twentieth century, the adoption of the Budget Act, its initial implementation, and some precursors of macrobudgeting.

CHAPTER 2

Budgeting in Congress through 1980

It has long been recognized that Congress has a penchant for spending. Constituency interests, policy objectives, and reelection calculations created a collective action problem—demands for greater spending than available resources could support. At various stages in congressional development, formal and informal "guardianship" institutions were devised to countervail such spending pressures and to keep them in rough balance with appropriate revenue levels. As the emphasis on spending or imposing fiscal discipline has shifted over time, Congress has altered rules dealing with the budget in an attempt to establish constraints.

The appropriations process had been the most important means for determining what government spent since the Civil War. Although not always satisfactory, this process largely kept the budget in balance or surplus through the beginning of World War I. The appropriations process exemplifies traditional budgeting, where specialized subcommittees carefully review the many complex parts of the federal budget. For many decades, this process also indirectly controlled the overall size of the budget by restraining excessive spending growth. The statutory debt limit, adopted in 1917, was one of the first congressional enactments that explicitly addressed macrobudgeting.[1] It was never able to act as a restraint on deficit spending or borrowing, however, since it was enacted ex post facto after taxing and spending decisions that required borrowing had already been made.

Concern that Congress was not doing an adequate job in controlling spending was in part behind the passage of the Budget and Accounting Act of 1921 which created the executive budget and initiated a period of steady growth of the president's influence over the nation's finances.[2] After 1920, the authorization and appropriations process was strengthened, but Congress still never considered the budget as a whole.[3] Along with assuring the adequate funding of government programs and the distribution of benefits to members' districts, the appropriations process developed norms to protect the public purse and restrain spending. When the appropriations process failed to restrain spending beginning in the 1960s, a variety of other institutions were tried as well, such as imposing spending ceilings. When these methods failed to provide either a stable process or satisfactory outcomes, a new budget process was created in 1974 that would provide the basis for macrobudgeting, a new stage in the evolution of congressional budgeting. This new set of rules and institutions did not replace authorizations and appropriations. Because of the "stickiness" of congressional institutions, the new process was superimposed on the old, creating a hybrid system with inherent tensions between making decisions on the parts of the budget and making decisions on the whole.

Appropriations, even after passage of the Budget Act, still conform more closely to the norm of universalism where near-unanimous, bipartisan coalitions form to distribute tangible benefits to congressional districts.[4] Macrobudgeting, in contrast, has produced sharper divisions in Congress. One reason for the difference may be that the opportunities for logrolling are decreased in budget resolutions and reconciliation bills. These macrobills are vast in scope and highly visible, with higher stakes. Although congressional budgeting was dominated by the appropriations process until the end of the 1970s, there were several kinds of legislative votes in budgeting that may be seen as precursors to the kinds of alignments that developed over budget resolutions: votes to recommit appropriations bills to committee and votes on the debt limit. Both of these types of policy decisions framed budget questions differently, were highly symbolic, often evoked partisan rhetoric, and provided a chance to criticize the majority party, the president, or both.

This chapter examines the development of congressional budgeting through 1980, beginning with the appropriations process and how by the 1970s it had proved unsatisfactory to members. Next, the adoption of the Budget and Impoundment Control Act of 1974 is reviewed, concentrating on the changes in congressional rules and institutions. The operation of the "new" budget process after 1975 is then analyzed in terms of how the new rules were implemented, what role parties played, and whether significant changes in the relationship with the presidency occurred.

The Appropriations Process

The Evolution of the Appropriations Process

As the norm of the balanced budget changed in symbolic meaning over the years, the process for approving taxing and spending necessary to maintain a balanced budget also underwent changes. Congress originally organized its taxing and spending process around the House Ways and Means Committee, established in 1802, and, to a lesser extent, the Senate Finance Committee.[5] This system faltered with the complexities of the Civil War, and in the late 1860s, the House and Senate Appropriations Committees were created. The committees increased their power to reduce executive branch requests in 1876, strengthening their role as guardian of the federal Treasury.

In the 1880s, however, pressure from members to increase federal spending on rivers and harbors, grants to railroads, land-grant colleges, and other programs led to a fragmentation of the appropriations power. By the late nineteenth century, the House Appropriations Committee was responsible for only half of federal spending. The process had become more fragmented and specialized: eight separate committees considered spending requests directly from agencies, and government spending was approved through many separate bills. Brady and Morgan argue that reforms in 1880 and 1885 which decentralized appropriations resulted in less fiscal discipline and higher levels of spending.[6]

The fragmentation of the congressional system helped convince many that the president was inherently more "responsible" in budgeting, leading ultimately to the enactment of the Budget and Accounting Act of 1921.[7] That legislation created the executive budget and the Bureau of the Budget (changed to the Office of Management and Budget or OMB in 1969). While this legislation certainly strengthened the president, it was by no means an abdication of power by the Congress, which also acted to reduce the fragmentation of its spending power. In 1919 and 1920, Congress moved to reform its budget process by eliminating the ability of committees other than Appropriations to appropriate money. One study suggests that this institutional change, which strengthened the capacity of Congress to impose fiscal discipline and restrain deficits, resulted in less spending than would have occurred under the more fragmented system.[8] It did not, however, create what could be thought of as a centralized budget process since the Appropriations Committees still acted primarily through their dozen or so specialized subcommittees. These institutional changes in 1919 and 1920 were not particularly partisan. As Brady and Morgan observe, "[A]lthough over 80 percent of the (majority) Republicans voted for the reform, there was also solid Democratic support."[9]

The reforms of 1920 clarified responsibilities among authorizing committees and the Appropriations Committees.[10] The standing committees could not appropriate money, and the Appropriations Committees were prohibited from taking any purely legislative actions. The differences between authorizations and appropriations represented a focal point of conflict within Congress between the forces of advocacy and guardianship. Formulated by the standing committees of the House and Senate, authorizations are instruments for making substantive policy decisions, and they enable agencies to undertake certain activities.[11] Appropriations finance these authorized activities, and the Appropriations Committees as a rule appropriate less than the programmatic committees desire. The appropriators emerged more powerful from the 1920 reforms. Despite the decentralization of authority among its subcommittees, the Appropriations Committees were able to impose sufficient discipline to restrain spending. Except during the Depression and World War II, deficits were largely held in check well into the 1960s.[12] After massive borrowing to finance World War II, the federal debt as a proportion of GDP fell steadily until the early 1970s.

Early Attempts at a Congressional Budget

Despite the institutionalization of the appropriations process, after World War II, many in Congress believed that the process was too decentralized since the federal budget was never considered as a whole. The sentiment for a congressional budget was fueled by a desire to check the growing power of the president in budgeting that carried over from wartime practices and was enhanced by the enactment of the Employment Act of 1946. The Legislative Reorganization Act of 1946 made a number of major reforms in congressional institutions, including the creation of a congressional budget.[13] The Joint Committee on the Budget was established to receive the president's budget. It consisted of all of the members of the House Ways and Means, Senate Finance, and House and Senate Appropriations Committees, well over one hundred members.[14] This unwieldy panel was supposed to report a concurrent resolution by February 15, only a few weeks after receiving the president's requests. The resolution was to specify a ceiling on expenditures, estimated receipts, and the size of the deficit or surplus. In its first attempt in 1947, the Republican Congress tried to slash President Truman's requests by $6 billion but was unable to agree on a resolution. Despite divided government and Republican partisanship refreshed by a dozen years out of power, majority party leaders were unable to build a partisan or conservative coalition majority to agree on a budget to counter the president's.

Budget-cutting efforts reverted to the appropriations process. In 1948, Congress again proved unable to pass an overall budget. In 1949, now back under Democratic control, Congress moved the date for passage of the budget resolution to May 1. But by that time, most appropriations bill had already been reported or passed, and the budget resolution was again abandoned. Congress tried one last time in 1950, this time through an omnibus appropriations bill emanating from the House Appropriations Committee. The House successfully passed the bill in May, but the Senate did not complete action until August, well into the fiscal year. So many supplemental appropriations had to be passed the next year that the practice was abandoned. Attempts at a congressional budget were dead for a generation as Congress returned to the tried-and-true appropriations process.

Appropriations and Spending Restraints

The tension between advocacy and guardianship characterizes budgeting in both legislative and executive branches. Aaron Wildavsky concluded in his study of budgeting that the president's budget office serves as a guardian of the purse and overwhelmingly tends to reduce agency requests.[15] In Congress, as Richard Fenno described in his classic 1966 study of appropriations politics, it was the House Appropriations Committee that played the guardian role.[16] As Fenno found, even the language of appropriators reflected this mission:

> The action verbs most commonly used are 'cut,' 'carve,' 'slice,' 'whittle,' 'squeeze,' 'wring,' 'trim,' 'lop off,' 'chop,' 'slash,' 'pare,' 'shave,' 'shack,' and 'fry.' The tools of the trade are appropriately referred to as 'knife,' 'blade,' 'meat axe,' 'scalpel,' 'meat cleaver,' 'hatchet,' 'shears,' 'wringer,' and 'fine tooth comb.' . . . Budgets are praised when they are 'cut to the bone.'[17]

Fenno argued that the House Appropriations Committee developed strong internal norms to foster its role of protecting the taxpayer from waste and excess spending whether from the White House or from authorizing committees. New members were socialized in this norm and were taught to laud the committee's record of reducing the president's budget requests. The norm of bipartisanship was strong on the committee, strengthening its position when spending bills were taken up on the floor of the House. Few minority reports were issued and little partisanship was displayed in voting for final passage.[18]

Subcommittee chairs were very senior members from safe districts, socialized in the norms of budget cutting. Senior members with safe seats were better able to resist pressure from interest groups and "vote against the district" in favor of larger national interests when necessary. Most markups were held in closed session, far from the view of media, interest groups, and constituents. Membership on subcommittees was determined by the committee chair and ranking minority member, allowing them to ensure that certain members without direct political interests were included.[19]

The Senate Appropriations Committee, which constitutionally can only follow the House in raising revenues and appropriating money, played a somewhat different role. In examining appropriations actions taken between 1947 and 1962, Fenno (1966) found that the Senate committee often restored some of the cuts in agency appropriations made on the House side. This led to their characterization as a "court of appeals" in the appropriations process.

Has the tendency for budget cutting and restraint in the traditional appropriations process been overemphasized? Perhaps. In the case of the House Appropriation Committees, the actual cuts in the president's budget were relatively minor. Despite the budget-cutting bravado, the committees moderated the tension between guardianship and spending desires by operating in a narrow, "safe" zone: granting less than requested but more than in the previous year.[20] Appropriations Committee members were equally if not more concerned with the goal of providing sufficient funding for government programs to satisfy constituency demands and the preferences of other members of the House. Despite a selection process that seemed to temper advocacy, there is evidence of program advocacy along with guardianship. Despite the record of bipartisanship in committee and on final votes, there was a record of partisanship on recommittal votes.

Recommittal votes provided members with an occasional opportunity to emphasize party differences. Particularly for Republicans when in the minority, the motion to recommit an appropriations bill provided an opportunity to show opposition to big government and excessive spending by the majority Democrats. In contrast to the record of lopsided bipartisan votes on final passage of appropriations bills, recommittal votes were usually closely contested party votes. Fenno wrote on these votes, "Minority party members . . . are less concerned with the flow of legislative business than with making a record or, perhaps, embarrassing the majority party."[21] Republican and Democratic Party leaders opposed each other on 90 percent of the recorded recommittal votes on appropriations bills.[22] This pattern would manifest itself even more strongly in voting on the debt ceiling, another opportunity for making a party statement.

The appropriations process was not a guarantee against deficits because decisions on revenues were not formally coordinated with spending at any point in the process. Rather, from the end of World War II through the mid-1960s, informal coordination between the tax-writing committees, the appropriations committees, and party leaders was largely effective at preventing large deficits given the nation's steady economic growth and the relative stability of the policy agenda. Although budgets were rarely in strict balance, and deficits increased during recessions, deficits were simply not much of a problem. Reflecting the absence of such concerns during this period, the word *deficit* does not appear in the index of either Wildavsky's or Fenno's book. But deficits would emerge as a greater problem because of shifts in the political and economic environment and declining performance of existing institutions.

The Decline of Restraint

The system of restraint through the appropriations process, while never perfect, began to unravel in the late 1960s and early 1970s. Budget deficits increased significantly between 1966 and 1975. In retrospect, the deficits of this era do not seem particularly large or chronic. In comparison with the preceding decades, however, it appeared that fiscal discipline was in serious decline. That decline was the result of many factors, including the slowing of economic expansion, the growth of entitlements, greater spending pressures within Congress, and institutional changes within the Appropriations Committees and Congress itself.[23] The fiscal dividend that the country had enjoyed in the postwar period dwindled as inflation increased and economic growth slowed. Spending pressures grew as the Johnson administration pursued an increasingly expensive war in Southeast Asia as well as an ambitious domestic agenda. This led to a deficit of $25 billion in FY 1968, constituting 3 percent of the nation's GDP, seen as unacceptably high by members of both parties. The war in Vietnam increased conflict between the Congress and the presidency, a conflict that gathered steam with the election and inauguration of Richard Nixon.

As the resources available for increased spending programs declined, spending advocates in Congress sought ways to avoid the discipline of the appropriations process. One of the most effective means to bypass the

Appropriations Committees was to create entitlement programs and other so-called backdoor spending mechanisms. These legislative actions by the authorizing committees created permanent appropriations, shielded from annual review. Mandatory obligations such as Medicare, Medicaid, and Social Security became the fastest-growing elements in the federal budget. This had the effect of rapidly shrinking the share of federal spending that fell under the jurisdiction of the Appropriations Committees, which by 1974 had fallen to 45 percent of outlays.[24] Even this overstates their degree of discretion since a growing portion of appropriations going through the committee were mandatory as well. Not only was Appropriations' piece of the pie smaller, but the norms of fiscal restraint in both committees were waning.

Budgeting was affected by the congressional reforms of the 1960s and 1970s discussed in chapter 1.[25] Several of the reforms had significant effects on diluting the guardianship of the appropriations process.[26] The House Appropriations Committee was enlarged and "liberalized" by the addition of new, younger Democratic members. In 1967, Democrats enjoyed a 30–21 majority over Republicans. Ten years later, reflecting the Democratic Caucus's desire to establish a 2–1 plus 1 majority, the ratio had grown to 37–18.[27] Many of the new members were liberals. The committee became even more fragmented by weakening the power of subcommittee chairs, the so-called College of Cardinals that had once been so dominant. Pressure for change came both from the House Democratic caucus and from the newer, more individualistic members. The thirteen subcommittee chairs had long been among the most conservative Democrats in Congress, often from the South. The caucus weakened the committee (and enhanced its own influence) by requiring the election of subcommittee chairs by the full caucus. The power of the Appropriations Committee Chair was also weakened as he became little more than first among equals.

One of the most important changes was in the method of establishing subcommittee membership. Instead of being assigned to subcommittees by the chair and ranking minority members, members were able to select their own assignments. This shift in the selection process tended to remove the disinterested members who served as critics and budget cutters and replace them with program supporters. The shift from assignment to self-selection removed this important barrier to all-out advocacy on the part of the House Appropriations Committee subcommittees.

Reforms that promoted greater openness in Congress also had an impact. "Sunshine" provisions adopted by the House required that committee sessions be open to the public unless the committee formally voted to meet in executive session. Between the late 1960s and 1975, the closed sessions of the

House Appropriations Committee dropped from 100 percent to 11 percent.[28] The hard bargaining that once took place behind closed doors, where members could argue for budget cutting against the economic self-interest of the district, was conducted in the glare of television lights. Constituents, lobbyists, the media, and even a few members of the public were watching.

The level of unity, internal integration, and bipartisanship slipped as well in the face of these internal changes. Once-rare minority reports became more commonplace in the 1970s. Once-infrequent floor amendments to appropriations bills became more frequent. The success of those amendments depended primarily on whether they were designed to increase or to cut spending, with those that increased spending four times more likely to pass.[29] The results of all of these changes were soon apparent. Despite continued adherence to the creed of reducing executive requests, the record of budget cutting by the Appropriations Committees was substantially poorer by the 1970s. Despite the fact that the committees were only responding to pressures from the other members of Congress, there was growing dissatisfaction with the appropriations process. Other methods were sought to deal with growing deficits.

Attempts to Limit the Deficits, 1967–1974

As upward pressure on spending mounted, Congress turned to a tax increase and expenditure caps to restrain deficits.[30] Congress enacted spending limits in 1967, 1968, 1969, 1970, and 1972 but to little avail.[31] In 1967, as a weapon against inflation and as a way to stem the budget deficit, President Lyndon Johnson proposed a 10 percent surtax on income taxes. After many months of negotiation with legislative leaders, the tax increase was made contingent on the adoption of a spending limitation. The spending cap that was finally passed in 1967 was nearly useless since it exempted mandatory spending, trust funds, permanent appropriations, and Vietnam War costs. The tax surcharge failed. In 1968, the House Ways and Means Committee held the president's tax increase hostage until the president could craft a more meaningful spending limit.

Both the surcharge and a new spending cap were finally passed as part of the Revenue and Expenditure Control Act of 1968. The spending cap exempted Social Security, interest, veterans' benefits, Vietnam War costs, farm subsidies, and public assistance.[32] Despite some $8 billion in cuts in nonexempt spending, because of growing entitlements and mandatory spending and no enforcement procedures in the legislation, actual outlays outstripped the statutory limits. Nonetheless, the FY 1969 budget, with the additional revenues, produced a slight surplus. This would be the last balanced budget for thirty years. The problems with spending ceilings were repeated under President Nixon in 1969 and 1970 when caps for total spending were enacted but soon exceeded. Congress tried various vehicles to control spending, attaching spending limits to a supplemental appropriations bill and a continuing resolution.

The disarray and dissatisfaction in Congress over growing spending, deficits, and hostility to the presidency in the face of its own shortcomings in dealing with the budget came to a head in 1972. In July 1972, President Nixon demanded that spending for FY 1973 not exceed $250 billion.[33] Nixon lambasted the lack of spending discipline in Congress and threatened to make the cuts himself if Congress failed. The cap was tied to an extension of the statutory debt limit (see below), but the House and Senate could not agree on whether to grant the president discretion to make the cuts.[34] The final version of the bill included contradictory provisions both establishing and invalidating a spending limit. It had become clear that the appropriations process was not up to the task of restraining spending or reducing deficits, and Congress seemed incapable of establishing discipline through any other methods. As part of the 1972 spending limit, Congress established a Joint Study Committee on Budget Control to examine serious reforms in their budgetary system.

Congressional Budget Reform

Perceived Defects in Congressional Institutions

The authorization/appropriations process had other perceived problems besides the undesirably large deficits that had resulted. Members of Congress were dissatisfied with their inability to make decisions on overall budget totals which limited their ability to influence fiscal policy. No mechanism for debating national priorities existed, a particular peeve for liberal members eager to reallocate resources from the military to domestic needs. The appropriations process itself had deteriorated, evidenced not only by the loss of jurisdiction over spending but also by the members' inability to approve spending bills in a timely fashion. Between 1972 and 1975, not a single appropriation bill was passed by the start of the fiscal year on July 1, and several bills simply were never passed at all.[35] Members were also unhappy with the information they had at their disposal to make decisions, especially as they aimed to challenge the budgetary power of President Nixon. It was the growing perception on Capitol Hill that OMB was suppressing information and providing highly suspect budget estimates designed to advantage the president. All of these factors, plus growing outrage over Nixon's impoundments, led to a bipartisan coalition supporting comprehensive budget reform.

The Bipartisan Budget Reform Coalition

The Budget and Impoundment Control Act of 1974 was enacted after eighteen months of review, drafting, revision, and balancing of various institutional, policy, and party interests. Some reformers wanted to create a process explicitly designed to restrain spending and curb deficits, but this was only one set of interests represented. Budget process reform legislation reflected the tension within Congress between program advocates and budget guardians, particularly between appropriators and authorizing committees.

The Joint Study Committee primarily represented House and Senate Appropriations Committees, House Ways and Means Committees, and Senate Finance Committees, thus creating divisions within the majority Democratic Party. These four committees were particularly concerned with enhancing spending control, curbing backdoor spending, and imposing greater discipline on the authorizing committees. In this sense, they were hawkish on deficit reduction and envisioned a budget process oriented toward spending control. To achieve this goal, the Joint Committee designed a budget process that would preserve the existing committee structure and superimpose an additional process over the existing one. Many of the provisions they designed would ultimately be enacted into law, but several key changes were made that weakened the emphasis on guardianship and deficit control.

Under the Joint Study Committee's recommendations, each house would have its own Budget Committee that would formulate resolutions shaping the overall parameters of the congressional budget. A Congressional Budget Office (CBO) was proposed to improve congressional information. A timetable for budgeting would be imposed on the process, and the start of the fiscal year would be moved to October 1 to give Congress more time to complete its business. The first resolution, to be passed in the spring, would set binding totals for budget authority and outlays by administrative units. Backdoor spending would be curtailed, and an early deadline for the adoption of authorizing legislation would be established.

The Joint Committee reported their recommendations to Congress in April 1973, and the recommendations were taken up by several House and Senate committees where the interests of the authorizing committees and more liberal members were better represented. In the House, the Rules Committee took jurisdiction over the legislation and considered an alternative bill introduced by Representative Jamie Whitten (D-MS), second ranking Democrat on Appropriations, along with the Joint Study Committee's plan. Whitten, who had co-chaired the Joint Committee, shifted gears by proposing that the first resolution would contain only targets, not binding totals, and that functional totals rather than agency accounts would be used, reducing the constraints that the budget resolution would impose on Appropriations Committee actions.[36] These two critical changes were adopted by the Rules Committee.

On the Senate side, the Government Operations Committee reported a bill, but the main direction of budget reform legislation in the Senate was provided by Majority Whip Robert Byrd (D-WV) and the Rules Committee. Their version further weakened the antispending orientation of the process in two ways. Reflecting the concerns of the authorizing committees, Byrd's bill loosened provisions limiting backdoor spending. Reflecting the concerns of the Appropriations Committees, the optional reconciliation process that followed the passage of the second resolution could reconcile differences in the budget resolution and committee-approved spending by raising revenues or by simply changing the totals in the resolution, rather than requiring the rescission of previously passed spending actions.[37]

Further compromises were struck in the House-Senate Conference Committee in 1974. Despite weakening the spending control orientation of the new process, all of the existing congressional interests in budgeting accepted greater restrictions on their discretion. The creation of the Budget Committees and the budget resolutions imposed new restrictions on authorizing committees and appropriators alike. But several key changes from the Joint Study Committee's original recommendations left the new process more neutral than anti-spending or anti-deficit.[38] First, existing backdoor spending was grandfathered in: restrictions would apply only to new programs. Second, the fact that the first resolution contained only targets rather than binding totals significantly reduced the restraint imposed. Third, the use of functional subtotals rather than agency accounts maintained greater maneuverability for appropriators and meant that floor amendments did not have to be consistent with the guidelines in the resolution. Despite the widespread lip service paid to the cause of deficit reduction and spending control, the institutional changes proposed in the final bill did not simply orient the process to spending restraint. Allen Schick concluded:

> What has emerged, therefore, is a process that is neutral on its face. It can
> be deployed in favor of higher or lower spending, bigger or smaller

deficits. Its effects on budget outcomes will depend on congressional preferences rather than on procedural limitations.[39]

The process of compromise and balancing institutional interests within Congress was successful in satisfying overwhelming majorities of both parties. The Budget and Impoundment Control Act passed the House by a vote of 401–6 and passed the Senate by a vote of 75–0. President Nixon signed the bill in July 1974, less than a month before his historic resignation.[40] The bill reflected a bipartisan consensus that Congress needed to strengthen its budgetary powers to check the inflated powers of the president and to restrict his impoundment authority. But underneath the unanimity, the budget reform coalition was a tenuous and temporary alliance of Democrats who wanted to realign national priorities and Republicans who wanted to force members to go on record to approve deficit spending. That coalition would disintegrate when the majority party had to make real decisions on taxing, spending, and deficits.

The Congressional Budget Process

The Budget Act would radically change the way Congress does business, and over the next thirty years it would become critical in reshaping the entire legislative process. The process has subsequently undergone many formal and informal changes, but the original blueprint is an essential starting point. The budget process as initially enacted was based on a strict calendar of steps that many doubted Congress could maintain, even with an extra three months at its disposal. Table 2–1 examines the original timetable for action. The process began with the arrival of the president's budget in January. The House and Senate Budget Committees separately held hearings on economic conditions, fiscal policy consequences, and national budget priorities. They took testimony from the administration, other members of Congress, independent experts, and interest groups. By March 15, the authorizing committees were required to submit their "views and estimates," stating the amount of budget authority and outlays likely to be authorized in the coming year. Independent budgetary analysis was provided by the CBO, which is required to submit a report by April 15.

By April 15, the House and Senate Budget Committees were required to report their version of the first concurrent resolution on the budget to their respective chambers. A concurrent resolution was chosen as the vehicle for the congressional budget since it does not require the signature of the president to

Table 2–1
Original congressional budget timetable

Action to Be Completed	On or Before
President submits annual budget message to Congress	15 days after Congress meets
Congressional committees make recommendations to budget committees	March 15
Congressional Budget Office reports to budget committees	April 1
Budget Committees report first budget resolution	April 15
Congress passes first budget resolution	May 15
Legislative committees complete reporting of authorizing legislation	May 15
Congress passes all spending bills	7 days after Labor Day
Congress passes second budget resolution	Sept. 15
Congress passes budget reconciliation bill	Sept. 25
Fiscal year begins	Oct. 1

take effect. As such, it has sway only over subsequent congressional actions and does not in itself create budget authority or outlays. Under the original plan, May 15 was the date when the authorizing committees were required to report all legislation recommending new budget authority. Legislation reported after that date could be considered only if Congress adopted an emergency waiver. May 15 was also the deadline for the adoption of the first resolution which had to target:

1. total outlays (what could be spent during the fiscal year)
2. total budget authority (what could be spent in the current and subsequent fiscal years)
3. total revenues
4. surplus or deficit
5. public debt
6. subtotals by functional category (e.g., defense, health, education, etc.)

Prior to the adoption of the resolution, neither house could consider any revenue, spending, entitlement, or debt legislation. When the House and Senate versions of the resolutions did not agree (virtually always), differences had to be resolved in conference. An accompanying statement provided for the distribution of allocations to committees of the totals included in the resolution. This created the problem of "crosswalking," that is, translating the functions such as "agriculture" and "health" into agency and department appropriations accounts. The period between May 15 and September was designated for the appropriations process. Operating under the targets of the first resolution, the appropriations subcommittees engaged in their normal review of agency operations and approval of their budgets for the coming fiscal year. To help determine whether these spending decisions were in concert with the budget resolution, CBO engaged in a complicated scorekeeping process.

By the seventh day after Labor Day, Congress was to have completed action on all bills providing new budget authority. The second concurrent budget resolution was to be passed by September 15, reaffirming or revising the totals in the first resolution in light of the action of the spending committees. If the second resolution was at variance with these actions, the Budget Committees could produce a bill reconciling the totals with the previously enacted legislation. Reconciliation was to be completed by September 25, five days before the start of the fiscal year. The Budget Act prohibited Congress from adjourning for the session until the second resolution was approved. After passage, it was out of order to consider any legislation that would exceed the approved totals or reduce revenues. Congress could at any time approve a third or subsequent budget resolution amending previous decisions.

The process seemed complicated and cumbersome, and many were pessimistic about its successful implementation. Yet Congress for the first time would explicitly engage in macrobudgeting: approving aggregate totals for revenues and expenditures and voting on the size of the deficit or surplus. Congressional leaders agreed to a trial run in 1975 with full implementation in 1976. Unlike the bipartisan coalition that approved the Budget Act in 1974, subsequent actions by party leaders and voting patterns would reflect sharp partisan differences.

Budgeting in Congress, 1975–1980

Implementing the Process

By the time Congress first put its budget process to the test, Gerald Ford was in the White House. With Ford being unelected and relatively unpopular after the pardon of his disgraced predecessor, the resurgent Democratic Congress wanted to display its ability to help set the priorities of the nation. Ford was also hampered by the poor performance of the nation's economy. In 1974, unemployment averaged 5 percent, but the consumer price index (CPI) surged ahead by a postwar record of 12.2 percent, pushing the so-called misery index (inflation rate plus unemployment rate) to 17.2 percent. Inflation was spurred by the oil boycott organized by the Organization of Petroleum Exporting Countries (OPEC), and by worldwide food shortages. The economy slipped into the worst recession since the Great Depression, with unemployment peaking at 8.9 percent in April 1975.[41] The deficit soared to $53 billion, 3.5 percent of GDP, in FY 1975. It would be even greater the next year. While much consternation about the deficit was expressed, Democratic Party leaders were more concerned with the traditional approach of providing fiscal stimulus to get out of the recession.

Into this economic confusion and political uncertainty the congressional budget process was launched. In the House, the first Budget Committee chair, Brock Adams (D-WA), struggled to get majority support for the first budget resolution. The House Budget Committee (HBC) was less independent than its Senate counterpart because House reformers had made assignment to the committee temporary: members could serve only four years out of ten. Assignment to the committee was heavily influenced by party leaders and voted on by the Democratic caucus.

The first budget resolution taken up by the House contained a projected deficit of $70 billion, the largest in history to that date. As it was taken up on the House floor, Republicans and conservative Democrats lambasted the record deficit.[42] At the same time, liberal Democrats criticized the resolution for not providing enough stimulus to bring the economy to full employment.[43] Lacking any support from Republicans, the Budget Committee had to make the budget resolution generous enough on stimulus and social programs, and stingy enough on defense, to build a coalition of liberal Democrats. The first budget resolution passed the House by a narrow 200–196 margin, with only three Republican yea votes. Republican opponents were joined by sixty-eight conservative, mostly southern Democrats of the 265 House Democrats voting. Republican Party unity (percentage of members voting for the party position) on the vote was 98 percent compared to 74 percent for Democrats. This initiated a pattern of voting in the House that would continue through the 1970s.

The situation was different on the Senate side of the Capitol. With weaker majority party leadership, the institutionally more independent Senate Budget Committee (SBC), constituted with the same powers as other standing committees, took a more bipartisan approach in trying to shape the parameters of subsequent taxing and spending actions. This was made possible in part because of a bipartisan alliance between SBC Chair Edmund

Muskie (D-ME) and ranking minority member Henry Bellmon (R-OK). Within the committee, Republicans and Democrats both participated in determining the totals and subtotals, producing a resolution calling for a deficit of $67 billion, $6 billion below the House figure. While senators also complained about the record deficit, the bipartisan alliance in committee translated into a comfortable 69–22 margin of victory for the Senate's first-ever budget resolution in early 1975. Because Republicans voted 19–18 in favor of the resolution, and Democrats 50–4, final passage was not a party vote even under the 50 percent criterion. Ninety-three percent of Senate Democrats voted with the party, while Republicans were nearly evenly divided. The Conference Committee came up with a compromise resolution calling for a deficit of $69 billion, closer to the Senate figure.

House-Senate Differences

In addition to partisan voting and the participation of minority members in committee, House-Senate differences in using the budget process to impose spending restraints developed as the appropriations process operated for the first time under the targets. Adams and House Democratic leaders continued to proceed cautiously, concerned most about protecting the fledgling budget process. Muskie and Bellmon challenged several pieces of "budget-busting" legislation on the floor of the Senate and prevailed on several notable occasions. These were largely isolated cases, however. In the fall, few changes were made in drafting the second resolution since the totals largely reflected the actions of the spending committees. Despite the fact that the final vote in the House was a narrow two-vote victory, in late 1975, Congress had passed its first comprehensive budget.

What explains the House-Senate differences, particularly in terms of institutions and partisanship? Some scholars have argued that senators are more insulated from constituency pressures than House members because of their longer terms and larger geographical areas.[44] Since the SBC was constituted as a regular standing committee where members can accrue seniority, there were greater incentives for members to work to restrain partisanship and enhance the power and reputation of the committee. Divisions on the HBC were fostered by the selection of members. At the outset, Democratic Party leaders generally selected committee members who were reflective of the mixed preferences of the caucus, while Republicans chose members who were more conservative than the median Republican.[45] This meant that the HBC had three conservative southern Democratic committee members who voted with their own party in committee only 16 percent, 11 percent, and 5 percent of the time respectively.[46] In contrast, the lowest party support score for Republicans in committee was 89 percent. Subsequently, beginning in the 95th Congress in 1977, House Democratic leaders appointed more liberal members to the committee and removed two of the three southern conservatives. Republicans continued their pattern. The result was what Republican and Democratic members called "the most partisan committee in Congress."[47]

In contrast, members of the Senate Budget Committee were more representative of the ideological stance of their respective parties. Differences between the House and Senate were also attributable to informal leadership factors. The collegiality and cooperation between Muskie and Bellmon played a major role in establishing support for the committee and the budget process. In the House, ranking HBC Republican Delbert Latta (R-OH) set a precedent by using the budget process to attack majority Democrats and enhance the reputation of the Republican Party. Democrats were primarily concerned with writing a budget that could command majority support in the House.

Voting Patterns

Table 2–2 compares votes on the first concurrent resolution on the budget in the House and Senate during the first six years of the congressional budget process.[48] Each of the four caucuses produced a consistent voting pattern over this period. House Republicans tended to vote overwhelmingly against the resolutions, with the percentage of members voting with the party ranging from 85 to 98 percent. In contrast, although three of the six votes could be categorized as party votes using the 50 percent criterion, Senate Republicans showed virtually no party unity, dividing nearly evenly between yes and no votes. House Democrats had less solid party cohesion than their Republican opponents, with some 70 to 80 percent of Democrats voting with the party. There were two distinct blocs among the Democrats. The defection of from 44 to 68 members made passage of budget resolutions in the House rather tenuous. Senate Democrats were solid in support, averaging around 90 percent voting with the majority.

The election of Democrat Jimmy Carter in 1976 and the return to unified control after eight years of divided government had no discernible impact on the House-Senate differences or partisan divisions in Congress on budget measures. Carter was blamed for the first defeat of a budget resolution in the House in 1977. Confusion over the president's support for an amendment to increase defense spending undermined liberal support for the bill without

Table 2–2
Votes on first budget resolutions, 1975–1980*

	Date	Vote Yes–No	Republicans Yes–No	Democrats Yes–No
House	1975	200–196	3–128	197–68
	1976	221–155	13–111	208–44
	1977	213–179	7–121	206–58
	1978	201–197	3–136	198–61
	1979	220–184	9–134	211–50
	1980	225–193	22–131	203–62
Senate	1975	69–22	19–18	50–4
	1976	62–22	17–16	45–6
	1977	56–31	15–17	41–14
	1978	64–27	16–19	48–8
	1979	64–20	20–15	44–5
	1980	68–28	19–22	49–6

*Votes on committee report, first concurrent resolutions, as amended.

gaining any Republican or conservative support. The first resolution for FY 1978 was overwhelmingly defeated, 84–320. House Budget Committee Chair Robert Giaimo (D-CT) was furious. "It is not the Georgia legislature," Giaimo fumed at a press conference. "You don't just call up from downtown . . . and say, 'write a budget resolution.'"[49] The committee regrouped with the help of new House Speaker Thomas P. "Tip" O'Neill and created a liberal Democratic majority to narrowly enact a modified resolution.

The process faltered in the House again in 1979, in part because of the growing concern with reducing the deficit. Conferees on the first resolution reported a budget that reduced the deficit below the $30 billion in Carter's budget. In May, the resolution was defeated on the House floor because of the defection of liberals who claimed that their support for the budget process had been taken for granted for years. Led by the congressional Black Caucus, liberals revolted against the erosion of social welfare funding in the budget. A second Conference Committee made at least symbolic concessions in terms of the balance between defense and social programs, and the resolution finally passed. Serious divisions erupted again in September 1979. For the first time since the budget process was implemented, a second resolution was defeated on the House floor, and Congress could not pass a resolution before the start of the fiscal year. Only three of thirteen appropriations bills had passed. It took conferees until November to finally enact the congressional budget.

Growing Concern with Budget Deficits

Analysis of floor debates over budget resolutions in the House reveals four recurrent areas of conflict between 1975 and 1980. First was the issue of the size of the federal budget and its overall rate of growth, of primary concern to Republicans. Second was the classic question of guns versus butter: the balance of defense spending in the budget compared to money spent on domestic needs and stimulus to maintain full employment, a concern of Democrats. Third was the question of taxes. Particularly after 1978, Republicans, beginning to articulate a supply-side philosophy, argued that taxes were too high and were stifling economic growth, and they accused majority Democrats of a "tax and spend" philosophy. Finally, a great deal of debate dealt with the size of the deficit and its detrimental effects on the nation. This was an issue primarily for Republicans but also for a significant number of Democrats.

The concern with deficits seemed to grow in prominence throughout the late 1970s, particularly after the 1978 midterm elections—despite the fact that deficits actually *fell* between 1975 and 1979. The tenor of the congressional debate reflected concerns in the nation as a whole and concerns and events in the individual states. In particular, Republicans lauded the passage of Proposition 13 in California, which rolled back property taxes, as indicating a growing a tax revolt in the nation. In the next several years, a number of states followed suit, enacting a variety of tax and spending limitations. The environment was also affected by the campaign in the states to call a convention for the purpose of drafting a balanced budget amendment to the U.S. Constitution. By early 1979, some thirty states had approved legislation to convene such a constitutional convention. Although the budget process was not originally designed as a vehicle for fiscal restraint, by 1979, there was growing sentiment in Congress that deficit reduction should be its primary mission. There is some evidence that these developments in the states influenced the congressional agenda.[50]

In 1978, Representative Marjorie Holt (R-MD) introduced an alternative Republican budget, an amendment in the form of a substitute for the first budget resolution for FY 1979. It made substantial spending cuts, reduced taxes, and cut the deficit significantly. While Republicans had offered amendments to balance the budget in earlier years, they were used primarily as a means to portray majority Democrats unfavorably. The Holt amendment was more pragmatic and was taken seriously. It attracted fifty-eight Democratic votes and was defeated by only six votes, 197–203. The 1978 elections reflected a growing concern with high taxes and deficits. Republicans emphasized the theme of fiscal conservatism, and a number of Democratic incumbents defensively followed suit. Although the Democrats lost only three seats in the Senate and thirteen in the House, a change in the preferences of members was occurring. Many of the previous budget resolutions in the House had passed by fewer than thirteen votes, and a number of the newly elected Democrats had campaigned on a pledge of fiscal restraint and elimination of budget deficits. Under unified control of Congress and the presidency, Democrats were accountable for the size of spending, the level of taxes, and the size of the deficit.

The changing sentiment regarding the budget process and deficits was reflected in the use of the reconciliation provisions of the Budget Act. With the process largely moribund until 1979, Senator Muskie attempted to use reconciliation for the first time that year to roll back previously enacted spending. Because the standing committees in the Senate had exceeded the targets in the first resolution, the Senate Budget Committee voted on August 2, 1979, to report a reconciliation bill requiring seven committees to rescind $4 billion in FY 1980 spending.[51] Careful negotiations with the relevant committee chairs, including Appropriations and Finance, created bipartisan support for the reconciliation bill in the Senate. Although the savings were largely offset by increases in the defense number in the budget resolution, the reconciliation bill was touted as a deficit reduction measure and passed by a 90–6 margin. Across the Capitol, HBC Chair Robert Giaimo (D-CT), who had succeeded Adams, rejected the use of reconciliation, refusing to confront the powerful chairs of the spending committees. However, the Senate action paved the way for the first reconciliation bill the next year.

Democrats found themselves in an increasingly difficult budget situation in the election year of 1980. Inflation was raging, interest rates were rising, the economy was sliding into recession, and the projected deficits were once again on the rise. The deficit exceeded the previous record in FY 1980, reaching $74 billion, although at 2.8 percent of GDP it was smaller in real terms than it was in 1976. The sense that the deficit was out of control prevailed, however, since it was more than $40 billion greater than the amount specified in the budget resolution. Despite the concern with the deficits, there was growing pressure on President Carter and congressional Democratic leaders to make substantial increases in defense spending. The Soviet invasion of

Afghanistan and a growing perception of U.S. weakness abroad further confounded the budget situation.

The events in 1980 included an institutional change that would presage the battles of 1981 and fundamentally change the congressional budget process.[52] As concern with the deficit mounted, party leaders in the Senate decided to apply reconciliation to the first resolution. This change would be possible under the Budget Act's "elastic clause" which allowed for "any other procedure which is considered appropriate to carry out the purposes of this Act."[53] Using reconciliation at the beginning of the process greatly enhanced its effectiveness by reaching past spending actions as well as by controlling spending to be approved that year. It also had the effect of making the totals in the first resolution binding rather than targets. Republicans were enthusiastic about the idea, but it was the conversion of a number of liberal Democrats and the House majority leadership that ultimately brought about the change.

Both the House and the Senate Budget Committees included around $9 billion in reconciliation instructions in the resolutions they reported, requiring committees to either raise additional revenues or scale back spending. Democrats were divided over the tactic, but enough of them supported reconciliation to establish the precedent in a bipartisan fashion. Despite some instances of bipartisan cooperation to reduce spending, voting patterns remained partisan in the House. Republicans introduced legislation to cut taxes by 10 percent, following the lead of likely presidential candidate Ronald Reagan. It took a lame-duck session of Congress to finally enact the reconciliation bill. It passed on December 3, 1980, cutting $8.2 billion from the deficit.

Assessing the Early Budget Process

Simply meeting the timetable and procedural requirements of the Budget Act was no small feat. In general, more appropriations were approved in a timely fashion than before reform. The act was waived on a number of occasions, but not to the point of undermining the process.[54] With the Congressional Budget Office, the amount and quality of congressional information used to make decisions improved substantially.

The Budget Act also succeeded in balancing power between legislative and executive branches. The impoundment control provisions eliminated the massive withholding of funds witnessed during the Nixon administration, although the rescission and deferral processes proved cumbersome. In its first two years with the budget process under President Ford, Congress proved itself capable of making changes in the president's budget, cutting requests in some cases while adding substantially in others. During Carter's first year, congressional Democrats also proved they could accommodate a president of their own party by passing a third resolution in early 1977. Because of Carter's early blunders in the budget process, Congress remained eager to protect its own prerogatives throughout the rest of his term.

Despite the successes of budget reform, the overall impact of the new process on policies and budget priorities was marginal. Congress remained subject to the same budgetary constraints as the president in terms of the vulnerability of budget totals to economic changes and the growing inflexibility of spending because of entitlements. The relative budget shares of defense versus domestic spending changed little between 1975 and 1980, far less than it had during the previous five years. The impact of the budget process was particularly disappointing to those who saw it primarily as a mechanism of fiscal restraint. The rate of growth in outlays in both real and nominal terms was not reduced. Deficits as a share of GDP were larger on average under the budget process than in the previous decade.[55]

Majority party leaders and the Budget Committees, particularly the House committee, did not use the new rules to seriously impose discipline on the standing committees. In that sense, the committees largely accommodated the spending desires of other members of Congress. Until 1980, the binding second resolution was merely the sum of enacted legislation. While several notable votes were cast where the Senate was able to cut previously approved spending, on the whole, the overall numbers reveal that their decisions were very similar in content to those of the House.

The situation would change after 1981. Conflict between legislative and executive branches would increase, deficits would become chronic and even more divisive, and the congressional budget process would adapt in fundamental ways. Before turning to that analysis, I examine congressional attempts to restrain deficits by limiting the borrowing authority of the federal government.

Statutory Debt Limitation

If the federal government runs a budget deficit, it must borrow money to make up the difference, going into debt. For most of the twentieth century, Congress enacted statutes to limit how much the government can borrow. Ostensibly, a cap on borrowing should be a cap on running annual deficits, but it has not worked out that way. In testimony before Congress, a CBO official summed up the widely held perspective on statutory debt limits:

> Most analysts view the statutory limit of federal debt as archaic. . . .
> Voting separately on the debt is hardly effective as a means of controlling
> deficits, since the decisions that necessitate borrowing are made else-
> where. By the time the debt ceiling comes up for a vote, it is too late to
> balk at paying the government's bills.[56]

Evolution of the Debt Limit

Congress first acted to limit the borrowing authority of the Treasury in 1917
as part of the Second Liberty Loan Act as a means of consolidating the
Treasury's borrowing after the U.S. entry into World War I.[57] Until 1931, borrowing authority was virtually unchanged at a level of $43.5 billion. The exi-
gencies of the Great Depression and World War II greatly expanded the need
for federal borrowing, and few questions were asked during the war. After
World War II, Congress overwhelmingly approved a permanent debt ceiling
of $300 billion; it was lowered to $275 billion in 1946. This ceiling met the
nation's borrowing needs until the Eisenhower administration took office.
The debt subject to statutory limit since 1940 increased one hundred-fold, to
$5 billion by the 1990s.[58]

   The need to raise the statutory debt limit has become more and more common since the 1950s. The debt has risen faster; borrowing limits are reached
sooner and must be raised by larger and larger amounts. For example, the
limit increased only 2 percent between 1950 and 1955 compared to 120 percent between 1985 and 1990. In the early 1950s, the debt limit extension
lasted an average of thirty months. By the late 1980s, it was down to four
months. Since 1990, the debt limit has been extended for longer periods to
correspond to multiyear budget agreements. Because of the surpluses enjoyed
between 1997 and 2001, it was not necessary to raise the debt limit again
until 2002. But it has not yet been eliminated as a legal requirement.

Executive Oversight

The statutory debt limitation provided an opportunity to review and com-
ment on administration economic and budget policy and to oversee the
Treasury. Hearings gave members the opportunity to review specific borrowing practices and procedures and to question administration officials directly
on economic and budget policy. As one Republican representative observed

in the 1950s, "One of the reasons for the (debt) limit was so that we could reexamine the operations of the Secretary of the Treasury."[59] Legislators sometimes used the debt limit as a means to micromanage Treasury policy. In the 1970s, for example, Congress set a minimum interest rate on Series E savings bonds, increased the number of long-term bonds that could be sold above the statutory interest rate, and extended the maximum maturity of Treasury notes from seven to ten years.

Prior to the enactment of the Budget Act in 1974, debt limit bills were one of the few opportunities for assessing administration economic and budget policy. Unlike appropriations hearings, the debt limit hearings could be wider-ranging, allowing committee members to critique the overall economic philosophy and budget priorities of the administration. During the Kennedy administration, for example, during debate over extending the debt limit, fiscal conservatives criticized the administration for using the "federal budget as a tool for testing economic theories."[60]

The most common congressional response to administration requests to extend the debt limit as borrowing authority was about to expire was to reduce the amount of the extension. Although debt ceiling legislation became less important as a vehicle for executive oversight after the implementation of the Budget Act, Congress continued to give the administration less than it requested in the name of fiscal restraint, and it did so under both Republican and Democratic presidents. Of course, this was one of the main causes for the increasing number of debt limit votes in Congress. The House and Senate also tended to wait until the last possible moment to approve additional borrowing authority. On a number of occasions, disruptions in Treasury operations resulted. In the face of debt limit expirations, the Treasury has had to delay or postpone auctions, underinvest in Social Security and other trust funds, and, in one case, actually disinvest trust fund securities to meet the nation's bills.[61]

Debt Limit Voting and Party Control of the Presidency

Since the 1950s, the debt limit has provided an opportunity for political position taking, particularly for minority Republicans who made many impassioned speeches on the floor against the national debt and voted nay. Some members, like Representative H. R. Gross (R-IA), made a career out of his theatrical opposition to debt legislation and other measures related to deficit spending. In the 1970s, Congressman Ed Jenkins (D-GA) pointed out that the utility of debt extension votes for members depended on the party of the president:

> First of all, there is always the political aspect of it. I do not think any-
> one in this House has anyone writing them asking them to vote to extend
> the debt limit. . . . We really play a game with ourselves. When we have
> a Republican President in the White House, then many of the Democrats
> do not feel obligated to vote for the debt limit legislation. When we have
> a Democrat in the White House, few, if any, Republicans feel any obliga-
> tion whatsoever to vote for this legislation . . . [yet] all of us in private
> agree that this has to be done if the Government is going to continue to
> operate.[62]

Representative Barber Conable (R-NY), generally a moderate, spelled out
the partisan elements involved:

> I do not see any reason why on an issue of this sort, given its compara-
> tive lack of significance in terms of controlling the fiscal policy of the
> country, why the minority should be required to let those majority mem-
> bers who are from marginal districts have the benefit of voting against
> this bill politically, which you would have us deny to ourselves.[63]

However, analysis of voting patterns reveals that compared to Democrats,
House Republicans have overwhelmingly voted against debt limit extensions,
regardless of who was in the White House. The exceptions tend to be in the
first year after the presidency changed from Democratic to Republican.
Partisan patterns of support and opposition on debt limitation legislation
began to emerge during the Eisenhower administration. In 1953, Eisenhower
requested an increase in the debt limit because of the Korean War and defense
needs, but he was rebuffed by Senate Republicans who refused to report the
bill out of committee. Ironically, after the Democrats regained majorities in
the House and Senate, Eisenhower had an easier time extending the debt
limit.

Figure 2–1 summarizes party support and opposition on debt extension
votes between 1953 and 1990 in the House. House Republicans initially supported the requests of Presidents Eisenhower, Nixon, and Reagan after captur-
ing the presidency from the Democrats. In each case, however, support declined
steadily afterwards. For example, House Republicans supported Reagan in
1981 by a margin of 150–36. In every subsequent vote through 1990, however, a majority of House Republicans voted against the debt limit extension
despite the fact that the request came from a Republican administration.
Opposition was even more cohesive under Democratic presidents. After 1962,
in all but one case, 90 percent or more Republicans voted against extending the

Figure 2–1

Party support for debit limit extensions in the House, 1953–1990: percentage voting for extension.

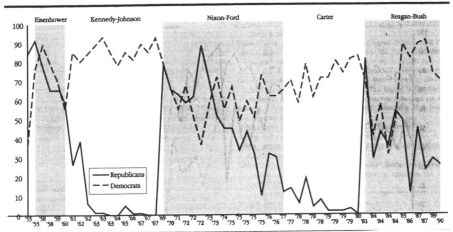

Source: Lance T. LeLoup and Linda Kowalcky, "Congress and the Politics of Statutory Debt Limitation," *Public Administration Review* 53 (Jan./Feb/ 1993): 25.

debt limit under Democratic presidents. House Democrats display a less cohesive pattern. Although support was less under Republican presidents, around 60 to 70 percent of House Democrats supported debt limit increases.

Figure 2–2 shows a somewhat different, less partisan, pattern in the Senate. Both parties showed less support for a president of the other party, but support in general was higher from Senate Republicans compared to their House counterparts. For example, about half of the Senate Republicans supported debt extension legislation under Kennedy, Johnson, and Carter. In contrast to the House, some 70 to 80 percent of Senate Republicans voted in support of the requests of Nixon, Ford, Reagan, and Bush. However, Senate Democrats' voting behavior changed notably after they lost their majority in the Senate in the 1980 elections. They took some solace in their new minority status in 1981 by exacting a measure of revenge on their Republican colleagues who they felt had grandstanded against the debt limit during the Carter administration. Democrats stood around the chamber with arms folded, waiting to vote until at least fifty Republicans voted in the affirmative. Overall, between 1981 and 1986, Democratic support for the debt limit ranged from zero to 40 percent in the Senate. When they reassumed the majority and the responsibility for governing in 1987, support returned to the 70 percent level, comparable to that of earlier periods.

Figure 2–2
Party support for debt limit extensions in the Senate, 1962–1990: percentage voting for extension.

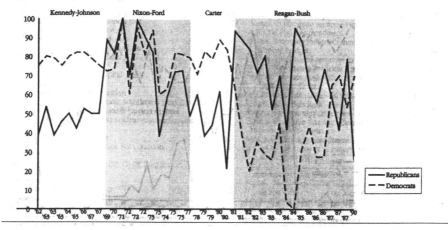

Source: Lance T. LeLoup and Linda Kowalcky, "Congress and the Politics of Statutory Debt Limitation," *Public Administration Review* 53 (Jan./Feb. 1993): 26.

Eliminating the Debt Limit Vote in the House

It was assumed that the congressional budget resolutions would be more effective in controlling deficits than the statutory debt limit since they were passed *before* the fact, not after. But, as we have seen, deficits still increased in the 1970s. In 1976, congressional leaders attempted to synchronize the statutory debt limit with the budget resolution and the government's new fiscal year. This and subsequent efforts failed, however, since the limit was reached sooner than expected or members would only support an extension of shorter duration. In 1978, the House Ways and Means Committee, which had jurisdiction over the debt limit, attempted to tie the limit directly to the budget resolution. The problem was that the concurrent resolution on the budget did not need the signature of the president, but the statute granting borrowing authority did.

In 1979, the House solved the problem by adopting an amendment by Representative Richard Gephardt (D-MO), eliminating the separate House vote on the debt limit. His amendment provided that the debt limit approved as part of the budget resolution would be inserted in a joint resolution deemed to be passed by the House. It was then automatically sent to the Senate to await final approval and the signature of the president.[64] Support for the change was strong, even attracting some Republican votes, as a vote to strike the amendment was defeated 132–283.[65]

Without the Senate adopting a similar change, however, separate votes were not eliminated in the House. If the Senate amended the joint resolution in any way, the House had to vote on the conference report. In cases where the limit was reached before expected, or there were delays in approving the budget resolution, separate House votes had to be taken. In 1981, two years after the Gephardt amendment was approved, the House cast twelve separate votes on the debt limit. The change did reduce the number of votes in the House compared to the Senate. Between 1979 and 1990, the House cast forty-eight roll calls on the statutory debt limit compared to eighty-one in the Senate.[66]

The Debt Limit as Must-Pass Legislation

The statutory debt limit is the ultimate "must-pass" legislation: Social Security checks would not be sent, agencies would close their doors, and the government could default on its existing debt if borrowing authority is not sufficient. Therefore, debt limit bills attracted a number of budget-related and -unrelated amendments. Initially, most amendments dealt with the mechanics of debt management or a reduction in borrowing authority. Since 1970, a wider range of amendments were proposed, in some cases to make the bills more palatable. In the early 1970s, on three occasions President Nixon tied large Social Security benefit increases to debt limit extensions.

Debt limit legislation was largely protected from amendment by party leaders in the House, and after 1979, the Gephardt amendment largely eliminated the problem of nongermane amendments. But in the Senate, debt limit legislation was not controlled by party leaders, and individual senators attached an assortment of legislation on them. Proposed amendments included invoking the War Powers Act, allowing school prayer, banning busing to achieve desegregation, freezing nuclear weapons, making money laundering a federal crime, and providing insurance to AIDS victims.[67] However, most of the nongermane amendments failed.

That was not the case for budget- and deficit-related amendments. Beginning in the late 1970s, the expiration of the statutory debt limit provided an opportunity to significantly change budget rules. Perhaps the most important was the Gramm-Rudman-Hollings mandatory deficit reduction bill that was adopted as an amendment to the debt ceiling in 1985 (see chapter 4). Other proposed rules changes would include constitutional amendments requiring a balanced budget, a federal revenue limitation, a limit on the president's rescission authority, a line-item veto, and a federal spending freeze.

Statutory limits on the national debt are a minor but instructive element in the evolution of congressional budgeting. They provided an early indication that explicit macrobudgetary votes in Congress had the potential to evoke sharp party cleavages. In particular, House Republicans found solidarity in enhancing their reputation as fiscal conservatives. The usefulness of the debt limit as an instrument for executive oversight or for challenging the policies of the president was greatly reduced after the adoption of the Budget Act in 1974. But debt limit votes as must-pass legislation were used to advantage as a vehicle for changing budget rules and the congressional budget process.

Conclusion

House/Senate differences were quite pronounced in the late 1970s in terms of the actions of party leaders and voting behavior. The most cohesive and partisan of the four caucuses, shown in voting on both budget resolutions and debt limits, were House Republicans. These votes gave voice to party positions on the size and scope of the federal budget and, later, to the need to cut taxes. House Democrats were a less cohesive party in the 1970s, and that is reflected in their voting patterns. One-fifth or so of the members voted consistently with the Republicans. The substantial size of Democratic majorities in the 1970s allowed party leaders to write more liberal budget resolutions that could hold the remainder of the party together, although it was often difficult.

On the Senate side, Democrats were as cohesive as House Republicans but far less partisan in their approach. Senate Republicans were the least unified, with half following the approach of their House colleagues of partisan opposition and the other half cooperating (or collaborating) with the majority to influence the shape of policy. In the more individualistic Senate, the initiative of Muskie and Bellmon helped postpone the partisan divisions that would emerge in later years. The content of the budget resolution in terms of key indicators, such as size of the deficit and percentage increases in defense versus domestic spending, reflect the policy preferences of those who voted in support of the resolutions. The pattern in the House provided some previews of what more partisan budgeting might look like, particularly in comparison with voting alignments on appropriation bills. From 1975 to 1980, all but one or two regular appropriations bills were passed by large, bipartisan majorities that would not meet the 50 percent criterion as a party vote.

Congress engaged in macrobudgeting, but the new rules did not provide majority party leaders the capacity to reshape policy, to impose discipline, or to override members' policy preferences. Speakers Carl Albert (D-OK) and Tip O'Neill (D-MA) were not particularly aggressive in using the process to constrain powerful committee chairs. The budget process in the 1970s was primarily an exercise in adapting to the timetable and new rules.

The new budget process did not significantly alter relations with the presidency or change the way in which bargaining took place. Divided or unified government does not appear to have been consequential in determining whether the budget timetable was met or in establishing voting alignments in Congress, and it appears to have had only minor effects on the content of policy. Under Ford, Congress met deadlines as well as or better than it did under Carter, but the one-year experience under Ford may be too limited for us to draw firm conclusions. Voting alignments were consistent regardless of who was in the White House. Under unified control beginning in 1977, Congress initially attempted to be more accommodating to Carter, but the budget process did not seem significant to the president. Many of these trends would change after the 1980 elections.

CHAPTER 3

Congress and the Reagan Budgets, 1981–1982

The 1980 elections brought significant changes to the presidency and the composition of Congress, changes that would produce a shift in the direction of budget policy in the United States. The election to the presidency of a conservative Republican advocate of massive tax cuts, the emergence of the first Republican Senate in twenty-four years, and the reduction of the size of the Democratic majority in the House would have profound consequences. With a sufficient number of conservative House Democrats consistently voting with Republicans, the administration was able to establish a stable cross-partisan majority in Congress on budget issues for two years.[1] The enactment of the Reagan budget and economic plan was one of the most significant macrobudgetary changes of the last thirty years. Reconciliation, moved to the beginning of the process, demonstrated its potential to reshape congressional power relationships in the hands of a cohesive majority. Congressional budgeting rules and processes were used to advantage by the Republican administration.

The enactment of the 1981 Reagan budget plan changed the shape and composition of the federal budget in the ensuing decade, with declining income tax rates and indexing, increased defense spending, and a shrinking share for discretionary domestic programs. But the most dramatic result was the emergence of deficits. The year 1981 marked the beginning of a new political prominence for deficits on the national agenda. It also signaled a change in party positions on budget deficits. A balanced budget was no longer the ultimate aim for some Republicans—deficits could be used to leverage certain favored policy outcomes. Reagan believed that deficits could be used to curtail the growth of spending:

> There were always those who told us that taxes couldn't be cut until
> spending was reduced. Well, you know we can lecture our children about

extravagance until we run out of voice and breath. Or we can cure their extravagance simply by reducing their allowance.[2]

To the extent that deficits became associated with the Republican administration, Democrats became more hawkish about their elimination.

Formulating the Reagan Plan

The 1980 Elections

For years Ronald Reagan had criticized big government, high taxes, wasteful programs, and deficit spending. Like many other candidates before and after, he promised, if elected, to balance the federal budget, and he had argued since the mid-1970s that it could be done by eliminating waste, fraud, and abuse. During the campaign, he hammered the Carter administration on these issues and the need to increase defense spending because of the weakness of U.S. military power that he claimed had developed under the Democrats. What looked like a close election only a week before voting day in 1980 turned into a rout. Reagan won a landslide victory, carrying every region of the country and virtually every demographic group except blacks.[3] While the meaning of any election is complex and often contradictory, Reagan and his people were quick to claim a broad mandate for their agenda.

The elections would prove significant for members of Congress as well, building on Republican gains in 1978. In the 95th Congress (1977–1978) the Democrats enjoyed a 149 vote majority over Republicans. The 1978 elections cut that margin to 117. The 1980 election further sliced the Democratic majority in the House to 51 votes, meaning that Republicans needed to attract only 26 conservative Democrats to gain a working majority. The change was even more sweeping in the Senate. The 1978 midterm elections cut the Democrats' majority from 62–38 to 59–41. The 1980 election swept the Democrats out of power in the Senate as the Republicans picked up 13 seats to gain a 54–46 advantage. For the first time since 1957, the Republicans would control a house of Congress. Not only was party control between legislative and executive branches divided, but now party control of the two houses of Congress was divided as well. In terms of policy preferences, the 97th would be more conservative than the two congresses that had preceded it.

The Reagan Budget Team

That Reagan's ideology was identified as "Reaganomics" was some measure of its departure from the ideas that had guided the political establishment for years, including within the Republican Party.[4] In it broadest terms, it represented a promise to reduce the size of government, to cut taxes, to bolster the nation's defenses, and to balance the budget. During the campaign, Reagan adopted the supply-side notion of a massive tax cut, most prominently promoted by Representative Jack Kemp (R-NY) and Senator William Roth (R-DE). From the start, the endorsement of Kemp-Roth created a potential contradiction in his agenda: how to eliminate deficits while slashing government revenues.[5] The supply-side answer was that tax cuts would generate economic expansion, and government would grow out of the deficits.

After the election, the promises of the campaign had to be translated into a set of concrete proposals to submit to Congress. David Stockman, former Republican congressman from Michigan, would become the chief architect and point man for the Reagan economic and budget plan. Stockman was intimately familiar with the nuances of the federal budget and the intricacies of the congressional budget process. Only weeks after the election, Stockman drafted a twenty-three-page memo entitled, "Avoiding a GOP Economic Dunkirk."[6] He argued that the budget changes needed to be incorporated into the fiscal strategy to avoid an economic crisis. In particular, he predicted that without substantial budget cuts to accompany the tax cuts, massive deficits would occur, and chaos in the financial markets would result. Alert to the changing party ideologies concerning deficits, he warned of a divisive schism within the Republican Party between traditional budget balancers and supply-siders. Such a cleavage would threaten the governing effectiveness of the administration, he argued.

The Dunkirk memo, written in large part to convince the president to name him as Budget Director, propelled Stockman to the forefront of the group preparing the economic and budget plan. Before Christmas, while nominees to cabinet and subcabinet positions were still being scrutinized, Stockman was already preparing detailed plans to slash their departments' budgets. Many of the cuts had been formulated earlier when he was in the House. Even though he was not in the president's "inner circle," he faced little opposition within the transition group, most of whom, like Reagan, were less oriented to the nuts and bolts of budgeting. Donald Regan, former president of Merrill Lynch, was named Secretary of the Treasury. His emphasis was on taxes and the upcoming tax cut. Casper Weinberger, former OMB Director, was named Secretary of Defense. To head his Council of Economic

Advisors (CEA), the president turned to Washington University economist Murray Weidenbaum. A microeconomist, Weidenbaum was a strong advocate of deregulation and getting the government out of the economy. He would play a major role in developing the economic forecast for the administration. Also critical to the formulation of the budget and economic plan were Reagan's closest political advisors, Edwin Meese, James Baker, and Michael Deaver.

Congressional Leadership

With the Republicans taking control of the Senate, Washington witnessed a transfer of power that had not occurred in a generation. Ranking minority members prepared to assume committee chairmanships, mindful of the treatment they had received in past years in the minority. Senator Howard Baker (R-TN) assumed the post of Majority Leader. Pete Domenici (R-NM) became chairman of the Senate Budget Committee (SBC). Democrats wondered whether the bipartisanship in budgeting nurtured over the previous six years by Senators Muskie and Bellmon, both out of the Senate, would continue.

The stance of the Democratic Party toward the Reagan economic and budget plan would be determined primarily in the House of Representatives, where they remained in the majority. Speaker Tip O'Neill organized the Democratic opposition to Reagan with less margin for defection than he had had in prior years. The "boll weevils"—conservative Democrats, mostly from the South—could hold the balance of power between the Republicans and more liberal Democrats. Democrat Phil Gramm of Texas, an old ally of Stockman, openly embraced supply-side tax cuts and many of the administration policies. Leadership of several key committees changed as well. Dan Rostenkowski (D-IL), a close ally of O'Neill, became Chair of the Ways and Means Committee. Moderate James Jones (D-OK) was narrowly elected by the caucus to head the House Budget Committee. The Democrats had to decide how and how vigorously to oppose the agenda of the president in a political environment that seemed to favor him.

Administration Proposals and Strategies

The transition team agreed that timing was of the essence. The plan had to be assembled and sent to Congress quickly while the president enjoyed his honeymoon and before entrenched interests had time to mobilize their congressional allies against the budget cuts. Stockman above all recognized the tension between fiscal restraint and the forces that propelled congressional spending. He originally suggested attaching a package of cuts to the debt ceiling bill that was coming up only weeks after the inauguration, but Republican leaders in Congress discouraged that suggestion.[7] Instead, Senate leaders and Stockman agreed to package the cuts in a reconciliation bill that would be moved to the beginning of the process, a strategy that would prove decisive. They also agreed to extend the scope of reconciliation to authorizations as well as entitlements to put permanent constraints on the congressional appropriators and make sure the cuts stuck. By making the cuts first through reconciliation, administration strategists and their congressional allies were able to convince traditional budget-balancing Republicans that the cuts would be sufficient to allow the big tax cuts without worsening the deficits. They would also need an optimistic economic forecast to make the numbers work.

The Reagan budget revisions would include some immediate changes in the current FY 1981 budget, major changes in the FY 1982 budget already submitted by Carter, and a set of multiyear tax and spending commitments through FY 1985. The package would include cuts in discretionary domestic spending and entitlements, a substantial increase in defense, and a cut in taxes over three years—all this while projecting a balanced budget by 1984. Each component had its own particular set of actors within the new administration and on Capitol Hill, with Stockman in charge of making it all come together. He was focused on discretionary spending cuts that he had been compiling for years. The administration purposely formulated their list of cuts before many high-level executive appointees were in place so that loyalty to the blueprint for cuts would not be compromised.

Entitlements presented higher political risks. The president was particularly sensitive about Social Security given its popularity and his own checkered record of support. Senate Republicans, Stockman, and others believed that the real spending problem could not be solved without curtailing the growth in entitlements. But Reagan's political advisors were worried about the Democratic advantages on this issue and wanted to be sure that their program was not perceived as penalizing the poor or elderly. They believed that the entitlement cuts should come at the margins rather than taking direct aim at basic benefits or cost of living adjustments (COLAs).

Along with tax cuts, the defense buildup was perhaps the top priority of the president, who in the campaign had effectively convinced Americans that the United States had fallen behind the Soviet Union in military might. Public opinion polls showed that nearly two-thirds of Americans wanted more defense spending. As a result, cost-conscious OMB had relatively little impact on this part of the plan. As opposed to the fine-toothed comb used to find cuts in domestic spending, the defense buildup was negotiated in terms of the percentage of real growth rather than specific programs. In his last year in office, President Carter had already called for a 5 percent increase in real growth, so, politically, the administration would have to do more. As one critic of the process later observed:

> The largest peacetime increase in defense in history was the product of an agreement between a few key Republican senators and the administration. . . . This approach contrasted with the approach taken in nondefense areas in which the entire gamut of domestic programs, as well as each foreign aid program, was subject to the line-item pruning of David Stockman. . . . The task of adding the extra money was simply assigned to the three military departments, all of which had long-standing shopping lists.[8]

Stockman unsuccessfully challenged Weinberger because of the president's strong predilections, but he contributed to the problem by making a mistake in the estimates.[9] Finally agreeing to an annual rate of real growth of 7 percent for FY 1983 and beyond, he did not take into account the "get well" package for defense for FY 1981 and FY 1982 that had already been agreed to. Building on this higher base, the annual rate of real growth in the president's requests to Congress was actually over 10 percent between 1980 and 1986. This decision would set the stage for many future confrontations between the Budget Director and Secretary of Defense when deficit projections worsened.

The tax cut was the cornerstone of supply-side philosophy. It would take the form of a 30 percent across-the-board cut in income taxes, the same as the Kemp-Roth proposal, for a cut of 10, 10, and 10 percent over three years. Taxes would also be reduced for business, such as by accelerating the time in which investments could be depreciated, to give society's producers more incentives to invest.

These points were raised on February 5, 1981, when Reagan went on television, only two weeks into his presidency, to prepare the nation for his budget and economic plan, even as Stockman was finalizing the details. In his "audit" of the U.S. economy, Reagan argued that the tax cut would actually increase revenues because of the amount of economic growth it would produce.[10] Finally, he held up two charts for the cameras, the first showing taxes and spending diverging into growing deficits under current policy, and the second showing them converging in several years into a balanced budget under his plan.

The speech was well received by the American public. The president spoke in general terms as his team developed the more specific elements of the plan that would be announced in less than two weeks. The administration needed an optimistic economic forecast—not one showing that the plan increased deficits, but one that would be credible. Weidenbaum, Stockman, and the other key advisors crafted a set of assumptions that Weidenbaum later called "extremely optimistic," but not "off the wall."[11] The forecast called for a robust recovery in late 1981 and 1982 with real economic growth at over 5 percent, double the historical average.

Even with the "rosy scenario" economic forecast, Stockman's numbers showed the package coming up some $40 billion short.[12] The solution was the infamous "magic asterisk": unspecified savings in future years from waste, fraud, and additional program cuts.[13] On February 18, Reagan presented his plan to a joint session of Congress and a prime-time national television audience. His package, under the revised economic assumptions, would slash spending by $41 billion and would reduce taxes by $54 billion for FY 1982.[14] He promised that the program cuts would be fair, preserving a "social safety net" for the truly needy. Among the programs targeted were food stamps, public housing, dairy price supports, federal employment, and mass transit; other grant programs would be reduced and consolidated into block grants. Two prominent campaign promises were not met in the outline of the package: the proposal to index tax rates to limit "bracket creep" and his promise to balance the budget in his first year. Projecting a deficit for FY 1982 of $45 billion, the goal of balancing the budget would not be achieved until 1984.

On March 10, the administration completed its economic and budget plan and submitted detailed budget revisions to Congress. Only defense was slated for increases. The administration claimed that its proposals would reduce the growth of spending to 6.2 percent compared to 11.6 percent under the Carter budget; revenue growth would be sliced from over 17 percent to 8.3 percent.[15] The ball was now in the hands of members of Congress who faced an intensive lobbying blitz from the administration to move quickly on the plan.

The Budget Resolution: Gramm-Latta I

Initial Senate Action

In the majority for the first time in a generation, Senate Republicans were eager to support the president, but they had some ideas of their own about the solutions to the nation's budget problems. Even before the budget resolution was approved, SBC Chair Domenici decided to move the spending cut agenda by delivering a reconciliation resolution outlining the cuts. On March 19, the Budget Committee reported out a bill instructing Senate committees to cut $36.4 billion from the FY 1982 budget, several billion more than in the president's plan.[16] In a surprising show of unity, the bill was reported by a unanimous vote of 20–0, with Democrats—acknowledging Reagan's popularity—deciding to let his proposals have a chance. This bipartisan unity carried through to the full Senate, which was debating the reconciliation bill on March 30 when Reagan was wounded by would-be assassin John Hinckley. Turning back a number of amendments to restore cuts made by the committee, the Senate voted to approve the bill on April 2 by a vote of 88–10.

Privately, however, Senate Republicans were frustrated in their attempts to achieve even greater savings by cutting entitlements, including Social Security. Domenici and his allies wanted to freeze COLAs, saving nearly $90 billion over the next five years. In a private meeting with the president on March 17, Reagan told the senators that he opposed the plan and asked them to join him in opposition.[17] The disappointed GOP senators abandoned their plan, but within a few months, as the numbers appeared more problematic, the administration would reconsider and propose a Social Security cut of its own.

Only a week after approving the reconciliation bill, the administration suffered a setback in the Senate, despite the president's soaring popularity after the assassination attempt. Marking up the budget resolution for FY 1982, the Senate Budget Committee opposed the proposed level of budget deficits by defeating the president's plan 8–12, with three Republicans joining the nine committee Democrats. During markup, committee Republicans were taunted for "no longer worshipping at the shrine of the balanced budget."[18] The three defectors opposed the $54 billion deficit projected in the Senate version. Democrats tried unsuccessfully to get the committee to use the less optimistic CBO forecast which would have made the deficits even bigger. Domenici adjourned the committee for the two-week Easter recess and a chance to regroup his troops.

House Action

The sustained Democratic opposition to the Reagan plan would come from the House. Although they were willing to concede much of the president's proposal, the majority party wanted to put their own imprint on the final version of the budget. Beginning with the concurrent budget resolution rather than reconciliation, the HBC began markup in early April. The main point of contention was the commitment to a three-year tax cut. House Democrats, because of worry about future deficits, wanted to limit the tax cut to only one year in this budget. The administration was adamantly opposed and issued orders to its supporters not to compromise or accept any amendments. "No administration has ever made such demands," Jones complained. "It is not the job of Congress not to think."[19] The HBC bill would reduce the FY 1982 deficit to $26 billion, even using more realistic economic assumptions. Reducing the tax cut allowed the Democrats to restore funds for a host of programs, including Medicaid and food stamps. Facing a Democratic alternative with a lower deficit, many thought that the president's plan was in trouble.

During the Easter recess, members went back to their states and districts to sample public sentiment. Support for the president's program remained strong. While Reagan recovered from the shooting, his administration continued the hard sell of the president's version of the budget. Tip O'Neill took a two-week trip to Australia and New Zealand, a move that later drew sharp criticism from his own party. One unhappy Democrat recounted, "We had the momentum going for our budget. . . . then Tip goes off on a junket. Meanwhile the White House is at work, they put on a real campaign, and we had only a half-baked effort."[20] The Reagan administration had assembled a highly experienced team of veterans to staff the legislative liaison office.[21] When Reagan met personally with wavering legislators, he was given detailed instructions on how to approach each member, including possible incentives. Meantime, the president continued to be extremely popular with the American people. When he appeared before a joint session of Congress in late April to appeal for his economic and budget plan, he received a thunderous ovation. "That was almost worth getting shot for," he joked.[22]

House Democrats were growing pessimistic about their chances as the floor debate on the budget resolution began. The main alternative was a version of the president's plan drafted by Stockman and Gramm. Democrat Gramm cosponsored the bipartisan substitute budget resolution with Delbert Latta, ranking Republican on the Budget Committee. The alternative became known as Gramm-Latta and was backed by the administration. It succeeded in reducing the deficit proposed by the president the month before to $39 billion by making additional spending cuts and using yet another set of economic assumptions. Several other budgetary "tricks" were used to get the crucial deficit number down. The Strategic Petroleum Reserve was moved off budget, and additional savings for "waste" were proposed.[23] Democrats lambasted these gimmicks and the use of further economic sleights of hand. On the Senate side, Domenici reversed the earlier defeat and reported a budget resolution that contained all of the crucial elements of the president's program. Republican defectors were brought back on board along with three Democrats by lowering the projected deficit through unspecified future savings. The stage was set for the first crucial votes on the Reagan plan.

Adoption of the Budget Resolution

As the House debate began, the Democratic leadership had all but conceded defeat. Despite their protests that the plan was the fiscal equivalent of believing in a free lunch, Gramm-Latta was adopted by a comfortable margin of 253–176 on May 7.[24] Sixty-three Democrats joined the unanimous Republicans in providing the victory. The final House resolution called for a deficit of $31 billion in FY 1982 and called for a balanced budget by 1984. In its first five years, the nonbinding first resolution had not played a significant role in shaping the policy actions of the spending committees. But it would in 1981 since it contained reconciliation instructions requiring the authorizing committees to come up with $36.6 billion in cuts by June 15.

Although his committee's plan was defeated, HBC Chair Jones pledged to enforce the reconciliation instructions in the resolution. If committees failed to meet the mandated cuts, the House Rules Committee would make the necessary statutory changes. Nonetheless, the Democratic leadership knew that the real battle—the vote that actually made the painful cuts—would come when the reconciliation bill itself came to the floor in June. They lost the first round but would have another chance.

With the outcome never in doubt, the Senate enacted their version of the budget resolution on May 12 by a vote of 78–20. Typical of the reaction of many Senate Democrats was that of Minority Leader Robert Byrd (D-WV). Although opposing many of its provisions, Byrd had announced before the vote that he would support the measure to give the administration its chance to govern. The Senate resolution called for a deficit of $51 billion and called for some $6 billion in cuts from entitlement COLAs. Despite the differences in the two versions, agreement was quickly reached in conference on a final resolution.

One of the main differences in the totals stemmed from discrepancies in the economic assumptions each body used, particularly interest rates. The House adopted the optimistic OMB assumption that interest rates would fall to 8.9 percent in FY 1982 (compared to the rates of over 15 percent that then existed). The Senate assumed a more reasonable 12 percent rate. Conferees simply split the difference at 10.5 percent.[25] The House and Senate passed the conference report by May 21. The authorizing committees were already struggling with the $37 billion in cuts to existing programs mandated by the budget resolution.

Gramm-Latta II: The Reconciliation Bill

The Administration's Social Security Proposal

Many Republican senators, a few Democrats, Stockman, and several other administration policy people still believed that the deficit problem would never really be solved without addressing entitlements. That inevitably led back to Social Security. Although Reagan had stressed the "social safety net" and had turned down the Senate Republicans less than two months earlier when they wanted to cut COLAs, the president was approached in May again. Stockman was becoming more concerned about how high the deficits might really be, and even Social Security's most ardent supporters agreed that the system would go bankrupt in 1982 if nothing were done.

The administration proposals to bail out Social Security and reduce the deficit in the process were developed by Health and Human Services (HHS) Secretary Richard Schweiker, who was eager to do something about the funding crisis. Stockman pushed the proposal he had originally omitted from the budget package: to raise the penalty for retiring between the ages of 62 and 65, making each retirement age actuarially equal, rather than in effect subsidizing early retirees.[26] Instead of 80 percent of benefits at age 62, retirees would receive only 50 percent of benefits. Other proposals included delaying and reducing future COLAs, phasing out the limitations on outside earnings, tightening up disability requirements, and eliminating "windfall" benefits for those who had worked only a few years.[27] The package would save $82 billion by 1986, and it even allowed the administration to promise that the 6.65 percent tax rate could be lowered by 1990.

The proposals were presented on May 11 to Reagan who approved them. But when the Legislative Strategy Group met later that afternoon, Reagan's political advisors panicked. Despite Schweiker's claim that there was some bipartisan support and Stockman's claim that they were essential to the economic plan, Baker and Darman tried to distance the president from them. They would be billed as a trial balloon from the Secretary of HHS and would be announced in Baltimore the next day. The ploy failed.

After the press conference, the outcry was loud and widespread. Speaker O'Neill called the proposals "despicable"; Representative Claude Pepper (D-FL) called them "the most fundamental assault ever" on Social Security.[28] Senior citizen groups were unanimous in their opposition. Nervous congressional Republicans repudiated the proposals. A week later, the Senate voted 96–0 to approve a resolution pledging to protect Social Security. Not only was the plan dead, but the Democrats had an issue that would carry well into the 1982 midterm elections. If the president had taken taxes and defense cuts off the table, the Democrats had taken Social Security off. Deficit reduction would be all the more difficult in the ensuing years.

The Reconciliation Battle

House and Senate committees complained publicly about the difficult task of meeting the budget cuts mandated in the resolution. A process of this magnitude had never been attempted before in Congress. Each committee worked on a baseline established by CBO and had to achieve the targets set in the budget resolution. Cuts covered three fiscal years, but only FY 1982 was binding. The administration had submitted detailed plans on how the savings were to be achieved, but committees were responsible only for arriving at the same total reductions. As a result, a number of the committees made changes in the administration's proposals. For example, the Ways and Means Committee adopted only $16 billion of the $30 billion in cuts specified by the administration, substituting a variety of alternatives to reach a total amount of $27 billion.[29] Stockman blasted the committee not so much for the shortfall but for not following the administration's "instructions." House Republicans and their allies threatened to propose a substitute bill. The "son of Gramm-Latta," or Gramm-Latta II, was born.

With a solid and loyal majority in the Senate, the authorizing committees essentially rubber-stamped the administration's proposed cuts. The battle would be in the House. The process in that body was particularly acrimonious as the authorizing committees struggled to meet the June 12 deadline to report their cuts. In the end, House Democrats gave the administration around 85 percent of the specific reductions they asked for. But it was not enough for the administration, and Stockman and Gramm proceeded with plans to offer a comprehensive substitute, effectively throwing out the painful work of the committees. Reagan and the administration lobbied hard for Gramm-Latta II. The president personally called all sixty-three House Democrats who had voted with him on the budget resolution.

Nonetheless, the House Democrats believed that, unlike the budget resolution, Gramm-Latta II would cut specific pet programs that members would fight to protect. They devised a divide-and-conquer strategy, agreeing to split the bill into six parts requiring six separate votes on the deeper cuts proposed by the administration. As the vote neared, O'Neill and the Democratic leadership believed they could muster enough votes to support their modified reconciliation package. On the evening of June 23, the Rules Committee voted 11–5 along party lines on a rule to consider the Omnibus Budget

Reconciliation Act of 1981 (OBRA-81) in six sections. Republicans were furious. The next day, in the one-minute speeches that precede legislative business, Republicans lashed out at the strong-arm tactics of the Democrats. The air was filled with epithets and accusations of "obstructionists," "king caucus rules again," "denial of rights," "a sham in the rules," "parliamentary dictatorship," "the tyranny of the majority," and "a Democratic wonderland."[30] Yet when the dust settled, it was the Democrats who were stunned and complaining about the destruction of the legislative process. By a vote of 210–217, unanimous Republicans and twenty-nine boll weevil Democrats reversed the Rules Committee, approving instead a rule that would consider the package as a whole, allowing one vote on the substitute amendment, Gramm-Latta II.

Stockman and Gramm worked furiously into the wee hours of the night to patch together the massive substitute bill. The bill was not even available until the next day, the day of the vote. It was so hastily prepared that the name and telephone number of a CBO staffer was accidentally written in the margin of the copies distributed to all members. Not even the sponsors were sure of what was in the final version, and members had only a few hours to review it. But the administration blitz was not to be stopped. Speaker O'Neill, in a rare floor speech, railed at the administration:

> I have never seen anything like this in my life, to be perfectly truthful. What is the authority for this? Does this mean that any time the President of the United States is interested in a piece of legislation, he merely sends it over? You do not have any regard for the process, for open hearings, discussions as to who it affects, or what it does to the economy? But because a man who does not understand or know our process sends it over, are we to take it in bulk?[31]

The House went on to approve the Omnibus Budget Reconciliation Act of 1981 (OBRA-81) by a vote of 232–193 and sent it to conference with the Senate. Conferees spent a month working out the differences. When the conference report came back to the House in late July, exhausted and defeated Democrats let it pass by voice vote. White and Wildavsky call Gramm-Latta II "the most sweeping legislation in modern American history."[32] It made cuts across a broad range of programs, reducing spending by an estimated $35 billion in FY 1982 and mandating nearly $100 billion in total cuts over three years. It reduced eligibility for food stamps, made cuts in welfare, narrowed eligibility for Social Security for college students, cut subsidized housing programs, reduced spending for school lunches, capped federal pay increases, reduced Medicaid payments, and created a series of block grants, consolidating and reducing total spending on hundreds of programs.

Ronald Reagan and the Republicans had won the second and most dramatic victory in his economic and budget plan. But as significant as those cuts were, they would not be enough to prevent deficits because of the third and final stage of the Reagan plan: the largest tax cut in American history.

Cutting Taxes: The Economic Recovery Tax Act (ERTA)

Competing Tax Plans

As with the budget resolution and reconciliation, congressional Democrats were willing to largely go along with the president on taxes, just not all the way. Most Democrats were in favor of some tax relief, particularly for the middle class, whose tax burdens had increased significantly with the high inflation of the 1970s. It was now the Democrats who were the party most worried about the impact of the tax cuts on the deficits and, as a result, did not want to lock themselves in to a three-year cut. House Democrats were determined to use any means possible to get their version of the tax plan through. That would mean using tax breaks—special provisions to benefit various interests—to woo members. But the administration would prove to be equally adept in a bidding war.

The administration originally engaged in negotiations with House Democrats to see if some compromise could be reached. The key player in Congress on taxes was Dan Rostenkowski (D-IL). Throughout the month of May and into early June, the administration expressed willingness to compromise with Rostenkowski and Democratic leaders. In the face of deficit worries, Reagan agreed to cut the original 30 percent across-the-board cut to 25 percent, 5–10–10 over the next three years. Most House Democrats wanted only a one-year cut, while Rostenkowski was willing to go for a 5–10 cut over two years. But the administration would not budge on the three-year cut. As they had with Gramm-Latta I and II, the administration decided to give up negotiations with Democratic leaders and formulate an alternative to the committee bill that they would offer as a substitute on the floor. The administration's package would be offered by Barber Conable (R-NY), ranking Republican on Ways and Means, and conservative Texas Democrat Kent Hance.[33]

The Conable-Hance bill would cut taxes in FY 1982 by $37.4 billion, some $17 billion less than Reagan's original proposals. It had reduced the amount not only by reducing the first year cut to 5 percent but by cutting back on some of the tax breaks for business in the original proposal. The accelerated depreciation provisions—the so-called 10–5–3 rules—were made less generous. But when business leaders reacted negatively, the administration strategists agreed to restore them after 1985, so the revenue loss would be beyond the three-year span of the budget. Other provisions of the revised administration plan included dropping the top rate on earned income from 70 percent to 50 percent, easing the "marriage penalty" in the tax code, liberalizing estate and gift taxes, expanding Individual Retirement Accounts (IRAs), and lowering taxes on Americans working abroad.

A Bidding War: "Hogs at the Trough"

The Reagan administration originally wanted a "clean" bill, bereft of the dozens of special-interest tax provisions that often plague tax legislation. But to counter the Democrats' bill, the administration gave up on this principle and opened up an all-out bidding war with the Democrats. David Stockman would later recount, "[T]he hogs were feeding at the trough."[34] Democrats were determined to make enough concessions in their bill to win wavering Democrats and perhaps a few Republicans. Rostenkowski's bill would cut $41 billion in FY 1982, more than the administration in the first year. But by defeating the three-year rate cut, their bill would lose less revenue over the long run. When negotiations with the administration finished, Rostenkowski switched from an across-the-board tax cut to one targeted at families earning less than $50,000.

While the administration was focusing on the House, Senate Finance Chair, Robert Dole (R-KS), took the opportunity to get tax indexing into the Senate bill. Tax indexing would tie tax brackets to inflation to eliminate "bracket creep," where taxpayers are pushed into paying higher rates even though their real income may not have increased. The Reagan administration supported indexing but did not include it in its original proposal. With deficit worries on the rise, indexing would result in even larger revenue losses. Once again, the solution was to push its effective date up to 1985, beyond the three years covered in the budget resolution. Indexing would become one of the most potent elements in ERTA.

As both the Senate Finance Committee and the House Ways and Means Committee marked up the tax bills, more and more deals were being made to win votes. Substantial tax breaks were dealt out to the oil industry to gain support of Texas, Oklahoma, and Louisiana Democrats. Tax credits for rehabilitating old buildings and woodburning stoves were handed out to entice

Northeastern Republicans. A tax credit for investing in television programs was tagged "the Gong Show amendment" by Dole.[35] Each amendment meant less and less revenue and bigger deficits over the coming years.

As the date for the floor votes on the tax bills approached, the Democrats still believed that their version had a chance. Those chances were probably dashed for good after Reagan made a nationally televised speech about his tax plan. "The plain truth is, our choice is not between two plans to reduce taxes, it is between a tax cut or a tax increase," the president said. "If the tax cut goes to you, the American people, . . . that money won't be available for Congress to spend."[36] Reagan asked viewers to telephone their members of Congress to express their support. Calls in favor of the president flooded the Capitol. A few days later, after more intense lobbying from the administration, the House passed the Conable-Hance substitute bill by a vote of 238–195. Forty-eight Democrats voted for the president's plan on July 28. The same day, the Senate version passed 89–11. The conference committee would hammer out the differences and remove some of the most egregious tax giveaways over the next week. On August 4, the Economic Recovery Tax Act was passed by both houses. Ronald Reagan had his third legislative victory in enacting his economic and budget plan.

The President's Impact on Congressional Budgeting

The enactment of the economic and budget plan was made possible by changes in the party composition of Congress, electoral considerations, and the policy preferences of members, but it was fostered by the strategies and actions of the Reagan administration. The president operated as if he had a mandate for change, even though public opinion on specific budget issues was mixed. For example, in 1981, the public preferred a balanced budget to a tax cut by a margin of 70 percent to 23 percent.[37] Although a large majority (over 60 percent) favored major increases in defense, most opposed specific cuts in domestic programs as well. Despite the disjuncture with public opinion on specific issues, overall support for Reagan and his general program was high. The president mobilized general public support for his program through his public appeals and the lobbying efforts of his congressional liaison office. His speech in favor of ERTA and the tax cuts was particularly effective. One analyst concluded that "everyone who saw the speech knew that it was a blockbuster."[38] Reagan himself believed that this speech had generated more support than any speech he had ever delivered.

The Reagan administration largely set the agenda of national politics during the first eight months of 1981, focusing congressional attention on the economic and budget plan. The social agenda, with controversial issues such as school prayer, was postponed to later years. In this regard, 1981 marked the beginning of new era of budgeting, where the federal budget increasingly became a major focal point for national politics and the main vehicle for policy change. The president made some concessions but was able to bargain within his congressional majority without resorting to the veto or veto threat. That would change in the fall of 1981. The administration was initially willing to deal on the tax bill but drew a line in the sand on its proposed budget cuts in Gramm-Latta I and II. Even on the tax bill, the president held firm at the end. William Lammers concludes, "[H]ad Reagan been more cautious, there would have been a different final package."[39]

Perhaps most significantly, the events of 1981 demonstrated that the new congressional budget process, designed to strengthen Congress vis-à-vis the president, could in fact be a powerful tool for presidential leadership given disciplined, supportive majorities in both houses. There would be a reaction against Reagan's legislative victories by House Democrats after they increased their majorities in the 1982 elections.

Dealing with Deficits

The Deteriorating Budget Situation

In August, President Reagan flew off to his California ranch, and Congress went into recess. But the FY 1982 budget was not history yet, as deficit projections ballooned only weeks after the vote on ERTA. The economic assumptions proved even more inaccurate than expected: inflation was falling and unemployment rising as the recession took hold. The projected $35 billion deficit was reestimated to over $100 billion that year. It became clear that entitlement growth, technical estimation errors, and economic factors could reshape budget numbers as much as tax bills or reconciliation.

In the face of the gloomy budget numbers, the administration went back to the Congress with a set of additional spending cuts. October 1, 1981, the first day of the fiscal year, arrived with no second budget resolution and no appropriations bills enacted. The administration tried to use the continuing resolution (CR) necessary to keep the government running to extract more spending cuts from Congress. Republican leaders in the Senate delayed action on spending bills while the House Democrats attempted to regroup.

The administration's credibility was damaged when William Greider's embarrassing interview with David Stockman was published in *The*

Atlantic.[40] In it, Stockman admitted that the administration had known all along that the numbers were cooked but had proceeded anyway. He suggested that supply-side economics was nothing more than the old "trickle down" theory of helping the rich. He acknowledged battles with Weinberger over the defense numbers and disparaged fellow Republican Delbert Latta, noting that he was "pouting" because his name came second on Gramm-Latta. The article almost cost the budget director his job, but a repentant Stockman was "taken to the woodshed" by Reagan and remained in his job.

When the first CR expired in November, Reagan vetoed the extension passed by Congress. This was his first veto as president and caused nonessential federal offices to shut down. Congress passed a three-week CR to avert the immediate crisis. The House and Senate then passed a massive omnibus appropriation bill funding the government through March 1982 and imposing an additional 4 percent across-the-board cut in domestic spending.[41] There was no chance of passing a meaningful second resolution, so Congress simply ratified the numbers in the first budget resolution passed in May, even though the figures were by then wildly inaccurate.

The Deficits

Perhaps the most controversial legacy of the Reagan budget and economic plan was the deficits that followed. The FY 1982 deficit reached $128 billion, and the next year, it reached a record-setting $207 billion, or 6.3 percent of GDP. The 1983 deficit meant that one of four federal outlay dollars was borrowed. The deficits remained near $200 billion and 5 percent of GDP through the middle of the decade, finally leading to the passage of Gramm-Rudman-Hollings, examined in the next chapter. It was a long way from the promised balanced budget.

Explanations of the deficits are controversial and generally partisan: They occurred because of the defense buildup; the large tax cut; the recession which increased the cyclical deficit; the failure to control the growth of entitlements, particularly Social Security, Medicare, and Medicaid; and the fact that the domestic spending cuts were unable to compensate for these other forces. The tax cut significantly reduced projected federal income tax revenues, an estimated loss over five years of over $700 billion.[42] Without other tax increases enacted in subsequent years to replace some of the cuts, ERTA would have left income taxes at 13.5 percent of personal income in 1988, compared to 18.5 percent without it.

The deficits were the result of more than the tax cut. C. Eugene Steuerle notes that much of the 25 percent reduction in individual rates simply overcame the effects of inflation in prior years.[43] Even in 1984, at their lowest point in the decade, individual income tax receipts never went below the level of 8 percent of GDP where they had stood as recently as 1976.[44] Steuerle concludes that "the major individual reform instituted in 1981 was not the direct reduction in tax rates, but the establishment of indexing of tax brackets, including, after 1984, what might be viewed as a zero bracket."[45] Indexing would make the problem of deficit reduction more difficult in the later years of the decade because receipts no longer automatically increased as general price levels rose.

Hamn, Kamlet, and Mowrey have found that the state of the economy and increased defense spending explained most of the variance in postwar U.S. deficits.[46] The cyclical portion of the deficits was a result of the budget's sensitivity to changes in the economy. Unemployment peaked at 10 percent in late 1982, accounting for over $100 billion of the deficit compared to an economy at 6 percent unemployment. The structural portion of the deficits that emerged in the 1980s was also a function of the large defense buildup undertaken in 1981 through 1985. Although the original $1.8 trillion buildup was never achieved, the defense budget went through five years of nearly unprecedented peacetime levels of real growth. When confronting the bad budget news only weeks after his three-part victory in 1981, Reagan told his closest advisors, "If it comes down to balancing the budget or defense, the balanced budget will have to give way."[47]

In addition to the tax cut, the defense buildup, and the recession, the deficits grew because the spending cuts were insufficient to stem the tide of red ink. In particular, the failure to curb entitlements, and health care costs in particular, kept mandatory spending on an upward trend. Defense spending increased by more than 50 percent between 1980 and 1983, growing to 25 percent of the budget and 6.3 percent of GDP. Domestic discretionary spending fell from 21 percent to 15 percent of the budget in little more than two years, dropping to under 4 percent of GDP. At the same time, entitlements continued to grow, up $119 billion, to nearly half of all outlays and 12.4 percent of GDP. The administration had succeeded in shrinking domestic discretionary spending, but in the face of large increases in entitlements and defense and falling revenues, big deficits were the result.

TEFRA 1982: The First Deficit Reduction Plan

Reagan would largely maintain his cross-partisan coalition in 1982, but the congressional budget process was different in several ways from the prior year. The FY 1983 budget submitted in January 1982 called for a deficit of $90 billion, only a fraction of the $208 billion it would actually reach.

Stockman later confessed, "I out and out cooked the books, inventing $15 billion per year of utterly phony cuts."[48] Even so, the deficit was too large for Congress to accept. As he had in the fall, the president turned to the veto and veto threat to cut spending, refusing to sign two supplemental appropriations bills in late spring of 1982.

The year 1982 would mark the beginning of a trend in the 1980s to rely on ad hoc negotiating groups and other forms of extraordinary resolution. In 1982, the so-called gang of seventeen, a group of negotiators representing the administration and the four congressional caucuses, tried to find some compromise package to reduce the deficit. Their efforts failed. Reagan at first remained adamant against a tax increase or curtailing the defense buildup; House Democrats opposed further domestic cuts and had effectively taken Social Security off the table. Both would have to compromise those positions because of the severity of the deficits.

After months of wrangling, the same coalition of Republicans and boll weevils united to pass a budget resolution in the House which was opposed by the Budget Committee and Democratic Party leaders. The Senate passed a similar plan, and conferees worked out the differences in a budget that attempted to cut $378 billion from the projected deficits over the next three years. Fearful of public reaction, members used budgetary tricks to make the deficits look smaller. Economic assumptions were manipulated, predicting lower interest rates and payments, and nearly $50 billion in deficit reduction was accepted in the form of unspecified management savings.[49]

While the deficit reduction package in 1982 supposedly cut three dollars of spending for each dollar of additional revenue, the largest single component of the deficit reduction package was a tax hike: the $100 billion Tax Equity and Fiscal Responsibility Act of 1982 (TEFRA). At the same time that the second year of Reagan's tax cut was going into effect, the president was convinced to accept a variety of other revenue-raising measures to stop the explosive growth of deficits. This was not a retreat, the president claimed. In a speech supporting TEFRA, he claimed that he was forced to accept some modest tax increases in order to get even larger spending cuts.[50] The president would later claim that the Democrats had reneged on the three-for-one deal, hardening his opposition to further tax increases to reduce the deficits.

In reaction to unhappiness with reconciliation in 1981, the spending cuts in 1982 were not voted in a single package. This represented a strategic victory for House Democrats who were able to limit the additional domestic cuts. The Appropriations Committees played a more significant role in 1982 than they had in 1981, although they still felt unjustly constrained by the budget process.[51] The House vote on the budget resolution in the House in

1982 was closer than in 1981, because thirty Republicans defected in response to the tax increases (see table 3–2). The vote in the Senate was much closer than the year before because Democrats, who had split in 1981, voted against the administration as a bloc in 1982.

The 1982 elections would eliminate the cross-partisan presidential majority for Reagan. With each party losing only one incumbent and one open seat, the Republicans maintained their 54–46 majority in the Senate. But in the House, the Democrats defeated twenty-two Republican incumbents and picked up six open Republican seats, increasing their majority to 103 seats.

As part of the growing deficit crisis, the president and the 98th Congress would have to deal with the impending insolvency of Social Security, a task that was postponed until after the 1982 elections. Both branches used another form of extraordinary resolution to solve this problem—a bipartisan commission.

The Social Security Bailout

In February 1981, CBO had predicted that Social Security would run out of money by 1983, even though President Carter and Congress had supposedly placed the program on sound financial footing only four years earlier.[52] Democrats had made the issue partisan, hammering Reagan with it in May of 1981 and using it effectively against Republican candidates in the 1982 elections. By fall of 1981, studies showed that unless remedial action were taken, the trust fund would run a deficit of $1.5 trillion over the next seventy-five years.[53] Seeking political cover for the tough decisions of raising taxes or lowering benefits, in September 1981, Reagan appointed a National Commission on Social Security Reform, headed by economist Alan Greenspan. The fifteen-member commission consisted of five members appointed by Speaker O'Neill, five by Majority Leader Baker, and five by the president.

The Greenspan commission included partisans on both sides of the issue, including elderly advocate Claude Pepper (D-TX).[54] They could not reach any consensus, and even after the elections, they remained as politicized as ever. Greenspan finally asked for direct participation by Reagan and O'Neill. With their support, secret meetings between Stockman, Senator Daniel Patrick Moynihan (D-NY), and O'Neill's personal representative led to the selection of a group of nine more moderate members of Congress and the administration who would meet in private and hammer out a compromise. In January 1983, this small group came up with a package of benefit cuts and tax increases that both Reagan and O'Neill could live with. It delayed annual

COLA increases for six months, raised the retirement age, restricted eligibility, and expanded coverage to new federal employees (which increases revenues and does not require payments for many years). Although the plan drew the criticism of groups representing the elderly, the bipartisan bargain held together in Congress. Although it did not solve the deficit crisis, the Social Security bailout created surpluses in the trust fund through the end of the century.

Parties and Budget Rules

Voting Patterns

Not only did Republicans replace Democrats after the 1980 elections, but they tended to be more conservative Republicans. The Democrats who remained were more liberal than in the preceding congresses.[55] This was part of the gradual trend in the 1980s and 1990s that would create congressional parties with greater intraparty cohesion and interparty conflict. Not only did the median Republican score decline, but the range and standard deviation of scores also declined, indicating fewer outliers in terms of ideology.[56] In power for the first time in a generation, Republicans knew that their ability to govern depended on their ability to vote as a bloc. How well they succeeded is shown in Table 3–1, which compares three key votes on the 1981 budget and economic package in the House and Senate. Republicans in both chambers voted with near unanimity with the party position and the president. This pattern was consistent for House Republicans within the 1975–1980 period, but it represented a change for Senate Republicans who had been divided. The more conservative budget policy was preferred by the Republican senators who had opposed the budget resolutions under the Democratic majority.

The Democrats present a different picture. Voting patterns by House Democrats were consistent with the previous five years, except that they were now voting against the resolutions. In much of the media coverage of congressional budgeting during June and July of 1981, Democratic leaders were portrayed as weak and ineffective for failing to craft a majority of their own. Perhaps the Democratic leaders in the House could have done a more effective job, and Tip O'Neill's trip to Australia may have been ill-timed. But comparing the voting patterns to those of the previous six years (see chapter 2), one sees no significant departure in the party voting alignments. The Democrats routinely had 20 to 25 percent of its members defect from the party position in the prior five years. The two most unified votes for

Table 3–1

Key votes on Reagan's economic plan in the House and Senate

Measure	Date	Vote	Republican	Democrats	Northern Democrats	Southern Democrats
House:						
Gramm-Latta I Substitute 1st Resolution FY 1982	5/7/81	253–176	190–0	63–176	17–144	46–32
Gramm-Latta Substitute Omnibus Reconciliation Bill of 1981	6/25/81	214–208	188–0	26–208	4–157	23–55
Conable-Hance Substitute Economic Recovery Act of 1981	7/29/81	238–195	190–1	48–194	12–151	36–43
Senate:						
1st Resolution FY 1982 Committee Report as Amended	5/12/81	78–20	50–2	28–18	14–17	14–1
Omnibus Reconciliation Bill of 1981 Committee Report as Amended	6/25/81	80–15	52–0	28–15	13–15	15–0
Economic Recovery Tax Act of 1981 Committee Report as Amended	7/29/81	89–11	52–1	37–10	24–8	13–2

Democrats were in 1976 and 1978 when 85 percent of Democrats voted with their party on a second resolution. In losing the vote on Gramm-Latta II, the reconciliation bill, Democratic defections dropped to 12 percent, the lowest since the budget process began.

Senate Democrats, like Senate Republicans, exhibited different cleavages in the minority compared to in the majority. Unified between 1975 and 1980 in voting for budget resolutions, in 1981 the Democrats generally went along with the president by a 2–1 margin. Only ten Democrats voted against ERTA. The president's proposals were popular, and most Senate Democrats wanted to be on the winning side.

Party Leaders and Party Differences

Aggregate party vote totals can conceal shifting votes by members within apparently stable totals. In fact, only ten Democrats cast inconsistent votes on the rule and final passage of Gramm-Latta I, and they canceled each other out, leaving totals nearly identical.[57] Despite the fact that majority Democrats in the House lost, they were extremely active in trying to maintain party discipline. Some of the larger vote margins may also be somewhat deceptive. Speaker O'Neill said just before the vote on Gramm-Latta I that "we'll either win it by five or six votes, or lose it by sixty, because if you start to lose it, the swing will come."[58] They lost by 77. The loss was less a failure of party leadership than a matter of numbers after the 1980 elections which cut the Democratic majority in the House to 51. The Republican budget "revolution" was less a change in voting behavior by Republicans and Democrats in the House and more a change in their shares of seats.

In their analysis of the 1981 budget plan, Brady and Volden emphasize the outcome to the presidential election and the shift in the "veto pivot" from Carter to Reagan: "No longer would the threat of a Presidential veto extend the gridlock region to the left: now the region would extend toward the conservative preferences of Ronald Reagan."[59] However, upon closer inspection of Democratic and Republican plans, one could argue that the policy differences between the competing packages in all three key stages were not that great. Both plans would have shifted budget policy significantly in the direction advocated by the president. Democrats were prepared to give the president most of what he wanted. For example, the Democratic reconciliation bill contained perhaps 85 percent of the cuts the administration requested. The major difference on the tax bill was mandating the third-year cut. And after the bidding war, the Democratic version of the tax bill would have reduced federal revenues by an estimated $706 billion over five years compared to $732 for the version of ERTA backed by the administration.[60] Within the apparent unity of Republican members were significant internal differences between supply-siders and traditional fiscal conservatives worried about deficits. However, the impulse to support the program of the Republican president prevented defections. What was unusual about 1981 and 1982 was the fact that a coalition of Republicans and Democratic defectors essentially wrested control of the budget process away from the official Democratic leaders of the House. It has not happened since under either party.

The differences in how Congress responded to microbudgeting and macrobudgeting in 1981 and 1982 are apparent again when one compares voting patterns on the budget resolutions to voting on appropriations. Of the eleven House and eight Senate roll-call votes on final approval of an appropriation bill in 1981, only two votes could be classified as a party vote under the minimum criterion of a majority of one party opposing a majority of the other.[61] These two cases were House Republicans opposing the State, Justice, Commerce Appropriation Bill by 69–104, and the Foreign Aid Appropriation by 84–87. On all other votes, both parties voted overwhelmingly for the spending bills. Despite the high level of conflict between parties on the budget resolution, the reconciliation bill, and tax cuts, individual appropriation bills continued to reflect traditional patterns of bipartisanship and consensus.

Budget Rules

While there is some dispute over who had the idea first, the decision to move reconciliation to the beginning of the process was instrumental in strengthening the congressional budget process and facilitating the enactment of the

Reagan budget package. The language of the Budget and Impoundment Control Act of 1974 makes it clear that reconciliation was intended to occur at the end of the process, related to the binding totals, not to the targets of the first resolution. It was possible to move reconciliation using the "elastic" clause of the act.[62] The other critical change, the application of reconciliation to authorizations, was accomplished by a precedent set the year before. Section 310 of the act provided that a budget resolution may specify the way in which budget authority "is to be changed and [may] direct that committee to . . . accomplish a change of such total amount." Senator Robert Byrd, one of the framers of the act, argued during the debate on Gramm-Latta II that reconciliation should apply only to spending authority, but the broader precedent had been established the year before when the Democrats were in the majority.

Reconciliation was extremely unpopular with committee chairs because it severely challenged their power and discretion. In a sense, reconciliation at the beginning reversed the normal legislative process. A majority on the floor threw out the work of the committees and forced cuts in programs under their jurisdiction. Because of the rules that govern its floor consideration, it would emerge in the 1980s as one of the strongest majoritarian institutions of the legislative process.[63] After 1982, it would be a tool of the majority party, not a cross-partisan majority.

Congressional Budgeting, 1983–1984

Budget rules continued to evolve in the early 1980s. The president's FY 1984 budget projecting a deficit of $190 billion was sent to Congress in January 1983.[64] Reagan opposed tax increases of any kind and refused to retreat on defense. With their larger majority after the 1982 elections, House Democrats refused to go along with further domestic cuts and took aim at the defense buildup. Reagan's FY 1984 budget was pronounced "DOA" or "dead on arrival." Disgusted with the process that had served him so well in 1981, two years later Reagan denounced the congressional budget process as "Mickey Mouse" and suggested that it be abandoned. The second resolution had been rendered moot in 1981 when reconciliation was moved to the beginning of the process. In 1982, Congress had agreed to simply declare the numbers in the first resolution binding if no second resolution was passed. The congressional budget was now specified in a single resolution.

Despite their strong party unity during the first two years of the administration, Republicans publicly showed some internal divisions by 1983. The

Table 3–2
Votes on budget resolutions, 1981–1985

	Year	Yea-Nay	Republicans	Democrats
House:	1981*	253–176	190–0	63–176
	1982	219–206	156–32	63–174
	1983	229–196	4–160	225–36
	1984	250–168	21–139	229–29
	1985	258–170	24–155	232–15
Senate:	1981*	78–20	50–2	28–18
	1982	49–43	46–2	3–41
	1983	50–49	21–32	29–17
	1984	41–34	40–3	1–31
	1985	50–49**	48–4	1–45

*Vote on first resolution.
**Vice President George Bush cast the vote that broke a 49–49 tie.

supply-siders preferred to tolerate the deficits rather than accept any tax increases, while the traditional fiscal conservatives believed that the deficits had to be brought down at any cost, including tax increases. Many Republican senators were upset with Reagan's intransigence and resented his attacks on their institutions. Their party split badly in 1983 as shown in table 3–2, which examines the votes on the budget resolutions from 1981 to 1985. The budget resolution in 1983 was adopted by a margin of 50–49, with twenty-one Republicans joining twenty-nine Democrats to pass a compromise resolution. A conference agreement was finally passed on June 23. In 1984 and 1985, Senate Republicans patched up their internal differences and returned to more cohesive voting patterns.

After the 1982 elections strengthened the majority enjoyed by House Democrats, the nature of the relationship between Congress and the president took on new characteristics as well. Most years were characterized by some sort of ad hoc budget summit between executive and legislative branches to reach final agreement on budget totals. At the time, changing congressional budget procedures and extraordinary means for resolving differences with the White House appeared to reflect procedural chaos. Many were critical of the process inside and outside of Congress. But in retrospect this period of evolution and experimentation can equally be seen as institutional adaptation and innovation as congressional Democratic leaders tried to strengthen their control of budgeting and increase their negotiating strength with the president.

The budget process went through a period of particular instability and uncertainty between 1982 and 1985. House-Senate negotiators were unable to reconcile their versions of the budget resolution for FY 1985 and finally gave up. Each chamber proceeded with appropriations using the figures and economic assumptions in their respective versions. Confident of reelection in 1984, Reagan increased his assault on the "big spenders" in Congress and refused to raise taxes to reduce the deficit. Walter Mondale's promise to raise taxes to cut the burgeoning deficits played into the incumbent president's hands. By the end of September 1984, no budget resolution and only four of thirteen appropriations bills had been adopted. Key authorizing bills had not cleared. By October 1, a massive continuing resolution was necessary to keep the government operating. This pattern was becoming more prevalent.

The omnibus spending bill became a vehicle for scores of bills that had been bottled up in the 98th Congress. Amendments included a comprehensive crime bill hundreds of pages long, foreign aid, aid to the Nicaraguan Contras, food stamps, public broadcasting, home rule for the District of Columbia, and dozens more. President Reagan threatened to veto the bill. After a four-day stop-gap bill expired, the president again sent nonessential federal workers home. A twenty-four-hour extension was enacted as Congress worked through the night. Senator Patrick Leahy (D-VT) pleaded to "free the Senate 100."[65] Finally, on October 12, after four temporary stop-gap bills, Congress adopted a massive continuing resolution for FY 1985. Massachusetts Republican Silvio Conte called the bill "753 pages of primal urge," but few were amused.[66]

The budget rules that seemed effective at imposing discipline seemed increasingly uncertain and ineffective in reducing record deficits. Committees and subcommittees found ways around budget resolution constraints. Supplemental appropriations were increasingly used to avoid the discipline of the budget rules. Fewer appropriations bills were passed on time, and an increasing number that did pass had no authorizations, in violation of House and Senate rules. Omnibus spending bills combining authorizations, appropriations, budget resolutions, and revenue measures were common. The second resolution was abandoned. Nonetheless, reconciliation, despite the conflict surrounding it in 1981, was used again in 1982 and 1984 and had become a critical element for establishing fiscal restraint in budgeting.

Despite consternation over the lack of orderliness in congressional budgeting, reconciliation and omnibus legislation strengthened those who controlled access to the bills: the party leaders and the few chairs of the money committees. The House moved to what some called the "four bill" system which encompassed most legislation: the budget resolution, the reconciliation bill, continuing resolutions, and supplemental appropriations.[67] The Senate was inevitably drawn into using the same legislative vehicles. Omnibus taxing and spending bills provided an instrument for more centralized budgeting and more effective negotiation with the White House. It also weakened committees and subcommittees, leading Congress away from the "subcommittee government" that had characterized the 1970s.

Member dissatisfaction with the situation led to calls for change. Task forces of both the House Rules Committee and House Budget Committees proposed formal revisions of the budget process. David Obey (D-WI) proposed institutionalizing a single omnibus appropriations bill. On the Senate side, a select committee chaired by Dan Quayle (R-IN) looked at ways to reduce overlapping jurisdictions between spending committees and the needlessly repetitive decision making. The most comprehensive review of the congressional budget process was conducted by Representative Anthony Beilenson (D-CA) whose House Rules Committee Task Force recommended a comprehensive revision.[68] But antagonism by the spending committees and their chairs created fears that the entire congressional budget process would happily be scrapped. The Budget Committees and party leaders kept formal reform proposals off the floor. The frustration would boil over the following year with the passage of a radical approach to deficit reduction and an overhaul of the budget process. The Beilensen recommendations, ignored in 1984, would prove critical in 1985.

CHAPTER 4

Legislating Deficit Reduction: Gramm-Rudman-Hollings, 1985 and 1987

Four years after Reagan's 1981 budget and economic plan was enacted by the House and Senate, and with the country nearly a trillion dollars further in debt, members of Congress seemed to be in near panic about deficits. Reagan's landslide victory in the 1984 presidential election had not created any new political alignment or solution for reducing the deficits. The voters made it clear that they cared much more about taxes than deficits. Reagan did not appear to be held accountable for the deficits and debt by the voters. Instead, he was rewarded for a recovering economy and his promise of low taxes. It was Democratic presidential candidate Walter Mondale who stumbled by acknowledging that he would raise taxes to reduce deficits. Both parties called the deficits a scandal but could not agree on how to reduce them. The president remained adamantly against any further tax increases and held tenaciously to his defense buildup. The Democrats wanted Social Security shielded from budget cutters and dug in their heels opposing further domestic program cuts. Out of this impasse came an "automatic" approach to force deficit reduction: set fixed deficit targets that would have to be met or impose mandatory across-the-board cuts in federal programs.

The Balanced Budget and Emergency Deficit Reduction Act of 1985, better known by the names of its sponsors as Gramm-Rudman-Hollings (GRH), was enacted with bipartisan support and was signed by the president in fall 1985. This chapter examines the Balanced Budget Act despite the fact that it did not make meaningful changes in long-term taxing and spending policy and despite the fact that it was revised in just two years and scrapped in five. Gramm-Rudman-Hollings is critical to the evolution of congressional budgeting for other reasons. First, it included the most important formal changes in budget rules since the 1975 Congressional Budget Act. Second, adopted by bipartisan votes in the House and Senate, it raises questions about the impact of party on macrobudgeting. In fact, GRH was a largely symbolic effort by primarily Republican legislators to show constituents that they were serious about deficit reduction which was too politically risky for Democrats to oppose. Partisanship is revealed in caucus strategies and in final negotiations where party leaders tried to design budget-cutting rules to protect their favored policies. The new budget rules adopted in 1985 affected party leaders and members in both houses, particularly in the Senate where historic limitations on debate and amendment resulted. Finally, the Balanced Budget Act was a uniquely congressional initiative, in some ways catching the Reagan administration off guard, but it had consequences for the ongoing evolution of presidential-congressional relations in budgeting, particularly under divided government.

The Political Context

The 1984 Elections

The 1984 elections produced a landslide of historic proportions for Ronald Reagan. He defeated Mondale by more than 16 million votes, 59 percent to 41 percent. Mondale carried only his home state of Minnesota, losing the electoral vote 525–13. Although the public overwhelmingly disapproved of the big deficits, Mondale had not succeeded in convincing the public that the deficits were the most important issue, or that he offered the more acceptable solution to reducing them. Mondale's message had helped raise public concerns about the deficit during the campaign to nearly 20 percent in the Gallup Poll as worries about the economy waned. But by election time, exit polls revealed that only 12 percent felt that the deficits were the most important issue, and of this group, Mondale was the choice by only a 52 to 48 percent margin.[1] In contrast, Reagan had succeeded in convincing the electorate that he would not raise taxes. Among those who cited taxes as the most important issue, Reagan carried the group by a whopping 80 to 20 percent.

The public wanted the deficits reduced in theory, but neither party's approach was supported in practice. Polls showed the public to be in favor more of defense cuts than of social program cuts, counter to the president's position; to be opposed to raising taxes; and to be strongly against cuts in entitlement programs. Republicans had succeeded in strengthening their reputation as the party against taxes, and Reagan used it to his advantage during the campaign. The Democrats continued to have clear identification with the public as the party that protects Social Security, Medicare, and, to a lesser extent, domestic programs. But the inconsistencies in public opinion contributed to the murkiness in party positions on deficits. The positions taken by congressional parties in negotiating GRH reflected their attempt to protect the issues they "owned" with the public.

The 1984 elections did not result in major changes in the composition of Congress. Republicans lost two Senate seats but maintained control 53–47. Democrats lost fourteen seats in the House, but maintained a majority of 253–182, a margin of seventy-one seats, still comfortable compared to 1981. In the House, William Gray (D-PA) replaced Jim Jones as Chair of the House Budget Committee. On the other side of the rotunda, Robert Dole (R-KS) became Majority Leader, replacing Howard Baker, who had retired from the Senate. In the White House, the triumvirate of Edwin Meese, Michael Deaver, and James Baker was replaced by Don Regan who took over as chief of staff. Baker moved to the Treasury, swapping jobs with Regan. David Stockman continued as budget director but would resign in the summer of 1985. The changes would do little to affect the basic differences between House, Senate, and White House on taxes, domestic spending, defense, and entitlements.

Ronald Reagan stated that tax reform was the top domestic priority of his second term. But, in contrast to 1981, the president did not try to speed a comprehensive reform through Congress in 1985. Instead, he waited six months for the Treasury to develop a proposal and let the Congress work its will in a bipartisan fashion. The sweeping bill that finally passed by wide margins in 1986 contrasted with the partisanship that continued to characterize budgeting. Why comprehensive tax reform did not conform to the more prevalent partisan alignments is discussed below.

Continued Budget Stalemate in 1985

Despite his landslide victory, Reagan's FY 1986 budget, like its recent predecessors, was pronounced by Democrats as "dead on arrival," a mere "opening bid." The assumptions in the president's budget were suspect to congressional Democrats who relied on the more pessimistic numbers of the Congressional Budget Office. The administration seemed content to let Congress come up with a way to cut deficits as long as it was not at the expense of defense or through tax cuts.

Both parties generally agreed that the deficits needed to be reduced by at least $50 billion in FY 1986 from CBO's projection of a deficit of over $225 billion. Senate Budget Committee Chair Pete Domenici and other Senate

Republicans continued to believe that real progress in curbing the deficits could not happen as long as entitlements were left off the table, despite the political risks involved. In April, in developing the Senate budget resolution, they got the president to endorse their plan which fixed Social Security and other entitlement COLAs at 2 percent for three years and guaranteed 3 percent real growth for defense while eliminating a host of domestic programs.[2] This would bring the deficit for FY 1986 down to $175 billion.

It was a hard sell on the Senate floor. Republican leaders, led by Dole and SBC Chair Domenici, continued to bargain within the Republican caucus to win a majority. The final version of the Senate budget resolution contained a one-year freeze on COLAs and no real growth for defense, but it promised 3 percent real growth for defense afterwards. The final vote was high Capitol Hill drama, as the Republicans barely gained a victory. Senator Pete Wilson (R-CA) was wheeled on a gurney onto the Senate floor from his hospital bed to cast the tying vote so that Vice President George Bush could cast the deciding vote for a 50–49 victory. The COLA limits on Social Security unified Democrats. Only one of forty-six Democrats voted aye, and four Republicans opposed the resolution.[3]

House Democrats, led by Claude Pepper and others, blasted the freeze on Social Security COLAs. Gray and the HBC reported out a resolution that matched the $50-billion-plus deficit reduction in FY 1986, but the resolution did so through steeper defense cuts while protecting COLAs. The House adopted the plan in late May by a vote of 258–170. Some 87 percent of House Republicans opposed the resolution, whereas 94 percent of Democrats supported it.[4] With such different approaches to deficit reduction, the House-Senate conference on the budget resolution remained stuck well into July. President Reagan entered the negotiations, undercutting the Senate Republicans by agreeing to give up the COLA freeze in return for higher defense spending. Having "walked the plank" by going on record in favor of cutting Social Security benefits, Senate Republicans were furious with the president.

Conferees still could not reach agreement. On July 16, the House voted to waive the Budget Act and proceed with appropriations bills without a budget resolution, using the numbers in their respective versions. Finally, on August 1, conferees agreed on a plan that most resembled the House version. It contained neither significant new revenues nor any entitlement cuts that directly affected beneficiaries. Most of the claimed $55 billion in deficit reduction (CBO estimated the savings at only $39 billion) came from domestic spending cuts and no growth in defense.[5] Few were happy with the compromise, but, eager to adjourn for Labor Day, both houses quickly adopted the resolution. Both Senator Ernest "Fritz" Hollings (D-SC) and Senator Warren Rudman (R-NH) opposed the compromise, while Senator Phil Gramm (R-TX) and his staff began reworking a deficit reduction approach he had toyed with some years earlier.

Forging a Mandatory Solution

The Gramm-Rudman-Hollings Plan[6]

Many Senate Republicans were dissatisfied with the compromise and were still smarting over the COLA vote that would be on their voting record forever. While most other members happily left town, Senators Gramm and Rudman were working independently with their staffs on more radical means of forcing deficit reduction. Gramm, who had helped shepherd Reagan's program through Congress in 1981 when he was still a Democrat and in the House of Representatives, had subsequently been punished by the House Democratic caucus which stripped him of his seniority. He promptly resigned from the House, switched to the Republican Party, and won the special election for his seat. In 1984, he was elected to the Senate from Texas, replacing the retiring Republican John Tower. Gramm had introduced legislation to force a balanced budget as early as 1979. In 1981, he introduced a bill that required the president to "sequester" funds by making across-the-board cuts if there were a deficit.[7] Rudman was frustrated with the Senate and morally outraged over the inability or unwillingness of Congress and the president to deal responsibly with the deficits.

Gramm had been working on this approach the longest, and when Rudman learned of his newest effort, he joined him. They recruited maverick Democrat Fritz Hollings of South Carolina to provide the appearance of bipartisanship. Hollings, who had chaired the SBC briefly after Senator Muskie had resigned, had long championed a budget "freeze" as a means to reduce the deficits. Their joint effort resulted in a plan that would set fixed deficit targets over the next five years and would require a mandatory sequester—across-the-board cuts—if Congress failed to meet those targets on their own. Congress would have five years to reduce the deficit to zero. The philosophy of the mandatory approach, as explained by the sponsors, was not actually to get to the point of mandatory cuts. Rather, the process was to create an alternative so unattractive that Congress would compromise to reach the targets on their own. If they did not, the automatic cuts were preferable to the huge deficits. When they introduced their mandatory deficit reduction plan as an amendment to the debt ceiling bill on September 25, 1985, they did not anticipate the extent to which the issue would dominate Congress for the rest of the year.

The debt ceiling as must-pass legislation was the perfect vehicle for GRH. No one in the Congress wanted to vote for what was then an obscenely high debt limit of $2 trillion. As we saw in chapter 2, the debt limit had proven to be an effective vehicle for riders dealing with the budget since the government would default without additional borrowing authority. The Gramm-Rudman-Hollings plan would not only provide some political cover for voting for the debt ceiling but also turn it into a positive action to reduce future debt. The alternative for members was to vote for the debt and against balancing the budget.

The original GRH amendment exempted Social Security from the mandatory cuts but specified that half of the cuts would come from other entitlements and federal retirement programs. The other half would come from discretionary programs, including both domestic programs and defense procurement. The amendment called for changes in the congressional budget process to facilitate the new approach, advancing the timetable and increasing enforcement mechanisms. To eliminate manipulation of economic and budget forecasts, their amendment provided for a baseline and for estimates developed jointly by CBO and OMB. This was truly a congressional initiative. Although there had been some discussion of a phased-in plan to balance the budget, the administration was now without Stockman, and the new White House staff lacked budgetary experience and expertise. When Gramm called the White House on September 12 to inform them of his plan, they agreed to the concept without much concern for details.[8]

The proposal took the Congress and the country by storm. Although most members, Democrats in particular, were dubious of such a mechanistic approach, deficit reduction was resonating in the country, and the $2 trillion debt was so large that opposing its reduction would be difficult. This was particularly good politics for the Republicans, who only weeks before were stewing about how to get the debt extension through the Senate. Suddenly, House Democrats found themselves on the defensive for criticizing a plan to deal with the deficits. Dole seized the opportunity, holding the debt legislation hostage until the Gramm-Rudman-Hollings amendment could be voted on. He kept the Senate in session on Saturday and Sunday, October 5 and 6, to force a vote, only the eleventh Sunday session in history.[9]

The original plan focused only on spending cuts if deficit targets were not met. Minority Leader Robert Byrd (D-WV) and Senator Lawton Chiles (D-FL) came up with a Democratic substitute for GRH to get revenues into the formula as well. Byrd said that the Democrats were "not prepared to bring the Sword of Damocles down on the poor, the young, the old."[10] His plan exempted means-tested programs and provided that if targets were missed, the deficiency would be made up equally from defense cuts, domestic cuts, and new revenues. Because of Republican opposition to the tax component, the proposal was defeated 59–40.[11] Gramm-Rudman-Hollings was now the only choice. The plan had not had a subcommittee or committee hearing, had not been subject to economic or other analyses, and had not been marked up or revised by senators. Nonetheless, on October 9, it was adopted by a bipartisan vote, 75–24, with twenty-seven of forty-seven Democrats, including liberals such as Ted Kennedy and John Kerry, joining forty-eight of fifty-two Republicans.[12] Even with the new deficit reduction scheme, the debt limit itself garnered only fifty-one votes the next day, with twelve senators not voting.

The House Response

House Democrats felt trapped. They too were frustrated with the deficits, but many detested Phil Gramm and thought that this mandatory plan was crazy. Speaker O'Neill fumed that GRH subverted the Constitution, but there was dissension in the Democratic ranks among younger members who felt that the leadership had failed to seize the initiative and had left them in an untenable position. Many were angry that the plan allowed Reagan to avoid all responsibility for deficits that they believed were largely his doing. As they analyzed the GRH proposal, opposition focused on five key points:

- *Disproportionate domestic cuts.* Critics believed that the Senate plan was unbalanced and unfair because the cuts would fall disproportionately on domestic social programs. There was scant sentiment to throw Social Security into the pot, but there was a sense among some that revenues and other exempt programs should be part of the mandatory solution.
- *Potential damage to defense.* The size of the cut that defense would take was in dispute, but some were worried that a sequester would be irrational, shielding slow-spending weapons procurement while endangering fast-spending categories such as personnel, operations, and maintenance. If the president declared a national security emergency to avoid mandatory defense cuts, it was not clear whether this would mean even bigger cuts in domestic programs.
- *Incapacitating fiscal policy.* The Senate-passed plan provided that

in the case of recession—negative or no real growth in GDP—for four consecutive quarters, the automatic cuts would be waived. Skeptics felt this was inadequate protection, however, and that GRH would hamstring the government's ability to use discretionary fiscal policy to manage the economy.

- *Excessive power to the president.* Many feared that GRH transferred tremendous budgetary power to the executive. Only a decade after the Budget Act restored significant legislative influence in budgeting, this was seen as an unconscionable abdication. The problem was that nobody really knew from the original language exactly how much discretion the president would have.
- *Dubious constitutionality.* GRH raised several constitutional issues. Members questioned whether it was constitutional for one Congress to bind future Congresses. It was also not clear whether a process involving CBO and the General Accounting Office (GAO) could constitutionally force the president to cut spending. Other questions surrounded the severability of certain provisions; for example, if one provision was found unconstitutional, would other parts remain operative?

Despite the legal and policy concerns, it was the political calculations that shaped the House Democrats' response. Representative Dick Gephardt (D-MO) and others convinced the top Democratic leaders not to bring the Gramm-Rudman-Hollings plan to a floor vote in its current form because they would lose. Instead, they would go directly to the Conference Committee and try to turn the measure to their advantage against the president and the Republicans. Since the separate debt limit extension vote in the House was eliminated in 1979, the House had already approved a new debt limit when it passed the budget resolution. On this basis, the leadership opted to go directly to conference with the Senate. In a strange reversal of the legislative process, the Conference Committee would be the first legislative committee to review the deficit reduction plan.

The First Conference Committee

By electing to go to conference directly, the Democrats conceded that some form of mandatory deficit reduction scheme would be enacted. The question was, Which party's policy positions—the reason for deficit gridlock in the first place—would be advantaged and which would be disadvantaged by the solution? The first meeting of the conference committee convened in October amidst hoopla, publicity, and emotion. The bulky committee, chaired by Senator Robert Packwood (R-OR), consisted of nine senators and thirty-nine representatives. Neither Gramm, Rudman, nor Hollings was on the conference, largely for reasons of seniority. Hearings of a sort were held for the first time, exploring constitutional issues, the role of CBO, the amount of power being ceded to the president, and the way the plan would actually work. Many Democrats remained openly hostile. House Judiciary Chair Peter Rodino wrote a letter pleading to protect legislative prerogatives in taxing and spending, noting, "It is troubling that Congress would so casually consider abdicating this power."[13] New budget director James Miller III testified for the administration in favor of the approach but raised a number of potential problems that needed to be resolved. Secretary of Defense Casper Weinberger was less enthusiastic, however, warning a reporter, "We can't have our defense and our security policy be a total prisoner of a rigid formula designed to reduce the budget."[14]

The conference broke down into four task forces after several weeks, focusing on economic issues, the sequestration process, revisions to the budget process, and constitutional issues. Some Democrats were working to ensure that the process would be so onerous as to force Reagan to accept a tax increase. Those on the fourth task force were concerned more with raising constitutional objections than with making the plan able to withstand a court challenge.[15] Meanwhile, without a revised debt ceiling, the Treasury announced that after November 1, it would begin to divest securities in the Social Security Trust Fund to keep the government running. By the end of the month, the Republicans were ready to disband the conference and had come up with a revised version of their own, taking care of a number of technical flaws in the original Senate version. Democrats caucused to come up with their own deficit reduction bill.

The Democrats crafted a version of GRH that would hit defense procurement hard and protect a long list of social programs from the cuts. It altered the deficit targets and allowed fewer cuts if real economic growth slipped below 3 percent. On November 1, the House took its first vote on GRH, passing the Democratic version 249–180 in a strict party line vote.[16] Even liberal Democrats who hated the plan voted for it to prevent approval of the Republican version. On November 6, the Senate passed their second iteration of GRH, introducing the Comptroller General of the GAO into the trigger process to certify the OMB/CBO figures and issue final sequester instructions to the president.

The main differences that remained surrounded the protection of Medicare; the FY 1986 deficit target; the question of whether to force an immediate sequester; the technical but critical question of scoring on budget authority or outlays; and the severability of any unconstitutional portion of the new process. Overall, much had already been agreed upon. The House and Senate had already established the broad outlines and many details of a radical new mandatory deficit reduction plan, including an overhaul of the congressional budget process that included many of the recommendations of the 1984 Beilensen Task Force. These provisions of GRH were virtually ignored in the media where the focus was on the imminent threat of government shutdown and potentially draconian budget cuts.

Compromise and Enactment

A second Conference Committee was named and began meeting after the Senate vote. The debt limit was still the insurance policy guaranteeing that mandatory deficit reduction would ultimately pass. Congress had failed to pass a temporary debt ceiling extension by November 1 to prevent the disinvestment of Social Security trust funds, much to the chagrin of many members. Now the Treasury warned of a default on November 15 without more authority to borrow. The stop-gap continuing resolution that funded federal agencies also expired on that date, leading to the possibility of shutting down most of the government. The second conference proved no more able to resolve differences between the two houses than its predecessor. As the date for default neared, President Reagan prepared to leave for Geneva to meet Soviet Union leader Mikhail Gorbachev. Neither party wanted the government to undergo an embarrassing budgetary crisis while the president was at a summit conference. As a result, congressional leaders agreed on a temporary debt ceiling and continuing appropriation that would fund the government through the beginning of December when the president would be back. While he was gone, private negotiations among four key legislators would break the impasse.

The logjam was broken in late November in private meetings among Majority Whip Thomas Foley and Caucus Chair Gephardt from the House, and Finance Chair Packwood and Budget Committee Chair Domenici from the Senate.[17] Away from the glare of publicity, the two sides offered several proposals and counterproposals that ultimately shaped the final compromise. First, and most critically, the Republican senators proposed that any sequester would be split 50–50 between domestic programs and defense. If the president canceled the defense cuts for national security reasons, then no cuts would be made in domestic programs. This solved the Democrats' biggest problem with GRH: making sure that Reagan's defense buildup would take a big hit if a sequester occurred. Foley explained that the deal was like "the kidnapping of the only child of the President's official family that he loves [the defense budget] and holding it in a dark basement and sending the President its ear."[18]

Pleased with this turn of events, Gephardt and Foley quickly agreed to the Republican offer and, in turn, conceded to the Senate on several other differences. The House agreed to drop its insistence that if one portion of the new process were declared unconstitutional, the entire process would fall. In addition, the House agreed to the Senate proposal involving GAO in the process to solve constitutional issues concerning the role of CBO. The Democrats were also successful at winning agreement for a deficit target for FY 1986 that would create the need for a limited sequester in March 1986 rather than wait until after the 1986 elections, as the Republicans wanted. The Democrats, who had been forced reluctantly into being party to the mandatory scheme, felt that they had gained significant leverage on the administration.

Facing yet another default and shutdown of government offices, conferees finally completed the compromise version in the wee hours of the morning of December 11. Later that day, both houses approved the Balanced Budget and Emergency Deficit Reduction Act of 1985 and extended the statutory debt limit to $2.079 trillion. During nine hours of sometimes emotional debate, proponents extolled the virtues of the plan, while critics such as Senator Moynihan called the bill a "suicide pact." In the end, the Senate approved GRH by a vote of 61–31.[19] Republicans voted for it by a margin of 39–9 while Democrats split 22–22. A few hours later, the House approved the conference report by a vote of 271–154; 153 Republicans and 118 Democrats voted for the bill.[20] Despite the bipartisanship, many members had strong reservations about the new law. According to one lobbyist, members voted "in abject fear that they're not going to be able to explain in a 20-second TV spot next fall why they voted against Gramm-Rudman."[21] Bad idea or not, its time had come.

Whatever misgivings he had, Reagan signed the bill the next day, noting that it was "an important step toward putting our fiscal house in order."[22] In his remarks signing the bill, he reaffirmed his commitment to continuing the defense buildup and his resolve against using tax increases to reduce the deficit. The president had been put in a difficult position. He had agreed in principle to the approach early on and needed the debt limit increase. It would be difficult to reverse course and veto the most prominent deficit reduction to emerge during his presidency. But many felt that the administration had been asleep at the switch, and they felt that they had not been included in the critical negotiations in November. Rookie Budget Director Miller was preoccupied with putting the FY 1987 budget together. Only the Defense Department had raised strong objections. CBO Director Rudolf Penner reflected afterwards, "The Democrats were so extraordinarily successful in amending the bill that I was amazed that Reagan signed the bill at all. He had the grounds to veto Gramm-Rudman as anti-defense."[23]

Hours after the bill was signed into law, Representative Mike Synar (D-OK) filed suit in federal district court for the District of Columbia, challenging the constitutionality of the law. He would later be joined in the suit by a dozen other members and a public employee union. The next year, he would find his challenge supported by an unlikely ally—Ronald Reagan's Department of Justice.

The Balanced Budget and Emergency Deficit Control Act of 1985

Gramm-Rudman-Hollings as passed by Congress and signed by the president maintained the basic framework devised by its sponsors in September. It established maximum deficit levels for both the president's budget and the congressional budget of $171.9 billion in FY 1986, $144 billion in FY 1987, $108 billion in FY 1988, $72 billion in FY 1989, and $36 billion in FY 1990, and it required a balanced budget by FY 1991. If the estimated deficit in any of those fiscal years exceeded the target by more than $10 billion, the mandatory sequester process would take effect, requiring across-the-board cuts in the eligible categories. For FY 1986, which was then already underway, a special set of procedures, a different timetable, and a cap on the amount of the sequester were established. In subsequent years, a revised budget process would take effect.

Revising Congressional Budget Rules

The deficit reduction plan not only shielded the debt limit extension; it also provided the vehicle for a thorough revision of the 1974 Budget and Impoundment Control Act. Advancing the timetable, moving reconciliation to the beginning of the process, dropping the second resolution, and strengthening enforcement procedures were among the most important changes. The changes would mean further shifts in the responsibilities and relative power of authorizing, appropriating, and budget committees as well as party leaders. Table 4–1 shows the revised budget and deficit reduction timetable that went into effect in 1986 for

Table 4–1
Revised budget timetable, 1985

Action	To Be Completed by
President submits budget	Monday after Jan. 3
CBO reports to Congress	Feb. 15
Committees submit views and estimates to Budget Committee	Feb. 25
Senate Budget Committee reports budget resolution	April 1
Congress passes budget resolution	April 15
House Appropriations Committee reports appropriations bills	June 10
Congress passes reconciliation bill	June 15
House passes all appropriations bills	June 30
Initial economic, revenue outlay, and deficit projections made by OMB and CBO	Aug. 15
OMB and CBO report tentative contents of sequester order to GAO	Aug. 20
GAO issues deficit and sequester report to the president*	Aug. 25
President issues sequester order	Sept. 1
Fiscal year begins, and sequester order takes effect	Oct. 1
OMB and CBO issue revised projections based on subsequent congressional action	Oct. 5
GAO issues revised sequester report to president*	Oct. 10
Final sequester order becomes effective	Oct. 15
GAO issues compliance report on sequester order	Nov. 15

Source: Balanced Budget and Emergency Deficit Control Act of 1985
*The role of the GAO in instructing the president to make budget cuts was ruled unconstitutional in 1986.

FY 1987 and beyond. Many of the key dates in budgeting were moved up, including the president's submission of the budget, which would be due on Capitol Hill on the first Monday after January 3. Of particular importance to the way Congress did business were the earlier dates for enacting the budget resolution (April 15), for reconciliation (June 15), and for passing appropriations (June 30). The old May 15 deadline for authorizations, long an irritant to standing committees, was dropped. In an effort to force itself to meet the deadlines, Congress adopted language to prevent adjournment for the Fourth of July holiday if spending bills had not been enacted.

Some of the most important changes in the budget process were designed to strengthen the enforcement of totals—to strengthen those in charge of fiscal restraint at the expense of the forces of spending. In its first decade, the budget process had often been circumvented, ignored, or thwarted by accounting gimmicks, rosy-scenario economic assumptions, and other tricks. GRH tried to close some of the loopholes:[24]

- Totals and subtotals in the budget resolution were made binding; previously they had been targets.
- To enable the Budget Committees and party leaders to better monitor compliance, committees were required to allocate outlays, budget authority, entitlements, and credits among its subcommittees. These so-called 302(b) allocations were then subject to enforcement on the floor; any legislation causing any subtotal to be exceeded would be subject to a point of order.
- No legislation providing new budget, entitlement, or credit authority could come to the floor until a budget resolution had been passed. However, bills taking effect in the subsequent fiscal year were exempted, as were appropriations bills, if a budget resolution had not passed by May 15.
- No budget resolution would be in order on the floor if it exceeded the maximum allowable deficit under GRH.
- In the Senate, waivers of these restrictions would require a three-fifths vote. In the House, waivers of conference reports, budget resolutions or reconciliation bills that exceeded the targets must also receive a three-fifths majority.

Another key change was the adoption of the so-called Byrd rule in the Senate.[25] Named after its sponsor, Senator Robert Byrd (D-WV), the Byrd rule prohibited extraneous materials from being attached to reconciliation bills. As reconciliation had become central to the budget process and to deficit reduction, it had become increasingly attractive as a vehicle for nongermane "Christmas tree" amendments. Byrd argued that:

> We are in the process of seeing . . . the Pandora's box which has been opened to the abuse of the reconciliation process. That process was never meant to be used as it is being used. There are 122 items in this reconciliation bill that are extraneous.[26]

The rule was originally adopted as an amendment to the reconciliation bill in October 1985. But since that bill was not formally adopted until April 1986, the Byrd rule was reaffirmed by a Senate resolution in December 1985. It would mean that one of the most critical must-pass bills in the budget process could not be used to get around deadlock on other measures. Although adopted only by the Senate, its provisions would affect the House since any nongermane amendments added in conference would be subject to a point of order on the Senate floor.

Gramm-Rudman-Hollings moved to make the budget more comprehensive with one notable exception: Social Security. This highly popular program was moved off budget and exempted from any across-the-board cuts, even though its trust fund totals were still included as far as calculating the deficit (which by 1985 had sizable surpluses tending to make the deficit smaller). Other programs, such as federal credit activities in the form of direct loans and loan guarantees, were now formally included in the budget.

The first formal revision of the Budget Act in eleven years strengthened and further centralized budgetary decisions. Budget Committees and the party leaders had new rules to increase their ability to constrain the actions of the authorizing committees and appropriators. One senior staff member observed:

> While nobody was paying much attention, the Budget Committees wrote into Gramm-Rudman their dreams of the ages. They adopted virtually all of the reforms of the Beilenson task force. This was an extraordinary coup for the Budget Committees—particularly the Senate Budget Committee, in expending and strengthening their powers.[27]

Despite these apparent changes to strengthen enforcement, program advocates and appropriators had proven innovative and clever in the past at avoiding discipline and would continue to do so.

The Deficit Reduction Process

The bipartisanship that had occurred in passing the Balanced Budget Act briefly concealed the pervasive partisanship that characterized budgeting in Congress by the mid-1980s. For shock value, House Democrats had wanted cuts in the FY 1986 budget to take place immediately after GRH was enacted, and they wanted to blame the Republicans for any pain and misery that resulted. In conference they consented to wait until March 1986 and to limit the maximum sequester to $11.7 billion. As a result, the legislation spelled out a process for FY 1986 that was separate from that for subsequent fiscal years. Because seven months remained in the fiscal year, only seven-twelfths of the "excess deficit" could be sequestered up to the cap.

The mandatory deficit reduction process for other fiscal years worked as follows. A joint CBO/OMB report would be issued in August, estimating the deficit for the coming fiscal based on assumptions specified in the law. The Comptroller General was then required to review the data, assumptions, and methodologies of the report, making a final determination of the deficit. If an excess deficit existed according to GAO, the president was required to issue a sequestration order by September 1. GRH allowed the president no flexibility in determining cuts except for a limited number of defense accounts in 1986.[28] Under the new rules, Congress had one month to find a way to eliminate the excess deficit. OMB, CBO, and GAO would then recalculate the deficit. If Congress could not agree on an alternative, or if GAO reported by October 10 that an excess deficit still existed, the president would be required to issue a final sequester order by October 15. The Comptroller General would then report to Congress on compliance with the order by the middle of November.

With so much at stake, the method for calculating and allocating the sequester order that was written into the formula was extremely important. Congress had ultimately agreed to keep score on the deficit using outlays, not budget authority. GRH introduced the concept of "budgetary resources" to categorize budget authority, entitlements, and borrowing authority upon which outlays are made. Therefore, the sequester order had to reduce budgetary resources sufficiently to produce the desired reduction in outlays.

Program Exemptions

Half of the mandatory cuts would come from domestic programs, but much of the negotiation over GRH had been over what programs to exclude from the process. It was a long list. While items such as interest on the national debt obviously could not be cut, Democrats had succeeded in shielding a number of programs from the GRH scalpel. Exempt programs included:

- interest
- Social Security
- railroad retirement
- veterans' compensation and pensions
- Aid to Families with Dependent Children (AFDC)
- supplemental security income (SSI)
- women, infants, children (WIC)
- child nutrition
- food stamps
- Medicaid

In addition, special rules were written for making the reductions in unemployment compensation, federal pay, student loans, child support enforcement, foster care and adoption assistance, and crop subsidy programs.

Programs with COLAs could be reduced only to the extent of that year's cost of living increase. But further limits on automatic cuts were written into law for Medicare, veterans' medical care, community health, migrant health, and Indian health facilities and services. Medicare cuts were limited to 1 percent in FY 1986 and 2 percent in subsequent years.

The other half of the across-the-board cuts were to come from defense. Those reductions would include some savings realized by adjusting the military retirement COLAs. The remaining defense cuts would be calculated by computing a fixed percentage reduction in defense outlays from new budget authority and unobligated balances. Outlays from existing budget authority, about 40 percent of total budget authority, were exempted from sequestration.

Would it work? Gramm-Rudman-Hollings was designed to end the deficit stalemate by providing punitive consequences for inaction by Congress and the president. On paper, House Democratic leaders and Senate Republican leaders had a speedier and tougher budget process with more enforcement muscle. The first test of the new process was the "dry run" of sorts on the FY 1986 budget. It would begin a session in which GRH would dominate the legislative process.

Mandatory Deficit Reduction in 1986

Reducing the FY 1986 Deficit

The second session of the 99th Congress began with more bad news about the deficit. Projections showed that it would exceed $220 billion, nearly $50 billion above the GRH target. CBO and OMB each reported their version of the $11.7 billion in cuts by January 1986, filling an entire volume of the Federal Register.[29] The relatively minor differences between the two reports were resolved by GAO. On February 5, a Republican resolution to force Congress to make cuts necessary to avoid the mandatory cuts was defeated, guaranteeing that the new deficit reduction process would go into effect.

The mandatory cuts for FY 1986 were calculated with agonizing detail using the complicated formula.[30] The calculations revealed how much of the federal budget had been taken out of the mandatory process. When all of the exemptions and special rules were applied, only 20 percent of outlays were subject to sequestration, hardly an "across-the-board" process. The cuts fell heavily on defense personnel, operations and maintenance, and procurement and research accounts. On the domestic side, the biggest cuts fell on independent agencies—education, health, housing, and natural resources programs. The percentage cuts were 4.9 percent in the eligible defense accounts and 4.3 percent in unprotected domestic accounts.

These cuts were much less severe than what would have been needed to reach the $172 billion target. CBO projected the FY 1987 deficit at $167 billion, $23 billion above the $144 billion target. CBO estimated that if Congress could not reach the target, cuts of 6.2 percent in defense and 8.4 percent in domestic accounts would be necessary. If the economy did not perform as expected, the deficit would rise to $194 billion, requiring cuts of 14.2 percent in defense and 20.9 percent in domestic programs.[31]

On the legal front, Synar's suit was decided in federal district court on February 7. The three-judge panel ruled that the automatic trigger mechanism was unconstitutional because the role of GAO violated separation of powers.[32] Because the case would be appealed to the U.S. Supreme Court, the decision had no immediate impact on the 1986 sequester or the new budget process rules under which the FY 1987 budget was being considered. It simply added to the doubts about the viability of the process among committee members struggling to meet the new February 25 deadline for views and estimates in order to pass a budget resolution by mid-April. On March 1, the sequestration took place, cutting $11.7 billion from the programs that were not exempted from the process.

Trying to Meet the New Timetable

The enactment of GRH was intended to signal to the public Congress's determination to do something about the deficits. As 1986 began, most members seemed serious about making the system work. In March, the Senate voted 61–33 not to exempt additional loans for farmers from the Balanced Budget Act's restrictions.[33] On March 19, Senate Republicans reported a budget resolution that met the target deficit in part through some new revenues, bringing a rebuke from Reagan. The SBC's action would be the only significant deadline in the new budget process that would be met that year

April 15 passed without the enactment of a budget resolution by either house. The Senate finally passed a bipartisan resolution on May 2, despite White House opposition to the taxes. They projected the deficit exactly at the GRH target of $144 billion. Following the Senate, the House passed a resolution with a deficit of $137 billion, achieving that figure primarily through defense cuts. President Reagan called the House budget a "radical anti-defense" plan and promised to oppose it. GRH had proven to be a mixed blessing for the president and a formidable weapon for congressional leaders, just as many Democrats had hoped. The 50–50 split between defense and domestic programs meant that House Democrats could get away with greater cuts in defense because the cuts were not as deep as they would be with a sequester. Reagan could use the veto at his own peril. House leaders, still fearing the tax issue, would not consider new revenues without some support from the White House. Despite the new timetable, the budget process was again stalled.

Lacking a budget resolution, the June 15 deadline for reconciliation was missed, and it was obvious that no spending bills would be passed by June 30. The prohibition against adjourning for the Fourth of July holiday was quietly waived on June 19. House and Senate conferees finally reached an agreement on the budget resolution on June 26, reporting a budget with a deficit of $143 billion based on spending of $995 billion and revenues of $852 billion. Reagan had won on taxes but lost on defense. No significant new taxes were included in the budget, but defense had been cut $28 billion below the president's request. As members left Washington, most of the work remained: reconciliation, another extension of the debt limit, and spending bills. Before the members returned, the Supreme Court would determine the constitutionality of the deficit reduction process.

Impact of New Budget Rules

Despite the fact that the accelerated timetable was not working, Gramm-Rudman-Hollings was having a significant effect on how Congress conducted its business. The Appropriations Committees found themselves under significantly greater constraints than ever before.[34] Under the 302(b) allocations to subcommittees, the full committees could not adjust subtotals internally to keep within the overall cap. This greatly increased dissension among committee members during markup. Scoring on outlays rather than budget authority also impacted the Appropriations Committees, since appropriations would be subjected to a point of order on the floor if they exceeded outlay allocations. This rule affected defense appropriations in particular because of the differences in the fast- and slow-spending programs. The Budget Committees and party leaders had more control over the committees with the 302(b) allocations, and they made it more difficult for subcommittee chairs to override cuts made by the Budget Committees.

The Balanced Budget Act affected the comprehensive tax reform package that Congress had been working on since 1985. The tax reform process presented a remarkable contrast to the budget process. Through a bipartisan process that included the House, Senate, and White House, tax reformers were able to agree on the most sweeping overhaul of the tax code in decades. This case is recounted in detail elsewhere, but several facets are relevant to the analysis of congressional budgeting.[35] Tax reform avoided the normal partisan divisions when Democrats agreed to not use it as a means to increase revenues to reduce the deficit. All agreed that the reforms would be "revenue neutral." Party leaders were able to maintain this stance during markup because of the new provisions of GRH.

The Balanced Budget Act did not specifically provide rules requiring that amendments must be "deficit neutral." But that was the effect of the super-majorities required to waive provisions combined with other requirements in the original Budget Act and the new law. Section 303(a) subjected amendments to a point of order unless the budget resolution was passed, and section 311 provided that no bill could reduce revenues or increase outlays. This combination of provisions had the effect of requiring "offsets" in any amendment, either in committee or on the floor. That is, when considering the Tax Reform Act, any provision that reduced revenues had to make that revenue up someplace else. This requirement reduced the number of amendments and enforced the concept of revenue neutrality. GRH had added another tool to the arsenal of those trying to impose fiscal restraint in Congress.

The Constitutional Flaw

The Balanced Budget Act, a response to the deficit stalemate between Congress and the president, raised the constitutional issue of separation of powers. This doctrine draws indistinct boundaries that have always allowed one branch to participate in the affairs of the other to some extent. In the 1970s, the U.S. Supreme Court followed a more relaxed interpretation of separation of powers.[36] However, in the case of *INS v. Chadha* (1983), the Court adopted a more formalistic and literal interpretation of separation of powers in striking down the legislative veto. This same constitutional interpretation was used by the Court on July 7, 1986, when it ruled in *Bowsher v. Synar* that Gramm-Rudman-Hollings violated separation of powers.[37] The ruling was restricted to the narrow question of the use of GAO as part of the trigger mechanism.

Both branches had to some extent anticipated constitutional questions surrounding the automatic trigger mechanism.[38] A fallback procedure was added to the law in case the automatic trigger provisions were invalidated. It provided that the joint report of OMB and CBO would be submitted to a Temporary Joint Committee on Deficit Reduction instead of to the

Comptroller General. This committee, consisting of the entire membership of the two Budget Committees, would be required to report a joint resolution in five days to both houses. Congress then was required to "certify" the cuts by voting on the resolution under special rules. That resolution, rather than the GAO report, would serve as the basis for the president's sequestration order.

In February, the three-judge panel of the DC District Court found the trigger mechanism unconstitutional because Congress had the power to remove the Comptroller General. In their opinion, Congress could not retain the power of removal of an officer performing executive functions. The court declined to rule on the plaintiffs' argument that GRH delegated excessive power to the executive branch since it was unconstitutional on other grounds. In obiter dicta, however, the judges concluded that the delegation made by the Balanced Budget Act was constitutional.[39]

The District Court's ruling was automatically appealed under a provision in the law that provided expedited review by the Supreme Court. By a 7–2 vote, the Court upheld the ruling of the lower court and concluded that the mandatory cuts imposed in March were unconstitutional. The majority opinion, written by Chief Justice Warren Burger, concluded, "The structure of the Constitution does not permit Congress to execute the laws; it follows that Congress cannot grant to an officer under its control what it does not possess."[40] In concurring with the opinion, Justices Stevens and Marshall wrote that GRH was unconstitutional because it delegated excess power to the Comptroller General to make national policy. In dissenting opinions, Justices White and Blackmun argued that the majority imposed an overly rigid interpretation of the separation of powers doctrine. They questioned striking down a critical federal enactment in order to preserve a sixty-five-year-old removal provision that was never exercised and that might itself be unconstitutional.

Repairing the Mandatory Trigger for Deficit Reduction

Avoiding the Sequester in 1986

When Congress returned from recess, Senators Gramm, Rudman, and Hollings were determined to repair the constitutional problem with the automatic trigger mechanism. Once again, the debt limit would be the vehicle for their efforts. Their initial solution was to eliminate the power of Congress to remove the Comptroller General. This option was blocked by opposition from Rep. Jack Brooks (D-TX), Chair of the House Government Operations

Committee which had oversight responsibility for GAO. Congress did move immediately on one front. Using a modified version of the fallback procedure, on July 17, by large majorities both the House and the Senate voted to certify the March 1 cuts that had been struck down by the Court.

When the Senate reported the debt ceiling extension, proponents had found a different "fix": empowering OMB alone to determine the spending cuts needed to meet the deficit targets. Under their proposal, GAO would still participate in formulating the estimates, but OMB would issue the final report to the president. The president's budget office would be limited in its ability to make changes in the report except to reflect changes in regulations or actions of Congress. The date for the president's budget, which had proved burdensome, would be moved back to February from the earlier date, and a provision was added to return to the original procedure if the Comptroller General were made an executive branch official. The measure was grudgingly accepted by the White House because of the restrictions on OMB, and it passed the Senate on July 30 by a 63–36 vote.

The repairs to GRH ran into trouble in the House, however, where majority Democrats were content to use the backup procedure. Members wanted to defer action until the August deficit estimates were released. Despite the attempt of Gramm and his allies to block the debt ceiling extension, a temporary extension without a new trigger mechanism was passed. The August deficit reestimates by CBO and OMB brought the usual bad news. On August 20, taking into account deficit savings already proposed by Congress, CBO projected the deficit at $170.6 billion, and OMB projected it at $156.2 billion. Without GAO to reconcile the differences, congressional leaders simply took the average: $163.4 billion. Taking advantage of the fact that a sequester would be necessary if the deficit exceeded the target by more than $10 billion, Congress simply decided to shoot for a $154 billion deficit rather than the $144 billion target. That meant that they had to come up with an additional $9.4 billion in cuts or new revenues to avoid a sequester.

Members wanted to avoid across-the-board cuts in the FY 1987 budget at all costs. By September, Congress had still not approved a reconciliation bill or any appropriations bills. An omnibus bill that reached the $154 billion deficit target was prepared to try to avoid sequestration. Revenues were increased by $2 billion by proposing the sale of government assets such as Conrail, actions that would actually increase the deficit in future years. Another $2 billion in savings was claimed by enhanced enforcement by the Internal Revenue Service. Representative George Miller (D-CA) deadpanned, "We're fine-tuning the smoke and mirror proportions—too much of one blinds you; too much of the other burns you."[41]

Congress missed the October 1 deadline for the deficit reduction package. Despite the new timetable, the critical budget decisions for FY 1987 were made in late-night sessions in early October, after the fiscal year had begun. Finally, a budget with a deficit of $151 billion was passed, within the GRH target range. Gramm and his allies tried unsuccessfully to block passage of a permanent debt limit bill that did not repair the constitutional flaw. They did succeed in limiting the extension to six months, however, so that in 1987, proponents would have another chance to renew the mandatory provisions.

The 1986 elections ended six years of Republican control of the Senate. When the 100th Congress reconvened in January 1987 to restructure GRH and reduce deficits, Democrats would control both houses of Congress.

Gramm-Rudman II: Reaffirming Mandatory Deficit Reduction

Missing the Original Targets

By the summer of 1987, deficit projections continued to expand. The FY 1988 deficit target under GRH was $108 billion. By mid-1987, projections showed that the deficit would go as high as $180 billion, making $108 billion virtually unreachable. The FY 1986 deficit, on which the five-year targets were based, had turned out to be $50 billion greater than expected, even with the limited sequester. Even the most ardent deficit hawks acknowledged that in addition to restoring the mandatory reduction process, the targets would have to be revised.

The debt limit was expiring, and Senate Republicans did not want to authorize more government borrowing without doing something about reducing the deficits. While the administration had supported GRH in 1985, two years later they were urging Congress to send the president a clean debt limit. Increasingly through the 1980s, the Treasury was forced to take extraordinary actions to prevent default, from postponing auctions of Treasury notes to disinvesting in Social Security trust funds.

Democrats and even many Republicans had little sympathy for Reagan's entreaties in 1987. The president had suffered a decline in public support as a result of Iran-Contra revelations. More central to the budget debate, members were exasperated with the president's continued assault on their institution. He continued to argue for a balanced budget amendment as the centerpiece of his proposed "economic bill of rights," even though the budgets he submitted to Congress were not in balance.[42] In July, Congress enacted another short-term extension and attempted to restructure mandatory deficit reduction.

Revising the Balanced Budget Act

Although the partisan motivations in 1987 were the same as they had been in 1985, the political calculus seemed to have changed. Little was said by proponents about the glaring failure to achieve the original five-year targets after only two years. Democrats were pushing stricter deficit targets than Republicans because of the impact on the defense budget. Democrats wanted to force the administration to compromise on new taxes in order to protect defense. The White House actively opposed many of the revisions being proposed on Capitol Hill.

In August, both OMB and CBO revised their January forecasts and showed deficits rising sharply through 1992 without major changes in policy. A sequester to reach the FY 1988 target alone would devastate both defense and domestic discretionary programs. Despite the accelerated timetable, GRH had made it irrational for members of Congress to make any tough choices before they saw the August estimates on which any sequester would be based.

In late September, after secret negotiations by a small group of members, the conference committee reached a compromise on the GRH reaffirmation act. The bill passed the House on September 22 by a vote of 230–176. It passed the Senate the next day by a margin of 64–34. The administration seriously considered a veto but reluctantly signed Gramm-Rudman-Hollings II into law primarily because it included the twenty-month debt extension that the president desired. This would leave the problem of the next debt ceiling to the new president in 1989.

New Targets and Budget Rules

The Balanced Budget and Emergency Deficit Control Reaffirmation Act of 1987 (GRH II) repaired the constitutional flaw by giving OMB responsibility for reporting deficits that exceeded the targets and for determining the actual cuts under the revised formula. It revised the budget timetable as well. OMB would report any excess deficit by August 25, and the final order to make cuts would be issued on October 15 if no legislation had been enacted to reach the targets. The date for a balanced budget was moved from 1991 to 1993 with the following annual deficit targets: for FY 1988, $144 billion; for FY 1989, $136 billion; for FY 1990, $100 billion; for FY 1991, $64 billion; for FY 1992, $28 billion; and for FY 1993, zero deficit. The $10 billion margin of error was allowed for all years with the exception of 1993.

While the cuts continued to be divided equally between defense and domestic programs with certain programs exempted, GRH II gave the president greater flexibility in determining where defense cuts would come. Under the new provisions, he could exempt all or part of cuts in personnel if an equivalent amount were cut in weapons procurement. In the face of the budgetary gimmicks and tricks used to reach the deficit target in 1986, GRH II put new limits on what could be counted as budget savings. Receipts from the sale of loans could not be counted; nor could Congress count savings by moving the date of a federal pay increase by a couple of days so that it would fall in the next fiscal year, as they had done the year before. Congress was now required to use a single set of economic and technical assumptions in an attempt to reduce the practice of using the most optimistic forecasts, or using different estimates in the same resolution as had been done previously. The revised version of mandatory deficit reduction expanded the baseline on which cuts would be imposed, allowing for inflation and increased program utilization.

GRH II also strengthened enforcement procedures in the budget process. It reinforced the Byrd rule against extraneous materials in reconciliation bills and restricted items that increase spending in future years in those bills. New rules made it tougher to waive the provisions of the process by requiring a sixty-vote majority rather than a simple majority in a number of instances.

The Crash and the Budget Summit

Black Monday

The financial markets were distressed at the abandonment of original targets and the acceptance of continued large deficits. The market had been dropping since August, but on Monday, October 19, 1987, three weeks after the new deficit law was signed into law, it crashed. The Dow Jones Industrial Average, the most common barometer of stock prices, dropped a then-unprecedented 508 points. A record 604 million shares were traded as prices plummeted in a wave of panic and computer-programmed selling. The index lost 23 percent of its value in a single day, far worse than the 13 percent drop in the famous crash of October 1929 that helped precipitate the Great Depression. Between August and October, the market lost 36 percent of its value, nearly $1 trillion in wealth.

Congress and the White House were sobered by the crash. Both branches quickly announced the formation of a budget summit to take more meaningful action to reduce the deficit. Congress had yet to clear spending bills and reconciliation for FY 1988. The summit would propose a two-year plan covering both FY 1988 and FY 1989, the last budget of the Reagan era.

The Summit Agreement

Despite the fears raised by the crash, none of the partisan cleavages over defense, taxes, and entitlements were resolved. It took several weeks for the summit even to get organized and for the imminent prospect of $23 billion in automatic cuts under GRH to force an agreement. On November 20, the day the automatic cuts took effect, congressional and administration negotiators arrived at the outlines of a compromise package. They agreed on a deficit reduction package of $30 billion for FY 1988 and $46 billion for FY 1989 comprising both spending cuts and new revenues.[43] Reagan had finally agreed to $23 billion in new taxes as part of the solution.

Yet even with the outline in place and with adjournment only days away, a final compromise was still difficult to reach. Last-minute disputes about Medicare cuts delayed final action. The deficit reduction package was contained in two bills: an omnibus appropriations bill and a reconciliation bill that included the revenue increases. The spending bill included all regular appropriations for the second year in a row. It was a massive 30-pound, 2,100-page document that provided over $600 billion to fund the majority of government programs. In this case, majority party leaders in the House failed to satisfy many of their caucus members because the bill included $14 million in aid to the Contras in Nicaragua. This amount was trivial in terms of the size of the bill but was politically explosive for Democrats. On December 22, the budget package narrowly passed the House by a margin of 209–208. Divided Democrats narrowly voted against the final version 116–128.[44] The Senate passed the bill easily, 59–30.

The reconciliation bill had a slightly more comfortable margin in the House and more typical partisan split, passing on December 21 by a margin of 237–181. Most of the new taxes it mandated were on corporations. The Senate followed suit in the early morning hours of December 22, sending it to the president. The summit agreement also included a preview of deficit reduction strategies to come: appropriation caps on domestic and defense spending. The Omnibus Budget Reconciliation Act of 1987 provided separate two-year limits on defense and discretionary domestic appropriations that would serve as the basis for committee allocations in the next year's budget resolution. In the Senate, it would take a three-fifths vote to override those caps.

After the scare of the market crash, a two-year budget pact had been reached, but many members remained dismayed at the chaotic budget process and the continuing problem of the deficits.

Conclusion

Congressional budgeting continued to evolve, often in a topsy-turvy fashion, through the mid- to late-1980s. One of the most important consequences of GRH was the rules changes to further centralize control of budgeting and the enforcement of agreements once reached. Under the new rules, the authorizing committees and the appropriations committees faced more constraints and were subject to specific allocations. House and Senate leaders were able to enforce totals more effectively through the Budget Committees and Rules Committee. Reconciliation was institutionalized. Rules were particularly enhanced in the Senate. The Byrd amendment introduced germaneness requirements on reconciliation bills. Revisions to the Budget Act in 1985 imposed the most restrictive rules on debate in Senate history, effectively prohibiting filibusters on any legislation creating the congressional budget.[45] The provisions requiring offsets made it harder for members or committees to push pet spending projects or tax breaks.

Had party differences been reduced and partisanship become less characteristic of macrobudgeting in this period? Mandatory deficit reduction had a bipartisan face with a Democrat and two Republicans as its cosponsors, and it attracted bipartisan support in both the House and the Senate. In the Senate, minority party members continued to participate in shaping budget legislation. Gramm-Rudman-Hollings II in 1987 was supported by a majority of both parties. The Tax Reform Act of 1986 was formulated by members of both parties and adopted on a bipartisan vote. The budget summit agreement in 1987 sharply divided House Democrats.

Even with some blurring of positions on deficits and occasional bipartisan cooperation, a strong case can be made that underlying partisanship remained undiminished. All three House votes and two of three Senate votes on budget resolutions from 1985 to 1987 were nearly party line votes. Through the entire 1980s, all Senate votes on the budget resolutions could be classified as party votes except in 1983 and 1986. Senate party divisions, unlike in the 1970s, became more similar to House voting patterns for the most part. Some bicameral differences persisted, however. In general, senators of both parties were more willing to compromise on key budget issues. Some Senate Republicans were willing to include tax increases in deficit reduction packages. Some Senate Democrats were willing to consider restrictions to entitlement growth. This was still much less the case in the House.

Being on the side of deficit reduction was politically important to members of both political parties. Gramm-Rudman-Hollings was intended to symbolize to the public a commitment to address the budget deficits, making opposition to the plan politically dangerous. Public opinion polls showed that by fall of 1985, 22 percent of respondents said that the deficit was the most serious problem facing the nation, making it the number one concern at that date.[46] Although public concern seemed to *follow* rather than *lead* congressional action, it was extremely difficult for members to vote against the Balanced Budget Act despite the concerns of members of both parties. Interviews with members and staff suggest that much of the support was *insincere,* particularly among Democrats. In the case of comprehensive tax reform, bipartisan support was more genuine. The law made sweeping changes to the tax code, but it did not tap into the divisions of macrobudgeting. The decision to make tax reform legislation "deficit neutral" changed the nature of the issue by taking tax cuts and entitlements cuts off the table.

Changes in congressional budgeting in this period also continued the evolution of presidential-congressional relations. While GRH reflected policy and electoral concerns over chronic deficits by members of both political parties, its adoption was also shaped by Democrats' opposition to Reagan's tax cuts and defense buildup and by Republicans' desire to restrain domestic spending and prevent tax increases. Both sides succeeded in shielding some of their policy priorities in GRH, particularly by keeping taxes out of the formula for Republicans and by exempting most entitlements for Democrats. Perhaps the main shortcoming in the mandatory scheme for the Reagan administration was the potential vulnerability of defense spending. The administration may have underestimated that threat, but the president was also under pressure to look as if he were doing something about the deficits. The administration regained important flexibility in imposing mandatory cuts in defense in GRH II, but the mandatory deficit reduction plan continued to serve as an institution that congressional Democrats could use to try to force the president to make concessions or threaten reductions in defense totals.

The growing regularity of budget summits during this period suggests that divided government in the 1980s affected the national budget process and the way Congress and the president negotiated budget policy disputes. Extraordinary resolution became the rule rather than the exception in presidential-congressional budgeting. In this regard, GRH is perhaps the most extraordinary means to resolve legislative-executive budget disputes ever devised.

Twenty years later, the Balanced Budget Act largely appears to have been a budgeting gimmick that failed. The most obvious failure was the fact that the initial targets had to be revised after only two years, and the process was abandoned after five years. It created incentives for Congress to avoid sequestration and exacerbated the use of budgetary tricks and illusions. For example, the $10 billion cushion on the targets was simply used to allow a larger deficit. Because only August budget forecasts would trigger sequestration, there were no reasons to make hard budget choices before that date, as economic and technical changes could simply wipe out any deficit savings. To manipulate budget totals, Congress proposed selling government assets, advancing revenue collections, and delaying outlays. All of these actions actually increased future deficits.[47]

On the other hand, even after GRH was abandoned, many of the less publicized rules changes left Congress with greater centralized control of decisions on budget totals, a single binding resolution at the start of the process, an institutionalized reconciliation process, stronger enforcement provisions once agreements had been reached, and more stringent limitations on debate and amendment, even in the Senate. When the deficits began rising again under the Bush administration several years later, Congress would finally abandon the mandatory approach and look to new rules changes to strengthen its position in budgeting.

CHAPTER 5

The Budget Summit Agreement, 1990

After eight years as vice president, George Bush believed that the partisanship over the budget and the deficit was destructive for the country. In his inaugural address on January 20, 1989, he extended his hand to the Democratic leaders of Congress. "We need compromise; we've had dissension," he said. "We need harmony; we've had a chorus of discordant voices," he continued. "When our mothers were young, Mr. Majority Leader, the Congress and the Executive were capable of working together to produce a budget on which this nation could live. Let us negotiate soon—and hard. But in the end, let us produce."[1]

Following up on this pledge, Bush reached a budget agreement with congressional leaders only months into office. However, the agreement would fail to check the forces propelling the deficit upwards, and eighteen months after his inauguration, the nation would face yet another budget crisis. By mid-1990, projections showed a deficit that would be as much as $160 billion greater than the Gramm-Rudman-Hollings target. It would lead to another struggle with Congress and, ultimately, to a new approach to deficit reduction.

Despite his embrace of bipartisanship and sentiments for a kinder and gentler nation, Bush had sewn the seeds of continuing partisan divisions by emphasizing the Republicans' best issue during the presidential campaign. His promise was dramatically repeated and repeated as he stumped the country: "read my lips; no new taxes." It was a promise that helped get him elected but prevented meaningful compromise with the Democratic Congress and ultimately proved impossible to keep. The budget summit in 1990 came up with the largest deficit reduction package in the nation's history—including new taxes—which was supposed to reduce the deficits by $500 billion over five years. The Balanced Budget Act was suspended as Congress focused more narrowly on the portion of the budget that it could actually control: revenues and discretionary spending.

The Omnibus Budget and Reconciliation Act of 1990 (OBRA-90) was one of the most sweeping budget packages of the past thirty years. The election of George Bush created another four years of divided government after eight years under Reagan. This chapter examines another major revision of congressional budget rules in the Budget Enforcement Act (BEA), including how forging such a large package of tax increases and spending cuts fractured party unity in Congress. Relations between Congress and the president continued to reveal extraordinary means to resolve macrobudgetary issues, including a failed bipartisan commission to resolve the deficit problem, and a summit and a "mini-summit" to finally arrive at the deficit reduction package. First, the changes in composition of Congress and the presidency following the 1988 election are considered.

The Bush Administration and the 101st Congress

The 1988 Elections

After trailing in many polls after the Democratic National Convention nominated Massachusetts Governor Michael Dukakis in July, Bush surged to a lead following his party's August convention—a lead that he would never relinquish. Party differences on budgetary issues played a prominent role in the campaign. Bush repeated the "no new taxes" pledge at nearly every campaign stop and attacked Dukakis as a liberal "tax and spend" Democrat. Nonbudget issues were important as well and helped polarize congressional Democrats after the election. Particularly divisive were Bush's attacks on Dukakis as soft on crime, responsible for furloughing dangerous prisoners as personified in the infamous Willie Horton television ads. When the votes were counted, Bush had won the election by 7 million votes, 54 percent to 46 percent. He carried 40 states with 426 electoral votes compared to Dukakis's 10 states and 112 electoral votes.

Among voters interviewed in exit polls, the problem of the budget deficit was mentioned most often (by one in four) as the key issue behind their vote.[2] Of this group, Dukakis was favored by 60 percent, but with the next three most important issues mentioned by voters, Bush was overwhelmingly favored. For example, of the 23 percent most concerned about national defense, 84 percent reported voting for Bush. Among voters most concerned about taxes, 70 percent voted for Bush. In general, Bush benefited from prosperity, peace, and the popularity of Ronald Reagan.[3]

Congressional Party Leadership

George Bush had short political coattails in 1988. In the House of Representatives, Democrats picked up five additional seats and enjoyed an eighty-five-seat majority. In the Senate, the Democrats added a seat, achieving a 55–45 majority. The administration would be dealing with many familiar faces and some new ones in the 101st Congress. The House Budget Committee was headed by Leon Panetta (D-CA), who had long been an advocate of budget reform and one of the key negotiators on the Democratic leadership team. Ways and Means was still headed by Dan Rostenkowski. The Senate Budget Committee was chaired by Jim Sasser (D-TN), and the Finance Committee by Senator Lloyd Bentsen (D-TX). George Mitchell (D-ME) had become majority leader after Robert Byrd (D-WV) opted to chair the Senate Appropriations Committee. The most critical change in congressional leadership did not occur as a result of the 1988 elections. It happened midway through 1989 when House Speaker Jim Wright (D-TX) and majority whip Tony Coehlo (D-CA) were forced to resign because of ethics violations. Tom Foley (D-WA) became Speaker and Dick Gephardt (D-MO) became majority leader six months into the Bush presidency.

The Bush Administration Team

The Bush budget team was headed by OMB Director Richard Darman, an experienced veteran of the budget wars of the Reagan years. Nicholas Brady was chosen as Secretary of the Treasury, and the White House Chief of Staff was John Sununu, former governor of New Hampshire. Sununu, who played a central role in the presidential campaign, had a reputation as shrewd, conservative, and extremely partisan, not the most likely choice to improve relations with Congress. President Bush's top economic priority of his first year in office was a cut in the capital gains tax. This issue would prove to be a major stumbling block to bipartisan cooperation with Congress.

The budget summit spurred by the crash of the stock markets in October 1987 produced a two-year budget agreement that claimed deficit savings of $76 billion over the period. As a result, 1988 had been a relatively peaceful year on the budget front compared to the previous six. The budget agreement that had been passed in December 1987 took another step in attempting to reduce the deficit: the creation of a bipartisan commission to find a long-term solution to reducing federal budget deficits.

Deficit Reduction by Bipartisan Commission: The NEC

Using the Greenspan Commission (1982–1983), which had helped solve the Social Security crisis, as a model, the 1987 budget agreement created the National Economic Commission (NEC).[4] Their charge was nothing less than breaking the stalemate between executive and legislative branches that had prevented satisfactory reduction of the deficits. The hope was that the blue ribbon panel would build on the progress made in 1987 and would arrive at more substantial deficit reduction that both parties could agree on.

Consisting of seven Democrats and seven Republicans, the NEC met throughout 1988. Co-chaired by Democrat Robert Strauss and Republican Drew Lewis, the NEC also included two ex-legislators; two former Secretaries of Defense; and high-profile representatives of labor, Lane Kirkland, and business, Lee Iacocca. Although Strauss and Lewis had reputations as pragmatists, ideologically, the two sides were relatively far apart.[5]

Congress gave the commission one year to complete its work and issue a report. Negotiators met for the first time in March 1988 and met sixteen additional times over the next twelve months. Despite its optimistic beginnings, the NEC made little headway. The same fundamental differences over the balance between taxes, defense, and domestic spending in deficit reduction, which had long divided the Democratic Congresses and the Republican presidents, also hung up the commission. The seven Republicans on the panel with the addition of Democrat Ashley formed a working majority that urged "spending restraint" to combat the deficit. The other six insisted that tax increases be part of the solution.

The NEC could not succeed in 1988 because of the presidential campaign. The six Democrats complained that the main obstacle to progress was George Bush's "no new taxes" pledge. Candidate Bush blasted the commission as a "stalking horse" for higher taxes. During the campaign, both Darman and Brady had urged Bush to abolish the NEC to avoid giving voters the impression that it would pave the way for a tax increase. Though he did not terminate the NEC, Bush made it clear after the election that he would not support any recommendations that included additional revenues.

The commission's chance to compromise was further diminished by a ruling on January 5, 1989, by U.S. District Judge Joyce Hens Green: the NEC had to hold its meeting in public under federal "sunshine" laws. Deprived of their ability to swap proposals in private, it became impossible for negotiators to move from preestablished positions. For example, when commissioners discussed a proposal to raise excise taxes on gasoline, they drew heavy fire from a variety of groups such as the American Automobile Association and a group called the Fuel Users for Equitable Levies (FUEL). The Executive Director of the NEC, David Mathiason, commented, "When it comes to real decision-making, they [commission members] don't want to go into a meeting that's public."[6]

As the commission's deadline approached, Bush asked for recommendations with or without consensus. He refused to extend their deadline. On March 1, 1989, the NEC issued three separate reports. The majority report, signed by the seven Republicans and Ashley, endorsed "no new taxes" and made no specific recommendations other than to urge "restraints" on spending in areas other than defense. The first minority report was a terse statement signed by five of the six remaining Democrats, lambasting the president for undermining negotiations and insisting that new revenues had to be part of any solution. The final report was an exhaustive analysis by Senator Moynihan on the danger of the deficits for trade, taxes, and the economy. The commission, launched with great fanfare, had met for a year at a cost of over $1 million and had come up with nothing. Leon Panetta lamented, "It's unfortunate. The hope was the commission would make some tough choices and then provide the political cover to help us put them into effect."[7] Unlike the Greenspan Commission which had facilitated the Social Security deal in 1983, the NEC could not find a basis for compromising party positions.

The 1989 Budget Agreement

Despite the demise of the NEC, the Bush administration followed through on its inaugural promises in taking a more bipartisan approach to its dealings with Congress. The Democratic leadership also wanted to reach an early and fair agreement that would free legislators from the incessant budget wars and allow them to work on other policies. Only weeks after Bush assumed the presidency, he offered to go to summit with congressional leaders to strike a deal early. The Gramm-Rudman-Hollings deficit target for FY 1990 was $100 billion. CBO had forecast a deficit of $147 billion, but negotiators decided to use the more optimistic OMB forecast that was $20 billion less. Although underlying policy differences had not changed, could constructive summitry bridge the differences?

The main negotiations were conducted by a group of five members of Congress and two administration officials. Darman and Brady represented the president, and House Majority Tom Foley was joined by the bipartisan leadership of the two Budget Committees: Panetta and Bill Frenzel (R-MN) from the House, and Sasser and Pete Domenici (R-NM) from the Senate.

Talks went on for nine weeks and intensified with daily meetings in Foley's office the week of April 10.[8] The main hang-up was the split between cuts in defense and cuts in domestic programs. The leaders eventually agreed to allow domestic spending to keep pace with inflation and provide a nominal increase in defense but below the rate of inflation. On April 14, President Bush and congressional leaders met reporters in the Rose Garden of the White House to announce their deficit reduction package of $28 billion, which would leave the deficit for FY 1990 at $99 billion.

The agreement was more a broad framework than anything else, since it left the actual cuts to subsequent legislative decisions. Senate Majority Leader Mitchell noted that "the most significant aspect of this agreement is its existence," and he warned that it was just the start of the process.[9] Speaker Wright complained that Bush's "no new taxes" pledge had severely hampered negotiations but that it was a good start. Some critics called it little more than an exercise in "least common denominator bipartisanship" that glossed over the real issues. The $28 billion was divided equally between spending cuts and new revenues (not new taxes). The spending cuts came in defense, Medicare, and farm price supports. The revenues were based on asset sales, user fees, IRS compliance, and $5.3 billion in unspecified new revenues. The administration wanted most of the latter to come from a reduction in the capital gains tax, which would increase revenue at first before losing revenue in future years. That idea was not well received in Democratic quarters and would prove a stumbling block to continued harmony.

Both sides agreed that 1989 would be a "slide by" year of sorts and that formulation of a blockbuster deficit reduction package would be delayed until 1990. After the Rose Garden agreement was announced, the House and Senate each passed their budget resolutions in a matter of weeks, in sharp contrast to the previous years. As they had in 1988, Congress operated under appropriation caps in international, domestic, and defense spending as well as a target cap for entitlement spending. The big question remained: how would they raise the $5 billion in new revenues?

The political strategy of the administration changed in the wake of the scandals that toppled Wright and Coehlo. With the House is some disarray after the sudden leadership change, Bush decided to make a full-fledged push for a reduction in the capital gains tax, a high priority among the business community. The budget process stalled as the Ways and Means Committee wrangled over the tax bill. Rostenkowski opposed the capital gains tax and, after some weeks, put together a bill without it. Conservative Democrats who favored the cut, however, led by Ed Jenkins of Georgia, fashioned a bill that would include the gains cut and would use it to pay for popular tax breaks.

The bill won in committee and later, to the surprise of many, on the House floor.

It would not fare as well in the Senate. Mitchell was against the bill and used his position as majority leader to bottle it up. Even though the dollars at stake were smaller than many of the previous budget fights, the battle was along familiar partisan lines. Darman led the administration's effort to get the capital gains tax cut, alienating many majority Democrats in the process. The deadlock lasted for months. In mid-October, Minority Leader Dole finally convinced the administration to admit defeat and drop their campaign in the Senate.[10] Congress finally cleared the reconciliation bill that implemented the deficit reduction package on November 22.

Democrats blamed Bush and Darman for polarizing the debate over capital gains and violating the spirit of the April agreement. The Republicans blamed the Democrats for trying to undermine the new president. Committee chairs and rank-and-file members complained that it showed that budget summits, which excluded them, did not work. But the next year, as a new deficit crisis unfolded, an executive-legislative summit would be necessary.

The 1990 Budget Summit

The FY 1991 Budget

The events of 1990 demonstrate the vulnerability of the budget to economic and technical changes beyond the immediate control of Congress and the president, and they illustrate how party polarization hampered negotiation over the deficit. As 1990 began, the budget picture looked promising. Bush submitted a FY 1991 budget in January that met the GRH deficit target of $64 billion. Only six months later, Congress and the president were looking at deficit projections as high as $300 billion, the highest ever. Bush was strapped by his "no new taxes" pledge: he faced the choice of breaking his promise, allowing GRH to wipe out as much as 40 percent of discretionary spending, or letting the deficit spiral out of control. He chose to break his promise and do something about the deficit, a decision that fractured Republican cohesion.

It appeared in January 1989 that Gramm-Rudman-Hollings might help Bush protect defense spending against Democrats eager to make deep cuts and cash in on the "peace dividend," following the end of the Cold War. At a minimum, he would be able to resist any defense cuts greater than those that would be required under GRH by simply letting the sequester take place.

Bush submitted a budget calling for approximately $1.2 trillion in outlays and a deficit of $64 billion.[11] The administration calculated the baseline deficit at $100.5 billion and therefore had to come up with some $35 billion in savings in its plan. It was premised on a set of optimistic OMB assumptions suggesting stronger economic growth and lower interest rates. CBO, assuming more modest growth and more stable interest rates, forecast a baseline deficit some $38 billion higher than the administration's forecast.[12] Both forecasts would prove to be too optimistic.

In addition to the rosy economic scenario, the Bush plan reduced the deficit to $64 billion through a combination of spending cuts and revenue increases, still claiming "no new taxes." He proposed eliminating some twenty-four programs unsuccessfully targeted by the Reagan administration, such as Amtrak, disaster loans, and the Economic Development Administration. He proposed a nominal increase in defense to $303 billion, 2 percent below the amount needed to keep up with inflation. He also proposed a $5.5 billion cut in Medicare. Most of his plan to reduce the deficit came from new revenues, the largest being the prized cut in capital gains taxes. Other revenues would come from asset sales, user fees, and IRS reforms. Reaction was along predictable partisan lines. Democrats claimed that the proposed budget was more smoke and mirrors, used unrealistic economic assumptions, and revealed the administration was not serious about deficit reduction.

The budget included an unusual introductory message written by Budget Director Darman.[13] He warned in more general terms about hidden "Pacmen" in the budget—a reference to the then-popular video game—lying in wait to gobble up federal revenues. He compared the budget to the Sesame Street character "Cookie Monster," always consuming more and more. While it irritated many of Darman's detractors, it contained a stark message about possible future liabilities of the federal government. Responding to the growing federal liabilities for failed savings and loan institutions (see the discussion later in this chapter), Darman showed that the potential exposure of the government could go as high as $5.8 trillion! This figure was a function of obligations for direct loans and loan guarantees, government-sponsored enterprises, and deposit insurance and other federal insurance liabilities. He reminded readers that there was virtually nothing in reserve to protect against failures in any of these programs that the federal government was legally obligated to meet.

The 1990 budget year was also accompanied by renewed attention to Social Security. The 1983 bailout had put the trust fund on sound financial footing; by 1990, the fund was running a surplus of $60 billion per year, a surplus that would approach $100 billion by the middle of the decade. Senator Moynihan (D-NY) provided another sidelight to the budget debate by proposing that the surpluses were too high and that payroll taxes supporting the program should be cut. Social Security, he claimed, was masking the true size of the deficit. His plan caught both sides by surprise but was quickly attacked by the administration. Treasury Secretary Brady called the idea "goofy," and Bush pledged in his State of the Union address not to "mess around with Social Security."[14] The issue of Social Security and the deficit would be one more dimension of the intensifying budget storm of 1990.

Crafting a Budget Resolution

The Democrats set out to fashion a budget resolution that reached the same $64 billion deficit as that of the president. The general plan was to cut more from defense to allow greater spending on a variety of domestic programs. This task was made harder when the CBO reestimated the deficit on March 5: a baseline deficit now projected to be $161 billion and a deficit of $131 billion under the Bush proposal. As the deficit worsened, it became increasingly apparent that some kind of summit would be necessary. Democrats were resistant, however, unless the president was willing to put everything on the table, including taxes.

The congressional budget resolution was fashioned to sharpen the Democrats' positions and serve as a starting point in the negotiations. In April, the House Budget Committee struggled to come up with a plan that could pass the committee. Finally, despite the Democrats' criticism of the Bush budget, they not only used some of the same gimmicks such as asset sales and enhanced compliance through IRS, but also adopted the president's original economic assumptions.[15] On May 1, the House passed a resolution 218–208 over the unanimous opposition of the Republicans who were joined by 34 Democrats.

Senate Democrats were more divided. SBC Chair Sasser opposed any summit with the administration until the Democrats had a unified bargaining position. To get a resolution out of committee, he was forced to ease the cuts in defense, protect farm programs, and leave a number of domestic cuts unspecified. The Senate plan called for $25 billion in savings through revenues and entitlement cuts. There was growing sentiment among a diverse group of senators to forego a resolution altogether in favor of going straight to summit with the administration. On May 9, Bush and congressional leaders agreed to high-level talks on a multiyear deficit reduction plan. On the other hand, House and Senate Appropriations Committees were eager for a resolution to pass so that they could begin their deliberations. This was particularly a problem in the Senate where spending bills were subject to a point of order without a budget resolution. The impasse stretched into June. The Senate finally passed a skeletal resolution that leaders described as "policy neutral" to allow appropriators to proceed.

The House was unwilling to go to Conference Committee because of the Senate resolution. Democratic Party leaders wanted to force the administration to make the first bid in the summit talks, but they also wanted to proceed with appropriations to prevent a year-end crisis. Finally, each house passed a so-called deeming resolution, determining that its own numbers were final in determining the parameters of committee allocations.[16]

Republican Division over Raising Taxes

The Democrats' main fear of a summit was that it was a trap that would allow the Republicans to blame them for any tax increases. Bush tried to reassure congressional leaders by promising "no preconditions" in the talks. But Democratic suspicions were seemingly confirmed when Chief of Staff John Sununu commented that the Democrats were free to put new taxes on the table and the president was free to take them off.[17] As a result, little progress was made through May and June among the seventeen legislators and three administration negotiators. Most of the first six weeks of summit meetings were spent in briefing sessions with OMB and CBO officials. The main accomplishment was an agreement on the size of the deficit reduction package that they would shoot for: $50 billion the first year, $500 billion over five years. Deciding how to achieve the savings would be much more difficult.

The outlook for the deficits kept getting worse. On June 20, CBO Director Robert Reischauer revealed that the FY 1991 deficit was now projected to be $232 billion because of a slowing economy and rapidly escalating costs of the thrift bailout.[18] Even Budget Director Darman conceded that the deficit would top $200 billion if the S&L bailout costs were included. Faced with these staggering numbers, President Bush made a monumental announcement on June 26:

> It is clear to me that both the size of the deficit problem and the need for a package that can be enacted require all of the following: entitlement and mandatory program reform; tax revenue increases; growth incentives; discretionary spending reductions; orderly reductions in defense expenditures; and budget process reform.[19]

"Tax revenue increases" meant that Bush had broken his "no new taxes" pledge. His statement had two immediate effects. First, it revitalized the stalled summit talks. Second, it incensed many congressional Republicans who believed that the president had sacrificed their best issue against the Democrats. The "no new taxes" mantra had become the defining issue of the Republican Party, and Bush's statement caused a major schism within the ranks. The House Republican Conference responded by passing a nonbinding resolution opposing the use of new taxes as part of the deficit reduction solution. Gleeful Democrats, for their part, agreed to proceed with making cuts in their favorite entitlements, even Social Security. At the same time, they advised the administration that new taxes had to be equitable and aimed at those families earning over $200,000 per year. Even congressional Republicans who supported the president balked at any increase in income taxes.

As summit negotiations bogged down again in July, it became apparent to both sides that the Gramm-Rudman-Hollings mandatory cuts would be devastating and had to be avoided at all costs. Even excluding the costs of the savings and loan bailout, the mid-session budget estimates revealed that a sequester of over $100 billion would be required to reach the deficit target for FY 1991. It would gut programs by requiring cuts as high as 43.6 percent in defense and 40.7 percent in domestic categories. Some solution had to be found. Congress recessed for a month on August 3, with both Republicans and Democrats hopeful that the threat of such cuts alone would force some compromise.

The Mini-Summit

The day before recess, Iraq invaded Kuwait, and budget worries were pushed off the front pages of the nation's newspapers. By the time Congress returned, the United States was engaged in a troop buildup in the Persian Gulf. Budget talks were now affected by the economic consequences of skyrocketing oil prices, additional defense needs, and possible war. In an attempt to insulate the summit from its many distractions, the talks were moved to Andrews Air Force Base outside Washington, DC. Yet the issues dividing negotiators had not been altered because of the change in venue. Republicans insisted on a capital gains tax cut; Democrats insisted on higher income taxes on the rich. Rank-and-file members of both parties were increasingly resentful of the closed, secret negotiations. As details of a possible deal leaked out, frustrated members who were excluded from the negotiations rallied against them. The New York delegation, for example, signed a letter promising to oppose any deal that included a provision to eliminate the deductibility of state and local taxes.[20] Rumors of massive cuts in Medicare had senior citizens groups organizing opposition. A group of conservative Republicans showed up wearing bright yellow "Junk the Summit" buttons.

On September 17, still far from a solution, talks were handed over to a group of eight negotiators. This mini-summit included House Minority Leader Robert Michel (R-IL), Senate Minority Leader Robert Dole (R-KS), Democratic leaders Gephardt, Foley, and Mitchell, and administration representatives Darman, Brady, and Sununu. Bush urged the negotiators to finish their business and produce a single package for an up or down vote by October 1.[21] With only a week to go until the start of the fiscal year, the country faced not only an impending war but massive GRH cuts and a complete government shutdown.

On Sunday, September 30, only hours before the start of the fiscal year, Bush and the seven negotiators emerged in the White House Rose Garden to announce that a deal had been reached. The new plan cut the deficit by $40 billion in FY 1991 and by $500 billion over five years. The cuts were real, the summiteers insisted—no smoke and mirrors. The cuts were also painful and unpopular. The deal attempted to take approximately one-third of the $500 billion savings from defense cuts, one-third from domestic cuts, and one-third from new revenues.

In a compromise on taxes, the package included neither a higher top income tax nor a capital gains tax reduction.[22] Most of the revenues came from energy taxes, excise taxes, payroll taxes, and corporate taxes, for a total of $148 billion. The domestic cuts came primarily from Medicare, slated for a $60 billion cut over five years. Defense would be cut by more than $100 billion over the same period. The agreement also included a thorough revision of the congressional budget process, including tougher new enforcement procedures to safeguard the savings. Gramm-Rudman-Hollings would be suspended for three years, and the fixed deficit targets, last set in 1987, were abandoned once again. The deal would go to Congress in the form of a new budget resolution to be followed by an omnibus reconciliation bill. Knowing that it would be a tough sell, the president and party leaders pledged unity and an all-out bipartisan effort to get it passed.

Breakdown of Party Unity

These key votes would take place only four weeks before the 1990 midterm elections. With politics on their minds, most members of Congress had been excluded from the negotiations. To many of them, the package announced at the eleventh hour confirmed their worst fears in facing the voters. The package was particularly divisive for Republicans. On Monday, Bush began calling Republican members of Congress from New York.[23] John Sununu tried to play hardball in a meeting with the House Republican Conference, threatening that Bush was prepared to embarrass Republicans up for reelection who did not support him on the budget. The move backfired. Immediately after the meeting, an irate Newt Gingrich (R-GA), the Republican Whip in the House, announced that he would actively oppose the summit agreement. His defection meant that supporters would not be able to use the whip organization that counts heads and lines up support. On the Democratic side, Gephardt and Foley tried gentler forms of persuasion, but still suggesting that the vote would be a test of party loyalty. The Speaker met privately with House committee chairs to enlist their support. Now desperate, leaders offered members some "flexibility" with the details of the package.[24]

On Tuesday evening, President Bush made a televised address to the nation to appeal for public support for the budget compromise. Following the practice Ronald Reagan had used so successfully in 1981, it was the first such appeal of his presidency. On Wednesday, Bush convinced Reagan to announce his support for the budget agreement. Republicans were summoned to the White House by the dozens to receive a personal pleading from the chief executive, but it did not seem to be stemming the firestorm. Republican critics labeled the plan the biggest tax increase in history. Democrats complained that it hit the middle class and the elderly the hardest and looked like five more years of Reaganomics.

On Thursday, October 4, the House debated the agreement all day and into the night. Dozens of members held back their votes, watching the totals unfold on the electronic tote boards. Democrats in particular watched to see if a majority of Republicans would support the president. With minutes to go, when it became clear that the Republicans would break ranks with Bush, Democrats cast their votes in droves against the package. In the early morning hours of Friday, an unusual bipartisan alliance in the House voted it down by a vote of 179–254. Both parties rejected it, Republicans opposing it 71–105 and Democrats voting against it 108–149.[25] Foley and Gephardt had managed to get only fourteen of the twenty-seven committee chairmen to support the agreement. Despite months of excruciating negotiations, the summit had been unable to resolve the nation's deficit crisis.

The defeat spared the Senate an equally difficult vote and plunged the country into an immediate budgetary crisis. Members had earlier agreed on a continuing resolution to temporarily fund the government through midnight, October 5. After the defeat, House leaders hastily assembled a second continuing resolution to keep agencies operating through October 12. On Saturday,

October 7, an irate President Bush vetoed the bill, stating that "responsible congressional action to reduce the deficit can be delayed no longer."[26] Government agencies were ordered to immediately shut down nonessential services, leaving lines of irate tourists locked out of popular Washington monuments and museums over the long Columbus Day weekend.

Bush relented the next day and signed a temporary funding bill and debt limit extension that would allow the government to operate as a new budget was being written. Congress quickly adopted a new budget resolution that provided essentially the same framework as the summit agreement but would allow congressional committees to change the details. Shaken by the budget defeat, Bush and his administration essentially turned the issue over to Congress. The president did not help himself politically the following week with a series of contradictory statements about taxes. He avoided reporters' questions during a morning jog, telling them to "read my hips," reinforcing an impression that he was abdicating leadership.[27]

Congressional Democratic leaders worked to put together a new package that could pass the House and Senate. This would involve taking Republican policy positions into account so that Bush would sign the final bill and so that the package could attract some Republican votes in the House and Senate. To appease liberal Democrats, taxes were shifted in part from the middle class to higher-income individuals and families, and the Medicare cuts were scaled back considerably. The process was much more open than the secret summit negotiations had been, and although the revised five-year plan closely resembled the original package, committee chairs and Democratic members were satisfied that their concerns had been taken into account. The reforms of the budget process were unchanged from the original agreement. After several more temporary funding bills, a package was reported. An all-night session that ended at dawn on October 27 produced a vote of 228–200 for the Omnibus Budget and Reconciliation Act of 1990 (OBRA-90). Bush supported the bill, and 47 Republicans and 181 Democrats voted for the measure. Later that day, the Senate passed OBRA-90 by a vote of 55–45, with Democrats approving 35–20 and Republicans dividing 19–25.[28] Hours later, with only ten days until the elections, members went home and the 101st Congress ended.

The Reconciliation Package

The final deficit reduction package could be considered a political victory for the Democrats. They had forced Bush to agree to new taxes, made significant cuts in defense and smaller cuts in Medicare, and were able to make other changes in the original summit agreement favorable to their positions. OBRA-90 was estimated to reduce the deficit by $42.5 billion the first year and by $496.2 billion over five years. Some of the major provisions included the following:

- *Defense cuts.* Reductions in planned spending for national defense made up the largest single share of the deficit reduction package: $130 billion below the 1990 baseline. Despite the magnitude of the cut, defense was reduced less than some had anticipated before Iraq's invasion of Kuwait. In addition, shifting cuts from domestic to defense spending would be prevented under the new budget process, discussed below.
- *Domestic discretionary cuts.* Programs in this category escaped the budget scalpel to a large extent. Programs would be allowed to grow with inflation to allow for new program initiatives for the first three years. Under the new discretionary appropriations caps, constraints on growth in domestic spending would be the most severe in the fourth and fifth years of the plan.
- *Entitlement cuts.* Most of the domestic cuts in the agreement came from entitlements. They absorbed $99 billion in cuts below the baseline over the subsequent five years. Although Medicare cuts were reduced from $60 billion in the original agreement to some $40 billion in the final package, they remained the largest domestic program cut. This was achieved by lowering reimbursement payments to providers and by increasing deductibles and copayments. Other major mandatory program cuts were imposed on farm support payments and income security.
- *Interest.* Because of the reduced spending and increased revenues, $68.4 billion of the deficit savings was accounted for by lower interest payments on the national debt over the subsequent five years.
- *Revenues.* Perhaps the most controversial aspect of the deficit reduction agreement was the $137 billion in new revenues raised by the budget agreement. The top personal income tax rate was raised from 28 percent to 31 percent. Personal exemptions were phased out and itemized deductions were limited for higher-income individuals. Tobacco and alcohol taxes were increased, and a 10 percent surcharge on luxury items such as boats was enacted. The cap on the amount of income subject to Medicare taxes was increased from $51,300 to $125,000, raising $27 billion over five years. The major concession to the Bush administration was keeping the capital gains tax at the old 28 percent level rather than raising it to the new 31 percent rate for taxpayers in that bracket.

OBRA-90 and the Budget Enforcement Act

The hard-fought budget agreement that had taken most of the year to reach not only made a number of important policy changes but once again revised the congressional budget process. Most significantly, the agreement suspended the Gramm-Rudman-Hollings mandatory sequester process after five years of failing to reach the required deficit targets. Perhaps the single greatest flaw of GRH was that Congress was held responsible for changes in the budget beyond their control—most notably, poorer-than-expected economic performance and increased entitlement spending through greater utilization and health care cost increases. Instead, Congress expanded on the experience of 1988 and 1989, creating separate appropriation caps for the three main categories of discretionary spending: domestic, defense, and international. While the new process contained deficit targets, they were not mandatory: Congress was held harmless from economic and technical changes. The emphasis shifted from deficit reduction to spending control, concentrating on maintaining budgetary discipline where Congress had direct responsibility.[29]

Discretionary Spending Limits

The Budget Enforcement Act (BEA) was contained in Title XIII of OBRA-90. It divided discretionary appropriations into three categories with separate outlay and budget authority limits for FY 1991, FY 1992, and FY 1993. In the final two years of the plan, discretionary spending would be constrained by a single cap. Thus, tradeoffs between categories would be prohibited in the first three years, largely to prevent domestic spending from being increased at the expense of defense. The defense category included not only Department of Defense spending but also defense-related activities such as the Energy Department's nuclear weapons programs. International programs included foreign economic and military aid, the State Department, and international financial programs such as the Export-Import Bank.

Under the BEA, discretionary spending limits were to be adjusted twice each year based on changes in budgetary definitions under the act and based on inflation.[30] Largely because of the efforts of Senator Byrd, the domestic caps allowed some modest growth in spending. In addition, the major reductions in total discretionary spending did not come until the fourth and fifth years, under a single cap, when defense could be raided. The three caps were held harmless from additional outlays resulting from Desert Shield (then Desert Storm), changes in economic assumptions or technical reestimates, costs associated with the savings and loan bailout, Egyptian debt forgiveness, and foreign contributions to DOD.[31] A potential loophole to the fiscal discipline was included in the BEA by specifying that any spending determined to be an "emergency" by both Congress and the president was exempted from the caps.

The "Mini-Sequester"

The appropriations caps were to be enforced by a new set of rules and procedures. Under the 1985 Balanced Budget Act, congressional budget resolutions covered only a single year. As we have seen, this created a huge loophole where Congress could simply shift additional spending or revenue-losing measures to future years. The BEA tightened enforcement by making the totals in budget resolutions and reconciliation bills binding over five years. If the spending caps were breached, excess spending would be eliminated by a "mini-sequester" within that category only. For example, if international program spending exceeded allowable authority or outlay caps, across-the-board cuts would be imposed on all accounts within the category. The law defined two kinds of sequesters, depending on how far along Congress was in the budget process. For budget-busting bills enacted before July 1, a "within session" sequester for the fiscal year would be triggered within fifteen days of enactment. Bills passed after July 1 that caused the caps to be exceeded would be subject to a "look back" sequester that reduced the discretionary spending limit for that category in the next fiscal year by the amount of the overage.[32]

The return to appropriations caps after nearly two decades reflected a notable shift in congressional philosophy and an increased institutional capacity to enforce such caps. Recall that Congress experimented with spending caps five times from 1967 to 1973 during the budget battles with President Nixon. In each case, the caps failed because of the autonomy of authorizing and the Appropriations Committees and the absence of enforcement mechanisms. After 1975, the functional subtotals in the budget resolution could have been considered caps, but they also were routinely breached by the spending committees. It was the experience after the 1987 budget summit that convinced negotiators that caps could work if sufficient procedural safeguards and enforcement mechanisms were included.

Pay-As-You-Go Rules

Another significant change enacted by the Budget Enforcement Act was new "pay-as-you-go" (PAYGO) rules as Congress attempted to extend some budgetary discipline to entitlements and revenues. While GRH had the effect of requiring that amendments to taxing and spending bills be "deficit neutral" in some cases, the BEA went further in codifying such rules and applying them to entitlements and all revenue bills. Under the new PAYGO rules, any action that increased entitlement eligibility or reduced revenues must be offset by spending cuts or tax increases elsewhere in the budget. This applied to changes that would occur as many as five years in the future. The provisions affected the total of all budgetary legislation, not just individual measures. The only exception was in the case of legislation deemed "emergency" by both branches.

PAYGO rules applied only to actions taken by Congress, not increases in entitlements or decreases in revenues that occurred under existing law. As such, they extended sequestration to revenues and entitlements for the first time. The BEA allowed the Budget Committees to issue reconciliation instructions to the Ways and Means Committee and Finance Committee to require an offset for a revenue loss or an entitlement increase. The impact of these provisions was somewhat different from the impact of spending caps in that these provisions focused on "deficit neutrality" rather than spending control since new entitlements could expand without limit if they were financed through new revenues.

Social Security received special treatment under OBRA-90. Under the new rules, the highly popular government trust fund was removed from all calculations under the BEA. The legislation instituted a Social Security "firewall" to prevent using trust fund surpluses from deficit reduction and to prevent expanding benefits or reducing payroll taxes.[33] Excluding Social Security from the official deficit made the deficit appear much higher.

Deficit Targets

The BEA retained overall deficit targets for five years, but the other provisions of the act made them essentially meaningless. The targets would be adjusted by the president each year to reflect changing economic and technical assumptions, emergency legislation, and other exempt items such as Desert Storm expenses and the S&L bailout. Even if economic conditions deteriorated during the consideration of the budget, the deficit targets, in effect, would be shifted upwards if the other rules have been followed. The law provided an opportunity to reassess the deficit targets and reinstate the mandatory GRH sequester procedures in early 1993, after the 1992 presidential election.

The Credit Budget

OBRA-90 and the BEA brought federal credit activity under the purview and discipline of the new budget process beginning with FY 1992.[34] Prior to this, credit activities were included only on a cash flow basis. Many had argued that this did not accurately reflect the real costs or liabilities to the government. Under the revised procedures, direct loans and loan guarantees would be recorded as an outlay at the time the loan was dispensed, more accurately reflecting the cost to the government. Discretionary credit programs under the jurisdiction of the Appropriations Committees were included under the discretionary spending cap.

Revised Budget Timetable

Once again, Congress revised the budget timetable to make it conform to the new process, although far fewer changes were made than in 1985. Five days before the president submits his budget, CBO is required to submit a "sequestration preview" in order to make comparisons with OMB estimates. The president must send the budget to Congress by the first Monday in February. OMB is required to explain differences with CBO, but its estimates of the discretionary spending caps and the deficit targets must be used by all parties during consideration and approval of the budget. Although estimates are to be revised in August, the initial OMB numbers are controlling so that Congress can proceed with more certainty and without the fear of an "August surprise" that would undermine previous work.

April 15 was established as the deadline for adopting the budget resolution, more feasible under the spending caps and new rules. If Congress would miss the deadline, the Appropriations Committees could proceed with their work based on the discretionary caps. Their bills are in order on the House floor after May 15, and the target date for adoption is June 30. Any supplemental appropriations enacted before July 1 that violate the caps are subject to a sequester fifteen days after enactment. In August, CBO and OMB must update their sequester estimates based on congressional actions. In a significant gain for the administration, under the BEA, compliance is determined by OMB; CBO estimates are only advisory. If congressional actions have exceeded the caps, Congress has until the end of the session to meet the targets.

Under the old Gramm-Rudman-Hollings procedure, Congress had only until October 15 to come into compliance with the deficit totals. Any actions to reduce the deficit after that date were not considered. Under the BEA, OMB does not issue its final sequestration report and the president does not order a sequestration until fifteen days after adjournment. The GAO must review compliance and issue a report thirty days later.

The Omnibus Budget Reconciliation Act of 1990 represented the largest deficit reduction package in history. The escalating deficits had become so serious that President Bush had compromised his campaign promise not to raise taxes, causing a serious split within the Republican Party. Party leaders in Congress now had additional rules to strengthen enforcement of the budget resolutions. Would they strengthen or weaken their ability to maintain party unity and develop a coherent party position in terms of budgeting? The summit process seemed to be redefining presidential-congressional bargaining. Did the failure of the first summit agreement strengthen or weaken the trend toward more reliance on interbranch summits and commissions? These questions are explored below, after considering the five-year experiment with automatic deficit reduction.

Abandoning Mandatory Deficit Reduction

Several studies have attempted to gauge the impact of the Balanced Budget Act during the five years it was in effect.[35] One of the act's main goals was to force the president and Congress to make more concerted efforts to reach deficit targets and avoid mandatory cuts. The deficit declined in FY 1987 to $150 billion, the first budget fully subject to the strictures of GRH. But this was largely explained by the enactment of the Tax Reform Act of 1986 which, despite its supposed revenue neutrality, actually resulted in additional revenues in 1987 of $22 billion to $27 billion.[36] In subsequent years, however, the deficit remained static at $155 billion in FY 1988 and $152 billion in FY 1989, before spiraling upwards to $221 billion in FY 1990 and to a record $270 billion in FY 1991.[37] These figures, too, are somewhat misleading because of external forces driving the deficit upwards, particularly the savings and loan bailout.

A better way to measure the impact of GRH is to compare the amount of deficit reduction contained in the president's budget before and after 1985. Using both CBO figures and OMB estimates, the total amount of deficit reduction was *less* after GRH than before.[38] According to OMB, the four Reagan budgets before GRH contained an average of $36.8 billion of savings. This fell to $30 billion in the next four Reagan budgets and to $34 billion in Bush's FY 1990 and FY 1991 budgets. Using CBO's estimates, the total amount of deficit reduction fell from an average of $25 billion before GRH to an average of $24 billion afterwards. Clearly, GRH did not increase the president's emphasis on deficit reduction.

Another goal of GRH was to force Congress and the president to seek long-term solutions to the deficit by setting out a five-year declining path to a balanced budget. In reality, the opposite occurred: both branches instead turned to short-term accounting gimmicks and optimistic assumptions in order to head off sequestration. After the passage of GRH, policymakers increasingly relied on overly optimistic economic and technical assumptions to reduce the apparent size of the deficit and also turned to one-time savings such as asset sales to reach the targets. For technical and economic reasons, in the four years before GRH, the actual deficits were greater than the deficit proposed in the president's budget by an average of $8.5 billion. For the six years after GRH, the actual deficits increased by an average of $53.5 billion over the figures presented in the president's budget because of economic and technical assumptions.[39] Although this average figure was driven upwards because of the rapid escalation of the thrift bailout in FY 1990 and FY 1991, the evidence clearly reveals increased reliance on optimistic assumptions to make the deficit look smaller.

After the passage of GRH, the utilization of one-time-only savings to lower the deficit for that year increased exponentially. This included accelerating revenue collections, selling government assets, moving agencies such as the Postal Service off budget, shifting pay increases by a day to fall into the next fiscal year, and altering retirement rules.[40] Before GRH, the permanent savings averaged $14 billion per year compared to only $3 billion annually in one-time savings. In the four years after, permanent savings averaged only $10 billion per year compared to $11 billion annually for one-time sales. Faced with fixed targets, Congress and the president turned to short-term expediency to avoid sequestration.

The 1985 Balanced Budget and Emergency Deficit Reduction Act received bipartisan support in part because both parties believed that the rules could assist in promoting their party's positions in terms of how to reduce the deficits. At the same time, both parties ran risks because defense and domestic discretionary programs would be cut disproportionately if a more broad-based package were not arrived at. For Democrats, that meant getting the president to accept higher revenues. For Republicans, it meant turning to entitlements as a source of cuts. However, *GRH failed to force greater reliance on either new taxes or entitlements as a source of deficit reduction*. Revenue increases constituted 64 percent of deficit reduction before GRH; this declined to 40 percent in the four years following its enactment.[41] Entitlements did not increase as a source of deficit reduction, either. The budget agreement of 1990 abandoned fixed deficit targets for floating targets and shifted the focus from deficit reduction to spending control. In enacting

OBRA-90, Congress exceeded the total amount of deficit reduction that occurred during the entire GRH era. The sequestration threat proved hollow, failing to force the president and Congress to raise taxes or cut entitlements.

Partisanship, Rules, and Budget Summits

The 1990 budget summit agreement represented the most significant compromise by the two parties of their core budgetary positions since 1981: for the Republicans, raising taxes; for the Democrats, cutting entitlements. One might find much to commend in making concessions to reach a deficit reduction package in the public interest, given the size of the deficits. From the perspective of the parties, however, the result was extremely divisive. More than a dozen years later, Bush's decision to agree to revenue increases was still being attacked by conservative Republicans.[42]

The original vote on OBRA-90 was bipartisan in the sense that both caucuses were opposed and splintered. The rejection reflects the limits of summitry and illustrates that party leaders, although strengthened, cannot stray too far from the policy preferences of members. This was most striking for Republicans because of the prominence of the "no new taxes" promise. The split in House Republican leadership, with Minority Leader Michel favoring the agreement and Minority Whip Gingrich opposing it, fractured Republican unity. Democratic leaders in the House were in favor of the agreement, but Democratic cohesion weakened when, out of concern that they would be blamed for raising taxes, a number of Democrats refused to support the agreement unless a majority of Republicans supported it as well.

What explains the change between the first vote and the second vote? From a macro perspective, the final agreement was fundamentally the same as the original package in terms of the relative proportion of revenue increases, defense cuts, and entitlement cuts. From a microbudgetary perspective, enough changes were made between the two versions to satisfy a number of Democratic committee chairs who had opposed the original agreement. Although Bush supported and signed the revised version of OBRA-90, it had become a deal that was associated more with the Democratic Congress than with the Republican White House. As a result, the second vote more closely resembled partisan voting patterns of the previous fifteen years, although with notably less cohesion. On the final vote of 228–220 on October 27, 181 of 255 (71 percent) Democrats supported the bill—73 more yea votes than on the first version. House Republicans voted against the final version of the bill 47–126, or 65 percent against. That represented 24 fewer votes for the amended version than for the original agreement. The Senate avoided a vote on the first version after the House defeated it. For the final version, both parties in the Senate were similarly splintered, with 64 percent of Democrats voting for it and 57 percent of Republicans voting against. While the final vote qualified as a party vote, one of the results of summitry was to weaken party unity.

Divided government continued to lead to extraordinary attempts to resolve partisan divisions over the budget and deficits. Unlike in 1983, however, a bipartisan commission failed to provide the basis for compromising and making hard choices. The NEC failed largely because of the nature of the appointments to the commission and a lack of commitment to that process by the executive branch and legislative leaders. By 1990, budget summits had become the rule rather than the exception, but the summit that year was the epitome of extraordinary resolution and unorthodox lawmaking.[43] Only 5 of 535 elected members of Congress had participated in the final negotiations in September. Despite leaks, the process was essentially shielded from their eyes and ideas. Even after ten years of divided government and a deficit crisis, this was too much for many members who were willing to break with their party leaders.

The revision of congressional budget rules in 1990 was unaffected by the negotiations in October. In general, the new rules did not do as much to strengthen majority party leaders as the Balanced Budget Act had five years earlier. They did strengthen enforcement of budget totals significantly, however, and made it harder for individual members and committees to avoid budget constraints. The appropriation caps left some room for maneuver within the totals but did not allow changes in relative budget shares. The PAYGO rules made tradeoffs explicit. Revenues and entitlements came under more restrictions than before, but sequesters would not occur because of economic trends, international events, or unforeseen crises such as the savings and loan bailout.

Budgeting under the Budget Enforcement Act

Even though OBRA-90 and the BEA represented an abandonment of fixed deficit targets, many doubted that Congress and the president could live within their strictures.[44] In 1991 and 1992, however, both branches respected the spending caps and PAYGO rules with few exceptions.[45] The Bush administration's supplemental requests in 1991 included increases for housing, nuclear weapons cleanup, Radio Free Europe, and other programs. So as not to violate the caps, the requests were accompanied by rescission requests in each of the three categories to offset the additional spending. Under PAYGO rules, extensions of unemployment compensation were financed through additional revenues and rescissions rather than breaking the caps. Despite the onset of a recession, Congress passed on opportunities to void the caps when the economy declined in two successive quarters, voting decisively to retain the spending limits.

The within-category sequester was used as well. Only four weeks after OBRA was signed, a drafting error was found in the foreign aid bill, exceeding the international program cap for 1991 by $395 million.[46] As a result, OMB Director Darman ordered a 1.9 percent sequester in all international programs. In April 1991, a seemingly insignificant transfer of $7 million from a defense to a domestic account was met with the threat of a within-session sequester. Later that year, a $2.4 million sequester was ordered when OMB ruled that the domestic cap had been exceeded by a supplemental.

The new budget process was also tested in terms of the designation of certain programs as "emergencies" exempt from budget cap discipline. In March 1991, a $42 billion supplemental to cover the costs of the Gulf War was exempt under the BEA. A second $5.4 billion supplemental, however, was subject to the new budget rules. OMB refused to accept the argument by Congress that additional funds for the U.S. Information Agency or veterans' programs constituted an emergency. Congress, in turn, refused to agree that increased military fuel costs not associated with the Gulf War were an emergency. Even some "motherhood" bills failed to gain an emergency designation: increases in life insurance and educational benefits for Desert Storm soldiers were turned down, as well as aid to local communities hard hit by the deployment.

The biggest threat to the new budget process followed the collapse of the Soviet Union. In the face of a growing recession and the end of the Cold War, leading Democrats introduced legislation, nicknamed "Operation Jericho," to tear down the budget walls separating defense and domestic programs.[47] Submitting his FY 1993 budget to Congress in early 1992, however, President Bush insisted on maintaining the walls. Any savings in the defense accounts would be used for deficit reduction, not for greater domestic spending. The House passed an unusual two-track budget resolution, one maintaining the caps, the other allowing significant transfers from defense to domestic spending. Reflective of a growing hawkishness on the deficit among conservative Democrats, such as Charles Stenholm (D-TX), the president and Republicans prevailed, and the "walls" bill was defeated in March, 187–238, repudiating the House leadership.[48]

Congress went on to cut the FY 1993 defense budget $4 billion below the Bush request and $11 billion below the 1993 cap. Congress also cut the foreign aid request by $1.3 billion. In a concession to the Democrats, the administration agreed to reclassify as defense spending $1 billion worth of programs such as job retraining and aid to school districts with military dependents, normally considered domestic spending. Despite the caps, President Bush was successful at passing a bill to aid the successor states of the Soviet Union after criticism from Richard Nixon, candidate Bill Clinton, and some members of Congress. The administration won support from congressional Democrats, who were worried about the recession, by promising to accelerate some $2 billion in public works spending and loan guarantees to localities. The package partially avoided the budget rules by committing $12.3 billion through the International Monetary Fund and taking the other $1.2 billion from within the existing international cap.

Despite a wide range of attempts to evade the discipline, often fueled by the Appropriations Committees, Congress largely obeyed the spending constraints mandated by OBRA-90 and followed the rules set down in the Budget Enforcement Act. More than fifty PAYGO provisions had taken effect, although many of them were minor.[49] In 1992, Congress completed action on all appropriations bills by October 5, allowing the earliest adjournment since 1988. In general, enforcement under the BEA was successful: within-category sequesters were ordered when caps were violated, PAYGO rules were followed, the "walls" between categories were protected, emergency exemptions were limited, and Congress had appropriated below the cap in defense and used the savings for deficit reduction. Yet, for several reasons, no one was celebrating the accomplishments.

First, the task would become even more difficult in 1993, as the discretionary caps began to bite. The 1990 budget agreement had allowed domestic spending to increase $40 billion between FY 1991 and FY 1993; that cushion would not exist for FY 1994 and FY 1995 unless the deal were renegotiated in 1993 after the presidential election. Second, a new wave of budget gloom had swept through Washington. Despite the tax increases, Medicare cuts, and discretionary discipline, the deficit was getting worse again, with projections showing it topping $400 billion in a few years. Only two years after the big budget deal, ravaged by the costs of deposit insurance and a deepening recession, the gap between spending and revenues would continue to increase without another dramatic round of deficit reduction.

What OBRA-90 and the BEA represented was a decision to make Congress accountable for the part of the budget over which it has the most short-term control: discretionary spending. The deteriorating deficit situation, however, demonstrated the limitations of this approach for deficit reduction. The extension of PAYGO rules to entitlements and revenues had little effect on curbing the growth of mandatory programs. As a result, the battle against budget deficits would have to be rejoined by a new administration in 1993, this time under unified party control.

CHAPTER 6

Clinton and the Democratic Deficit Reduction Plan, 1993

After twelve years of divided government, would unified control of Congress and the presidency under the Democrats facilitate solving the deficit problem? Although Bill Clinton had promised during the campaign to cut the deficit in half by 1996, it was his unrelenting focus on the economy, not deficit reduction, that got him elected president. Yet even before his inauguration as the 42nd President of the United States, the familiar scenario of growing budget deficits demanded Clinton's attention. Budget projections in late 1992 showed the deficits hovering at $300 billion and, if nothing were done, heading past $500 billion by the end of the century. The new administration, eager to reform health care and welfare, was forced to confront this problem first; deficit reduction would again drive national politics in 1993. Congress was battle-hardened from the budget wars. It had acquired through the Reagan and Bush administrations significant capacity in budgeting with rules and procedures that allowed party leaders to formulate alternatives and to negotiate with the administration. Would congressional leaders cede leadership back to the president or be willing to take on the unpopular choices needed to reduce the deficit?

This chapter explores the adoption of the Omnibus Budget and Reconciliation Act of 1993 (OBRA-93). Clinton, like Reagan in 1981, would attempt to seize the initiative to make significant policy changes in the first six months of his presidential term. Democratic leaders would work with the president in trying to build majorities for a number of unpopular tax increases and spending cuts, and they would succeed by the narrowest of margins. How would the congressional institutions and budget rules that had undergone so much change since the end of the Carter administration affect budget choices in 1993? Would a return to unified party control of government increase, decrease, or have no effect on congressional partisanship? What was the impact of the Democratic budget plan, and what was its political legacy?

137

Deficit Crisis Redux

What Happened to the 1990 Deficit Savings?

The Omnibus Budget and Reconciliation Act of 1990 (OBRA-90) claimed savings of nearly $500 billion in 1990 dollars. Yet three years after its enactment, deficit projections were actually larger than they had been before. In the fall of 1990, the Congressional Budget Office (CBO) estimated that the deficit would fall to $29 billion in FY 1995 as a result of OBRA-90. Three years later, the deficit for that year was estimated at $284 billion, an increase of $255 billion in three years. Republicans used this as compelling evidence against the tax increases OBRA-90 contained, blaming the increases for the recession and George Bush's 1992 electoral defeat.

The deficit situation worsened in the early 1990s because of the deterioration of the U.S. economy and technical errors in estimating revenues and entitlements, not because of inherent defects in the plan itself or a breakdown in the Budget Enforcement Act (BEA) designed to protect the savings.[1] Technical errors were the greatest culprit, adding $185 billion to the projected deficit in FY 1995 alone. Annual costs of Medicare, Medicaid, and other benefit programs were $85 billion greater than expected. Revenues for 1995 were projected to be $138 billion less than in the 1990 forecast, $102 billion because of the recession, and $36 billion because of errors in predicting what the new tax provisions would achieve. Conversely, the deficits did not grow because of policy changes made by Congress; only $2 billion of the revised FY 1995 deficit was attributable to purposeful actions to spend more or tax less. The BEA succeeded in holding the line on discretionary spending, even if it did not include any provisions for further policy changes if the deficits worsened. The bottom line for OBRA-90 was a net deficit savings of $482 billion in five years over what would have occurred if nothing had been done.[2] The deficit in 1995 would have been nearly $500 billion without OBRA-90.

Targeting the Deficits: Responsibility and Risks

The Clinton administration and congressional Democrats were jolted by the numbers they saw after the election. Both the Office of Management and Budget (OMB) and CBO were showing a deficit path veering upwards. On January 6, 1993, Bush Budget Director Richard Darman released the outgoing administration's final set of estimates. For the first time since the executive budget was created in 1921, the president did not submit a set of budget requests, instead leaving the decisions to his successor.[3] OMB figures added $189 billion to the deficit over what it had projected in mid-1992 during the campaign. But as bad as the new numbers were, congressional Democrats argued that they were deceptively low. Darman, they complained, could not resist manipulating the numbers one last time. The key year for measuring Clinton's campaign promise was FY 1997, the fourth year of his presidency. OMB projected a deficit of $300 billion, based on several controversial assumptions. Clinton supporters suggested that a more accurate number was $360 billion, making the task of cutting the deficit in half all the more difficult.[4] CBO's long-term budget outlook projected a deficit of $319 billion in 1997 and showed the gap between revenues and expenditures growing to as high as $650 billion (7 percent of GDP) early in the next century.[5]

Clinton had promised a new economic plan immediately after his inauguration. The schedule called for the unveiling of his economic and budget package in mid-February when he delivered the State of the Union address. During the transition, his new economic team immediately began to struggle with the need for deficit reduction and its political risks. The team included former Texas senator Lloyd Bentsen as Treasury Secretary, former HBC chair Leon Panetta as Budget Director, Robert Rubin as Chair of the National Economic Council, and Laura D'Andrea Tyson as Chair of the Council of Economic Advisors (CEA). Along with the president's personal advisors, they realized that they would have to temper Clinton's promises to stimulate the sluggish but expanding economy because of the growing pressures for serious deficit reduction.

The president faced a critical choice the day after his inauguration. Two and a half years earlier, the authors of OBRA-90 had set January 21, 1993, as the day the new president would have to choose between the fixed deficit targets of Gramm-Rudman-Hollings that had prevailed between 1985 and 1990, or the flexible targets that were established for 1991 to 1995. Preserving flexibility, the administration opted to retain the floating deficit targets.[6] Predictably, the decision was attacked by Phil Gramm and other Republicans. Gramm promised that he would follow his familiar strategy of using the statutory debt limit (which would expire sometime in April) for an all-out assault on the deficit in the form of a balanced budget amendment, with the help of H. Ross Perot and his United We Stand backers.

Several members assumed new leadership posts in Congress. In the House of Representatives, Democrats had chosen Martin Olav Sabo of Minnesota to chair the Budget Committee. A liberal, Sabo was less experienced in the arcane world of congressional budgeting than his predecessor, Leon Panetta. Members of the House Appropriations Committee hoped that in Sabo, a longtime member of the Appropriations Committee, they finally had a Budget Committee Chair more sensitive to their interests. In the Senate, the resignation of Lloyd Bentsen to take the reins at the Treasury elevated New York Senator Daniel Patrick Moynihan to the post of Chair of the Finance Committee. Deficit hawks within the Democratic Party had grown stronger in recent years. But while congressional support for the concept of deficit reduction was strong in principle, agreement on the specifics would prove highly problematic.

The Clinton Economic and Budget Plan

Stimulus, Investment, and Deficit Reduction

The Clinton plan announced to a joint session of Congress and a national television audience on February 17, 1993, was greeted by Democratic cheers and Republican jeers. The plan had three components: a short-term economic stimulus package, a long-term investment package, and a deficit reduction plan balanced between tax increases and spending cuts.[7] The $30 billion stimulus package was divided between $16 billion in new spending and $12 billion in business tax credits, with the remainder in loans and construction authority. The four-year, $160 billion investment plan combined new spending on infrastructure and on training and education and other social programs such as child care with additional tax incentives. These two components of the president's campaign promises were largely overshadowed by the largest piece of the administration's proposals: a package of tax increases and spending cuts to cut the federal deficit by $493 billion over five years. Spending cuts of $247 billion were matched by $246 in new revenues, a politically sensitive 1–1 ratio. The proposed spending cuts came from defense ($76 billion), discretionary domestic programs ($50 billion), entitlements ($76 billion), Social Security ($21 billion), and reduced interest payments ($24 billion). Proposed new revenues included higher personal income taxes for upper-income individuals ($126 billion), an energy tax based on BTU content ($71 billion), higher corporate income taxes ($31 billion), and a variety of other smaller measures. To protect lower-income families, the Clinton administration asked Congress to expand the Earned Income Tax Credit (EITC) which would cost $26 billion.

The reaction was partisan, with Republicans lashing out at the ratio of spending cuts to tax increases in what they labeled a "tax and spend" Democratic package. They immediately questioned counting an increase in the amount of Social Security income subject to federal taxes, which would bring in an additional $21 billion, as a spending cut as the administration had proposed. When the stimulus and investment packages were included, the deficit savings netted cuts of only $117 billion and tax increases of $207 billion, nearly the inverse of what administration officials had earlier advocated. Nonetheless, both the economic and budget plan and the president himself received high ratings in the polls. He received public support for the package from Fed Chair Alan Greenspan, and long-term interest rates continued to decline.

The Budget Resolution

The stimulus and investment packages designed to sweeten the deal would prove harder to sell than the deficit reduction proposals. The fast track for the president's proposals began with the congressional budget resolution. The short-term stimulus package was contained in a supplemental appropriations bill, with the bulk of the spending cuts and revenues lumped together in a reconciliation bill. The remaining one-third of the spending cuts would have to be made by the Appropriations Committees through regular appropriations bills. To deflect Republican criticism that spending cuts would never be enacted, the Democrats revised the budget schedule in order to vote on the full package of spending cuts in the budget resolution before bringing up the $16 billion stimulus bill.

The administration lobbied Congress hard for the budget resolution and stimulus plan as a parade of cabinet secretaries testified on the Hill. The president himself traveled to the Capitol to pressure both wavering Democrats and Republicans, bringing a birthday cake to House minority leader Michel and later dining on Big Macs and fries with Senate minority leader Dole.[8] The administration suffered a setback when CBO's analysis of the president's proposals found some $60 billion less in deficit reduction than claimed through 1998. To keep conservative Democrats on board, both the House and Senate Budget Committees, with the administration's support, added an additional $63 billion in deficit reduction, mostly in additional spending cuts. The Senate Budget Committee defeated over fifty Republican amendments, and both budget committees approved their budget resolution in strict party line votes. This was no guarantee of unanimous Democratic support throughout the process, however. The details, such as the increasingly unpopular BTU tax, would be debated and voted on later.

In the third week of March, the House of Representatives approved both the budget resolution and the president's stimulus package. The $1.5 trillion resolution passed 243–183 with only eleven Democratic defections, while the stimulus package was approved 235–190 with twenty-two Democrats voting against. Not a single Republican voted for either measure, a pattern that would repeat itself throughout the spring and summer. A week later, under the restrictive procedures of the budget process, the Senate approved the budget resolution by a vote of 54–45 sending it to conference. Only two Democrats joined the unanimous minority in opposition.

The Demise of the Stimulus Package

Unlike the budget resolution, the stimulus package did not fall under the protection of the budget rules which limited debate in the Senate. After repeated efforts at compromise failed, the Senate Republicans filibustered, as much to send a message that they should not be ignored as to elucidate their specific policy differences. After failing four times to get the sixty votes necessary to invoke cloture, the administration and Senate leaders conceded defeat at the end of April. The time had already passed for much of the spending to be obligated by summer, a key rationale of the short-term stimulus package. Clinton would eventually succeed in getting about half the money approved, such as the $4 billion extension of unemployment benefits that was approved the same day the stimulus package was abandoned.

Approving the Package: The "Near Death" Experience

The Reconciliation Process

Despite the defeat of the spending portion of the stimulus package, the administration continued to make progress on the deficit reduction package, most of which was contained in the largest reconciliation bill in history. Conferees had no trouble in agreeing on a budget resolution, and it was approved by both houses. The Democrats also faced the problem of the expiration of the statutory debt limit. Once again, Senator Gramm and others had threatened to use the must-pass bill as a vehicle for deficit reduction measures such as the line-item veto or a balanced budget amendment. Although the House automatically approved a multiyear extension with the enactment of the budget resolution, they had to go to conference with the Senate. The best the Democrats could do was to provide enough borrowing authority to cover the government's needs through September 30, 1993, an increase of $225 billion. Gramm and his allies were thwarted by a procedural maneuver by the Democratic leadership. Because of the early passage of the budget resolution, congressional Democrats were able to include the debt limit extension as part of the reconciliation instructions and more restrictive floor procedures. This protection would hold for the permanent increase in the debt limit as well, as long it was included as part of the reconciliation bill that contained the deficit reduction package.

The fate of the debt limit compared to that of the stimulus package was a demonstration of the impact of reconciliation and the budget rules. The deficit reduction plan was embodied in the $343 billion reconciliation bill, a measure providing binding instructions to committees. This bill was protected on the floor from nongermane amendments, from any amendments that would increase the deficit, and from a filibuster on the Senate floor. The only procedural "loophole" left after the 1985 revisions in reconciliation was the provision that allows opponents to offer a motion to strike, potentially allowing separate votes on controversial elements. Over the years, multiyear reconciliation bills had increased in size and scope, culminating in OBRA-90 and OBRA-93, Clinton's deficit reduction package.

House Passage: The Narrow Democratic Majority

As the House of Representatives prepared to take up the reconciliation bill, the most serious threat to passage seemed to come from oil-and-gas-state Democrats who felt that the BTU tax would be damaging to their constituencies. On the Senate side, David Boren (D-OK) proposed an alternative approach that would scrap the BTU tax and replace the lost revenue with an entitlement cap.[9] Boren's vote on the Senate Finance Committee was particularly crucial because the Democrats held a slim 11–9 majority on the committee, and the defection of a single Democratic senator would leave the committee deadlocked 10–10. The Boren alternative made things more difficult in the House where conservative Democrats feared "walking the plank" by voting for the BTU tax, only to have the Senate eliminate it in their version.

Administration lobbyists, including the president himself, pressured House Democrats to pass the bill, claiming that nothing less than the viability of Clinton's fledgling presidency was at stake. With their unanimous opposition, Republicans were ignored in the bargaining over details and the lobbying campaign. The challenge for the president and party leaders was to assuage more conservative Democrats while holding the liberal wing of the party that was already restive over the cuts in entitlements and social programs. The administration made concessions, promising that they would support reducing the energy tax by some $30 billion in the Senate version of the bill. They attempted to mollify deficit hawks by promising to further control entitle-ment growth.[10]

On the day of the House vote, May 27, head counts were still coming up short.[11] With all of the attention focused on Democrats opposing the bill, Democrats loyal to the president launched a counterattack. A petition was circulated demanding that any committee or subcommittee chair who voted against the bill be stripped of his or her position by the Democratic caucus. Within hours, supporters had gathered eighty signatures, enough to force a showdown in caucus if necessary. Several wavering subcommittee chairmen announced that they would support the bill. In the end, every committee chairman and all but eleven subcommittee chairmen would vote for the rec-onciliation bill.

The president spent the day on the phone calling likely "no" voters. The vice president met with small groups of opponents in his Senate office. After the defeat of the stimulus package, the administration proved to be single-minded, focused, and ultimately successful. In the end, they prevailed by six votes, 219–213. Thirty-eight Democrats and all 175 Republicans voted against the deficit reduction package. This was only half the battle as atten-tion turned to the Senate.

Senate Passage: More Cuts, Fewer Tax Increases

Although a Senate defeat of the budget package would be devastating to the Clinton presidency, passage was even less secure than in the House. Twenty Democratic senators were up for reelection in 1994, and the relentless ham-mering by Republicans on the tax issue presented them with real electoral problems. In a massive, $500 billion package affecting virtually everything the government does, it is easy to find something not to like. The problem for Majority Leader George Mitchell and President Clinton was to forge a com-promise package and sell it to Democrats on the basis of the viability of their party's presidency. Unlike many of the previous years when they had been full participants in budget making, Senate Republicans followed the pattern of unified partisan opposition of their House counterparts and were excluded from all bargaining.

The biggest stumbling block in the Senate was the president's proposed energy tax based on BTU content, and it was the first major element of the package to go. The Senate Finance Committee had jurisdiction over the major portion of the reconciliation bill, and all eleven Democratic members had to agree in order to move it to the floor. In committee, the BTU tax, which would have brought in $72 billion over five years, was replaced by a

4.3¢ per gallon gasoline tax that raised only $24 billion over the same peri-od. To keep the deficit reduction at $500 billion, the Finance Committee had to find nearly $50 billion in additional cuts or new revenues. The adminis-tration's concessions were aimed at conservative Democrats. Medicare was cut an additional $19 billion. Tax breaks for business were scaled back by $5 billion, and the EITC for the poor was reduced by $10 billion. The proposal to pump $5 billion into depressed urban and rural areas by creating empow-erment zones was jettisoned from the bill.[12] The committee version of the bill claimed $516 in deficit reduction over five years when discretionary cuts were included. By an 11–9 party line vote, the Finance committee approved the reconciliation bill on June 18 and sent it to the full Senate.

Senate liberals, led by Howard Metzenbaum (D-OH) and Paul Wellstone (D-MN), balked at the increase in Medicare cuts, threatening to withhold their votes. To keep them on board, Senate leaders agreed to amendments that reduced the additional Medicare cuts to $10 billion and restored tax incentives for small business. These and other changes lowered the total deficit reduction to $499 billion. The floor debate was unabashedly partisan, as a number of Republican amendments and a substitute bill that excluded any tax increases were debated and defeated. Minority Leader Dole ridiculed the package as "the largest tax increase in the history of the world" that would earn Clinton a place on "Mount Taxmore."[13] An almost gleeful Phil Gramm commented that he felt "like a mosquito in a nudist colony. The real question is where to strike first."[14]

As the eighteen-hour debate wound down in the early hours of the morn-ing of June 25, the outcome remained in doubt. In the end, six Democrats voted against the package, joining all forty-three Republicans, leaving it tied 49–49. For the first time since 1987, the vice president would cast a deciding vote. Al Gore, consulting the Senate manual as he presided, voted in the affir-mative to give the president a narrow 50–49 victory. Convincing Senator Bob Kerrey (D-NE), a former presidential opponent of Clinton who strongly opposed the gasoline tax, was particularly crucial to the victory. But Clinton had one more obstacle: reconciling the significant House-Senate differences and getting the compromise through both houses.

The "Conference without Walls"

Although much of the focus in July and early August during the conference and final floor consideration was on House-Senate differences, most of the original Clinton plan had remained intact. The balance of spending cuts to tax increases, significant increases in personal income tax rates for upper-income individuals, taxes on Social Security benefits, corporate income tax increases, removal of the cap on income subject to Medicare tax, and many other provisions were close or the same in both bills.[15] Yet the differences that existed were potentially fatal for the Democratic plan. The biggest difference in the competing versions was the energy tax, with many House Democrats still unhappy that they had been pressured to go on record with a vote for the unpopular BTU tax.

The thirty-eight-member House Black Caucus threatened revolt over the Senate changes. Angry at Clinton for his withdrawal of the nomination of Lani Guinier to head the Civil Rights Division of the Justice Department, caucus head Kweisi Mfume (D-MD) insisted that critical House provisions be maintained in the conference. In particular, the caucus wanted empowerment zones, the larger EITC, and smaller Medicare cuts protected. Without their support, no budget could pass the House.

There were countless other problems with the complex package, and there was no margin for error. Truckers organized a national campaign against the gasoline tax. Senior citizens campaigned against Medicare cuts and higher Social Security taxes. Virtually every group and every legislator cared passionately about some portion of the bill. When Senator David Boren (D-OK), who had reluctantly voted for the Senate version in June after the BTU tax was dropped, announced in late July that he would vote against the bill, the leverage of each individual senator became even greater. The administration and Democratic leaders not only had to find another vote to replace Boren but also had to hold on to the other votes. Senator Dianne Feinstein of California got an enhanced research and development tax credit. Senator Russell Feingold of Wisconsin was able to get a ban on bovine growth hormone in the bill.

The Conference Committee itself was a massive assemblage—with over two hundred members involved, it was what one observer labeled a "conference without walls."[16] Unlike the exclusive group of summiteers who had privately hammered out the original version of the 1990 budget agreement (which was initially voted down), the 1993 budget conference was a wide-open affair.

The Senate had greater leverage in the conference, not only because of the razor-thin margin of support in the first vote, but also because of the "Byrd rule" which banned extraneous matter from reconciliation bills. Senate Republicans hoped to use the procedure to challenge provisions of the conference report on the Senate floor in an effort to gut key provisions of the bill. Democratic leaders pursued a defensive strategy, consulting with the parliamentarian in advance, and striking or revising over one hundred items from the House version that might be subject to challenge.

Despite the hundreds of issues and participants, the outlines of the final version of the bill were falling into place by the end of July. After much negotiation, the Senate's gasoline tax was adopted. To recoup lost revenues, conferees agreed to make the income taxes retroactive to January 1, 1993, a move that led to cries of outrage from Republicans. Conferees came closer to the Senate provisions on income levels triggering higher taxes on Social Security benefits. Tax breaks for the working poor through the EITC were set at a level below the House version but higher than the Senate's. The higher corporate income tax rate of 36 percent contained in the House bill was adopted. Empowerment zone spending, at a reduced rate of $3.5 billion, was included in the conference report. With these and hundreds of other compromises, the conference report was completed. Although total numbers continued to be in question, it claimed a deficit reduction of $496 billion over five years, equally divided between tax increases and spending cuts. All that remained was to get majorities in the House and Senate to support it.

Final Passage

Votes were scheduled for the week of August 2 with Congress scheduled to adjourn for the summer on August 6. On Tuesday, August 3, President Clinton made a televised address to the nation. His speech stressed the importance of serious deficit reduction to the health of the nation and the necessity of shared sacrifice to accomplish it. "It has been at least 30 years since a President has asked Americans to take personal responsibility for our country's future," he opened.[17] Reminiscent of Ronald Reagan's appeals, Clinton used charts to try to convince viewers that he "would not balance the budget on the backs of older Americans while protecting the wealthy." The president's public appeal as measured by opinion polls was effective, and he was bolstered by the critical support of Fed Chairman Alan Greenspan. But his televised speech was followed on the networks by a blistering attack by Bob Dole who asked citizens to call Congress to demand that the package be voted down. Those calls overwhelmed supportive calls. A few more deals had to be closed as the final vote approached.

With the defection of Boren, the administration appeared to be one vote short in the Senate, with several others still wavering. Senator Dennis DeConcini of Arizona, despite facing a tough reelection fight the next year, provided that last vote.[18] As the price of the switch, DeConcini had negotiated a higher threshold for income that would be subject to Social Security taxes, and as a final concession, Clinton promised to issue an executive order creating a "deficit trust fund." Such a trust fund had been precluded from the reconciliation bill by the Byrd rule.

With the Senate now seeming more secure, attention turned to the House, which would vote first. As the debate began on August 5, support seemed to be slipping away. With liberals and the Black Caucus back on board based on conference compromises, some of the more conservative Democratic deficit hawks, led by Timothy Penny of Minnesota, began to waiver. In an eleventh-hour gesture, Clinton agreed to establish a formal entitlement review and promised to allow another round of spending cuts in the fall.

As the debate wore on in the House, whip counts continued to come up short. When the fifteen-minute period for House members to vote by electronic device expired, the board showed the vote deadlocked 210–210.[19] As the vote went back and forth, it came down to the last uncast vote, that of freshman Marjorie Margolies-Mezvinsky (D-PA). Told by party leaders that they would lose without her, she cast her vote for the package with what was described as "the terror-struck demeanor of someone being marched to her own hanging."[20] More narrowly than expected, the administration's deficit reduction plan passed the House, 218–216. Forty-one Democrats joined the unanimous Republicans in voting "nay."

The Senate took up the bill the next day, August 6. Even with the conversion of DeConcini, the outcome was in doubt until Bob Kerrey announced before the balloting that he could not cast the vote that would bring down the Clinton presidency. Republicans tried in vain to use points of order to remove provisions that they claimed violated the Byrd rule, and they failed in their challenge of the constitutionality of the retroactive tax increases. The final roll call produced a 50–50 tie. Once again, Vice President Gore cast the decisive vote to give his administration the narrowest of victories. Bill Clinton commented that "the margin was close but the mandate was clear."[21] On August 10, on the south lawn of the White House, 174 days after his address to a joint session of Congress, Clinton signed the plan into law.

The Deficit Reduction Plan

How Much Deficit Reduction?

At the time of enactment, proponents claimed that HR 2264, the 976-page Omnibus Budget Reconciliation Act of 1993, would reduce the deficit by an estimated $496 billion over five years through increased revenues of $241 and net spending reductions of $255.[22] As with most projections of multiyear budget aggregates, however, total savings depend on assumptions of a certain baseline as well as on estimates of the financial consequences of policy changes. During the deliberations of 1993, three different baselines were used at various times.

One of the main disputes centered on the baseline for discretionary spending in 1994 and 1995 which were capped by OBRA-90 but without specifying particular cuts. Critics claimed that the Democrats were double-counting $44 billion in discretionary cuts. In September 1993, when CBO and OMB recalculated the net deficit reduction produced by OBRA-93, they were as much as $72 billion apart. OMB calculated that the law would reduce spending by $256 billion and increase revenues by $250 billion for a total deficit reduction of $504.8 billion.[23] This was based on an "uncapped baseline" and assumed the Bush administration's 1992 estimates for defense. CBO, assuming compliance with the earlier discretionary caps, calculated the total deficit reduction at $433 billion: $241 billion in new revenues and $192 billion in reduced spending.[24]

Revenue Changes

- *Individual income taxes.* OBRA-93 imposed a fourth bracket, increasing the top marginal rate to 36 percent for couples with taxable income above $140,000 and for single filers above $115,000. At higher income levels, this top rate rises to 39.6 percent when a 10 percent surtax is added, and that rises further to 40.8 percent when the limitation on itemized deductions is taken into account.[25] CBO estimated that the new rates would produce $115 billion in revenue compared to OMB's estimate of $125 billion.

- *Gasoline tax.* The major congressional change in the Clinton plan imposed a 4.3¢ per gallon gasoline tax, raising approximately $32 billion over five years.

- *Social Security and Medicare taxes.* The new law made 85 percent of Social Security benefits fully taxable for couples earning over $44,000 and for individuals earning over $34,000 annually. This raised $25 billion over five years according to CBO but only $19 billion according to OMB. Eliminating the cap on wages subject to the 1.45 percent Medicare tax ($135,000 in 1993) raised $29 billion.

- *Corporate taxes.* The final version of the deficit reduction plan raised the corporate income tax to 35 percent for incomes over $10 million, raising $16 billion by 1998.

- *Business meals and entertainment.* The deductible portion of business meals and entertainment was reduced from 80 percent to 50 percent, raising $15 billion in new revenues over five years.

Spending Cuts

OBRA-93 reduced the deficit through cuts in mandatory entitlements and a freeze on defense and domestic discretionary spending. OMB calculated the five-year savings in entitlement spending at $71 billion compared to CBO's estimate of $77 billion.

- *Medicare.* The largest cuts came from cutting the rate of growth of Medicare by between $49 billion (OMB) and $56 billion (CBO). This was accomplished by reducing payments to hospitals, doctors, and other providers and by increasing the premiums for Medicare Part B.
- *Delay of COLAs.* Federal civilian and military retirees paid for part of the deficit reduction effort: cost of living adjustments were delayed, and the law eliminated the lump-sum payment option for retirees. These changes saved $12 billion.
- *FCC license auction.* OBRA-93 mandated that the FCC auction for commercial use a portion of the electromagnetic spectrum formerly reserved for government. OMB estimated that this would save nearly $13 billion, while CBO came up with a more conservative estimate of $7 billion.
- *Medicaid.* The Democratic plan as enacted repealed the requirement that states provide personal care services under Medicaid, and the plan limited payments to hospitals serving a high proportion of indigents. This would save $7 billion.
- *Student loans.* OBRA-93 changed federal law under the Family Education Loan program, formerly called Guaranteed Student Loan program, to begin a transition to direct federal loans to college students. States were also required to share in default costs. This was estimated to save $4 billion over five years.
- *Discretionary spending freeze.* The most significant spending cuts came in the form of a freeze on discretionary spending, maintaining and extending a set of discretionary caps through 1998. As noted above, this component represented the greatest disparity in estimating the impact of OBRA-93, with CBO counting only the $68 billion saved in FY 1996, FY 1997, and FY 1998, while the administration counted the savings at $108 billion over what discretionary spending would have been over five years with no caps. The overall impact of the caps was to freeze discretionary spending at nominal 1994 levels. With inflation around 3 percent, this equated to a cut

of approximately 10 percent in real terms by 1998. As discussed in more detail below, the discretionary caps imposed rigid policy constraints on both Congress and the president, ushering in an era of zero-sum budgeting for much of the federal government.

Changes in Budget Rules

The Balanced Budget Act of 1985 (GRH) and OBRA-90 had included a number of major changes in budget rules and procedures. Primarily because of the Byrd rule, OBRA-93 did not ultimately make major changes in budget rules, largely reaffirming the procedures implemented through the Budget Enforcement Act (BEA) enacted in 1990. Yet a number of changes were part of the negotiations over the 1993 budget plan. As we have seen throughout, negotiation over budget rules is important for several reasons. First, the results help determine how effectively party leaders can maintain control of the agenda and floor consideration in the House and Senate. Second, some of the rules have direct budgetary consequences and can limit congressional discretion and policy options. Third, in terms of bargaining and making concessions within the party to maintain a majority, certain procedural changes have been used as a bargaining chip in much the same way as taxing and spending provisions. The House adopted a number of budget process changes, but many were deleted in Conference Committee. These new rules were less oriented to helping party leaders than to achieving certain policy goals and serving the political interests of their proponents.

House-Passed Changes

The reconciliation bill passed by the House in May included a number of changes in the budget process, including several separate new titles: the Budget Enforcement Act of 1993, designed to extend and expand the provisions of the 1990 BEA; and the Budget Control Act of 1993, designed to control the growth of direct spending (predominantly entitlements).[26]

- *Extend discretionary caps, and end deficit targets.* The House bill extended the deficit targets only through 1995, eliminating one of the most prominent features of GRH. The bill extended the discretionary spending limits through 1998, opting for a single cap rather than the separate defense, domestic, and international caps that were enacted in 1990.

- *Extend BEA enforcement provisions.* The bill also extended the life of the enforcement mechanisms that had been enacted in 1990. PAYGO requirements that any legislation increasing the deficit be offset with additional revenues or spending cuts were extended until 2002. Other temporary BEA rules were made permanent, and a number of changes were made concerning the budget resolution coverage and enforcement.
- *Establish deficit reduction trust fund.* In an attempt to ensure that all the budget savings in OBRA-93 went to deficit reduction, the bill established a Deficit Reduction Trust Fund (DRTF).[27] Money in the trust fund must equal the amount of savings from OBRA-93 in that year and previous years and may be used only for the payment of Treasury debt obligations when they mature.
- *Create direct spending targets.* The Budget Control Act created a series of targets for "direct spending" through 1997.[28] The targets were to be established and adjusted by the OMB Director according to a series of requirements.

Senate-Passed Changes

The Senate also considered a number of changes in the budget process as part of their version of the reconciliation bill in June.[29] The bulk of the changes were introduced in the form of three amendments during floor consideration by Budget Committee Chairman Sasser (D-TN). Only one of those amendments—the one extending the provisions of the BEA and creating discretionary caps through 1998—passed. The others, including direct spending targets and a deficit trust fund, were rejected on procedural grounds. Several other amendments by other senators were also rejected. Senator Gramm unsuccessfully proposed an amendment that would extend deficit targets through 1998, but that would have followed the projected deficits in the Clinton plan, rather than bringing the deficit to zero.[30] In its final version, the Senate bill followed the House actions on spending caps, ending deficit targets in 1995, adopting PAYGO to the new totals, and extending temporary enforcement procedures, including a modified point of order against any budget resolution that violated the spending caps.

The Byrd Rule

The parliamentary rule that doomed most of the amendments on the Senate floor and ultimately favored Senate positions in conference was the Byrd rule.[31] The rule was originated by Senator Robert Byrd (D-WV) and adopted in October 1985, during the consideration of Gramm-Rudman-Hollings. Facing a massive list of nongermane amendments to the reconciliation bill in 1985, Byrd commented, "We are in the process of seeing . . . the Pandora's Box which has been opened to the abuse of the reconciliation process. That process was never meant to be used as it is being used. There are 122 items in this reconciliation bill that are extraneous."[32] The Senate reaffirmed the rule in a Senate resolution in December 1985.

The rule, by 1993, had become a complicated parliamentary technique allowing extraneous material to be struck from reconciliation bills through points of order. The Senate Budget Committee report noted in 1993, "'Extraneous' is a term of art. Broadly speaking, the rule prohibits inclusion in reconciliation of matters unrelated to the reduction goals of the reconciliation process."[33]

In general, a provision is considered to be extraneous if it meets at least one of the following:

1. It does not produce a change in outlays or revenues.
2. It produces an outlay increase or revenue decrease when the instructed committee is not in compliance with its instructions.
3. It is outside the jurisdiction of the committee that submitted the title or provision for inclusion in the reconciliation measure.
4. It produces a change in outlays or revenues which is merely incidental to the nonbudgetary components of the provision.
5. It would increase the deficit for a fiscal year beyond that covered by the reconciliation measure.
6. It recommends changes in Social Security.[34]

The Byrd rule proved effective in keeping extraneous material out of reconciliation bills. In eleven of the fourteen cases involving the Byrd rule between 1985 and 1993, extraneous matter was struck from the bill or not considered at all. The rule came to thwart budget reformers in 1993, however. To prevent challenges to the conference agreement when it came back to the Senate, Majority Leader Mitchell worked with the Senate parliamentarian to assure that no extraneous material would be included. Thus, only the essential components of extending the discretionary caps and enforcement rules would be included in the final version of OBRA-93. That left several key House and Senate Democrats unhappy and led President Clinton, in the final days before the vote, to promise to implement two of the failed reforms through executive order.

Clinton's Executive Orders

On August 7, 1993, Bill Clinton issued Executive Order No. 12857 establishing direct spending targets through 1997. Following essentially the House-passed version, the president committed to issuing an annual report on entitlement spending. If there were overages, the president would issue a report explaining the cause and "may recommend recouping or eliminating all, some, or none of the overage."[35] Executive Order No. 12858 established a Deficit Trust Fund in the Treasury to guarantee that new revenues and net budget savings achieved by OBRA-93 were used exclusively for redeeming maturing debt obligations of the Treasury that were held by foreign governments.[36]

The president kept his promise, and these two changes satisfied several critical members of the House and Senate. But neither "reform" would have any practicable effect on either deficit reduction or debt retirement. Neither the president nor Congress was under any obligation to compensate for increased entitlement spending. The order itself did nothing to eliminate the cause of growing entitlement spending, particularly health care costs. The deficit trust fund, similar to President Bush's proposed tax return check-off to reduce the deficit, simply requires the Treasury to manipulate funds used to retire debt while continuing to issue new debt as needed.

Despite the lack of new rules, OBRA-93 did nothing to weaken the hand of party leaders in controlling the agenda and protecting macrobudgetary legislation on the floor. Ultimately OBRA-93 had a significant impact on the deficit and on the scope of budgetary discretion in subsequent years. The discretionary spending caps locked the president and Congress into essentially zero-sum budgeting for much of the 1990s.

Budgeting under Unified Party Control

Clinton came to Washington after twelve years of Republican administration, ending divided government and promising to end the gridlock attributed to it. Winning the presidency with only 43 percent of the popular vote, Clinton was elected with a plurality that exceeded only that of Lincoln in 1860 and Nixon in 1968, also multiple-candidate races. Even considering his 54 percent of the two-party vote and a better than 2–1 majority in the Electoral College, Clinton's election did not have the look or feel of a sweeping mandate. Yet the voters had sent a message for the new president to focus on the economy and on domestic issues over foreign policy. The domestic issue that he focused on first was the deficit, requiring spending cuts and/or tax increases.

By 1993, electoral changes had gradually changed the composition of the congressional parties. Both parties had become more ideologically cohesive, and party voting in Congress had been on a steady upward trend. With the political realignment in the South, many conservative southern Democrats had been replaced by Republicans, and the Democrats that remained tended to be more liberal. Since the mid-1970s, votes on budget resolutions, reconciliation, and omnibus spending bills had been predominantly partisan. Yet Clinton could not automatically count on strict party discipline among congressional Democrats for a package that cut popular programs and raised taxes significantly.

In the final analysis, the Clinton deficit reduction package was a party victory. The most striking feature in 1993 was the unified opposition of the Republicans in both the House and the Senate. This was standard fare for the House, but in many prior years, the Senate Republicans worked with Democrats on budget resolutions and reconciliation, and a substantial number voted for these budgets. In 1993, political calculations and the nature of the tax package led the Senate Republicans to follow the pattern of their House counterparts. The lesson many Republicans took from Bush's defeat in 1992 was that his compromise on taxes cost him the election. The Republicans used the debate over the Democrats' deficit reduction plan to reestablish their party's anti-tax image. They were the unified loyal opposition.

The Democratic Party was less unified, consistent with patterns established over the previous eighteen years. To put it in some perspective, Tip O'Neill delivered a slightly higher proportion of House Democrats in a losing effort in the 1981 reconciliation bill than Speaker Foley, Majority Leader Gephardt, and President Clinton did in 1993. Yet the common conclusion in 1993 was that Democrats proved that they could govern; in 1981, that they were in disarray. However, the task of gaining support for the largest tax *increase* in history was perhaps more formidable than breaking party ranks to vote for the largest tax *cut* in history. In 1993 compared to 1981, the size of the Democratic majorities in each house allowed for more defections.

Building a winning party majority was far from automatic or assured. The president and Democratic leaders made a number of concessions to create their narrow victory. Despite the concessions, except for the BTU tax, the package remained largely intact, particularly in terms of the overall size of spending cuts and tax increases. The bargaining was done strictly among Democrats. It is apparent that many more Democrats, for political reasons, would have liked to vote against the deficit reduction package, but they were convinced that it was in their interest for the party's plan and the party's president to succeed.

Particularly striking in 1993 was the emphasis on an appeal to party by the White House and by congressional leaders. This was framed as a test of the Democrats' ability to govern, particularly facing unified Republican opposition. Party leaders used a variety of techniques to maintain sufficient party unity to prevail. At the extreme, the petition to strip committee and subcommittee chairs raised the possibility of using punitive means. In the end, committee and subcommittee chairs voted overwhelmingly for the plan. More common was the carrot, winning over wavering members with specific concessions ranging from reduced spending cuts to promises of presidential action by executive order.

Democratic Party leaders fostered broader participation in shaping the package, notably in the large Conference Committee. The defeat of the original deficit reduction package in 1990 had demonstrated the shortcomings of small, closed summits. But leaders also used the budget rules to prevent floor amendments or obstruction on the floor. Passing the budget resolution early allowed party leaders to make greater use of the protections afforded by reconciliation. Conversely, the rules also prevented members from making significant budget process changes in OBRA-93. The Byrd rule effectively stymied House attempts to further tinker with the process. On page after page in the section of the reconciliation bill dealing with the budget process, the following language appeared: "The House recedes to the Senate. The House conferees believe that the recommended changes in the House proposal are useful and important and therefore intend to pursue these changes in another forum."[37]

The transition from divided to unified government had a number of consequences, particularly when comparisons with 1990 are made. First, there was no need to utilize extraordinary means such as summits or bipartisan commissions in 1993. Second, the budget plan was adopted in a timely fashion, progressing through the budget timetable devised in 1974 and altered in later years. Third, as noted above, unified party control affected the content of the budget package. Deficit reduction packages under divided government, such as in 1982, 1987, and 1990, never relied on revenue increases for more than one-third of total savings. In the Democrats' 1993 plan, more than half of the deficit reduction came through higher taxes.

The deficit reduction plan was a significant accomplishment for the president and invited comparisons to Reagan in 1981. He, like Reagan, effectively focused the policy agenda. The president appealed to the public and convinced enough members of his own party to support a set of proposals that were much more difficult to sell than Reagan's big tax cut and popular defense buildup. Outside of budgeting, Clinton did not find Democratic majorities eager to do his bidding. The narrow budget coalition did not transfer to other issues that lacked the procedural protection of the budget rules. For example, the vote on the North American Free Trade Agreement (NAFTA) a few months later in the fall of 1993 found the president working with an entirely different coalition, one that put him in opposition to a majority of congressional Democrats. His problems with health care reform in 1994 further highlighted the limits of partisanship as a governing strategy and created a context for the midterm elections that would put an end to the brief period of unified government.

CHAPTER 7

The Balanced Budget Agreement, 1997

The Clinton deficit reduction plan and a robust economy would reverse the upward trend in deficit projections. But politically, Democrats were given little credit, and they headed into the 1994 midterm elections also burdened by a failed effort at reforming health care. The 1994 elections produced a Republican surge in Congress, ushering in a Republican majority in both House and Senate for the first time in forty years, majorities that they would hold for a decade. Once again, national government returned to divided government, this time with a Democratic president facing a Republican Congress.

The new Republican leadership, especially Speaker Newt Gingrich (R-GA), was given a great deal of credit for the electoral victory. Many of the newly elected Republican members of the House believed that Gingrich's "Contract with America"—ten major proposals that Republicans promised to act on within one hundred days if they gained control of Congress—was behind their sweeping victory. Republicans made a successful national partisan appeal to voters in a campaign where the issues of tax cutting and budget balancing were prominent in the Republican message. In addition, significant turnover in Congress after the 1992 and 1994 elections had changed the partisan and ideological composition of both the House and the Senate. In 1992, 110 new members were elected to the House, and 14 to the Senate. In the 1994 Republican sweep, 86 new representatives and 11 new senators were elected. By the time the 104th Congress convened in 1995, the parties had become even more ideologically divided. In the majority for the first time in two generations, Republicans were particularly eager to use the majority party leadership of Congress to dominate the policy agenda of government and to dominate the president. Republican leaders were particularly assertive in centralizing power in the House, in violating seniority in selecting committee chairs, and in limiting committee autonomy. In terms of budgeting, the Republicans inherited a set of rules and institutions that by 1995 had become a powerful tool for the majority party leaders.

This chapter examines the two and a half years of conflict between President Clinton and the Republican Congress that ultimately resulted in an agreement to balance the federal budget. Despite the continuing conflict, the final result was a *bipartisan* agreement between Clinton and Republican leaders. In the evolution of congressional budgeting, did this represent a genuine shift toward bipartisanship or, as in the case of Gramm-Rudman-Hollings, a temporary agreement of convenience? How was it possible to balance the budget under divided government when divided government had been assumed to be a major reason for deficits in the first place? We will see that, as in 1993, few significant changes in budget rules were adopted as part of the plan. Instead, congressional Republicans turned to votes on constitutional amendments to enhance their budgetary reputation.

Budget Deadlock, 1995–1996

Cutting taxes was important to the new Republican majority, but so was balancing the budget. Gingrich and Republican leaders believed that the election results presented them with a clear mandate, and they would act aggressively to implement it. House Republicans formulated a plan with nearly $1 trillion in spending cuts over seven years, including sharp reductions in Medicare, enough cuts to allow them to incorporate $350 billion in tax cuts during the same period. They would try to force the president to go along by threatening to shut down the government and default on federal debt if necessary. Although he gradually moved toward their position and agreed to seek a balanced budget, throughout 1995, Clinton used his main weapon, the veto and the threat of a veto, to counter Speaker Gingrich and the Republican tactics. Eighteen months after the battle over the FY 1996 budget started, there was still no agreement on a plan to balance the budget in seven years. Both sides were left to hope that the deadlock over balancing the budget would be resolved by the 1996 elections.

As the frenetic first one hundred days of the 104th Congress were ending, committees in both the House and the Senate were getting down to the business of crafting a comprehensive plan to balance the budget. The House Budget Committee, headed by Representative John Kasich (R-OH), and the Senate Budget Committee, chaired by Senator Domenici (R-NM), began hearings on the budget resolution for FY 1996. On February 6, 1995, President Clinton, chastened by the 1994 election results, submitted a cautious budget that included no major initiatives or deficit reduction. Republicans lambasted the president for abdicating leadership, claiming that he "took a walk" and "put up the white flag."[1] Not content just to shape the FY 1996 budget for the fiscal year that would begin on October 1, 1995, Republicans proposed a package of rescissions to cancel spending already approved for the current budget. In May, Clinton vetoed the rescissions bill, and the Republicans lacked the votes to override, a pattern that would be repeated over the next year. A greatly reduced compromise rescissions bill was finally approved in July.

The House balanced budget plan went to the floor in May. It was an ambitious attempt to make major reductions in government, including the elimination of fourteen federal agencies. The House plan would cut spending by $1.04 trillion, including $288 billion in Medicare reductions, and cut taxes by $353 billion.[2] The Senate plan was somewhat more modest, making tax cuts contingent on a plan that would actually balance the budget. Democrats attacked the bills, claiming that the Republicans wanted to balance the budget on the backs of the young, the poor, and the elderly. Still on the defensive, however, on June 13, Clinton put out his own plan for a balanced budget over ten years. Some Democrats attacked the president for capitulating to the Republicans, but he argued his plan would not harm society's most vulnerable. Republicans ignored the president's plan. After House and Senate versions passed by nearly party line votes, the budget resolution, which did not need presidential approval, went to conference. The Conference Committee worked out the differences between the two versions, and on June 29, the budget resolution laying out the Republicans' seven-year balanced budget plan was passed.

Implementation of the blueprint contained in the budget resolution would take place on two fronts. First, the thirteen individual appropriations bills containing discretionary spending that had to be passed by October 1 would provide Republicans an opportunity to make sharp cuts in existing programs. Second, the bulk of the balanced budget package would be contained in a massive reconciliation bill, encompassing multiyear cuts in entitlements and other spending along with tax reductions. With conflict at every stage, the pace was slow and the administration's resolve was growing. By October 1, only two spending bills had passed, and Clinton had vetoed one of them. Congress passed a six-week stop-gap spending bill as a big battle was shaping up over the reconciliation bill.

The Republican strategy was to try to force Clinton to approve their balanced budget plan by threatening to shut down the government for lack of money and default on the debt if he did not sign their bill. The statutory debt limit was set to expire in mid-November 1995.[3] The Republicans bet that rather than allow a first-ever default on federal debt, Clinton would accept their budget plan. They were wrong. As the November 13 date for the expiration of the temporary spending bill approached, Clinton stepped up his counterattacks on Congress for trying to blackmail him into signing the bill. The Republicans passed another temporary spending bill and a debt extension with provisions that he had promised not to accept. He vetoed both, and on November 14, "non-essential" federal employees were sent home as the government closed down for six days. The Treasury was able to manipulate funds in order to avoid a default on government bonds.

Republicans did win one important concession from the president. As they were negotiating over another temporary funding bill, Clinton agreed with the seven-year timetable to balance the budget as long as it included his priorities for health care, education, and the environment. Now, both sides wanted a balanced budget in the same timeframe—the only question was how to do it. This concession by Clinton would not make compromise any easier. The final version of the reconciliation bill passed Congress and was vetoed by the president on December 6. Clinton released a new budget plan of his own on December 7. As the stalemate continued, on December 16, the government shut down again and federal workers were sent home right before the holidays. Opinion polls suggested that the public was getting fed up with the divisions in Washington.

However, it was the Republican Congress rather than the president that seemed to be blamed for the budget deadlock. Clinton's approval rating shot up over 50 percent, the highest rate in two years, as support for Newt Gingrich and the Republicans tumbled.[4] The public saw Clinton sticking to principles and standing up for the little guy. News stories featured unhappy tourists locked out of national parks and monuments and disgruntled government workers not allowed to go to the office. To make matters worse, the stock market dropped over concerns with the budget deadlock. After the holidays, members of Congress returned to Washington, and, spurred by growing internal divisions over the political consequences of their strategy, the Republicans started to back away from their hardball tactics. Robert Dole, worrying about the negative consequences to his presidential bid, said, "Enough is enough. I do not see any sense in what we have been doing, frankly. Maybe I missed the point . . . If there is any point to be made, I think that point should have been made by now."[5]

Ironically, with concessions by the Clinton administration, the two sides were not as far apart as they had been earlier, and agreement seemed to be within reach. In November 1995, the White House and Congress were as much as $350 billion apart. By January 1996, this figure had lessened to $66 billion.[6] However, as yet another temporary spending bill expired, Republicans were desperate to avoid another shutdown. In essence, the Republicans gave up on getting a budget agreement. Newt Gingrich said, "I don't expect us to get a seven-year balanced budget with President Clinton in office."[7] Meanwhile, no budget had passed, leaving many agencies and departments in financial chaos. In the spring of 1996, half way into the fiscal year, fewer than half of the appropriations bills had passed, and the fourteenth temporary spending bill had to be passed to avoid another shutdown. An increasingly confident White House lambasted the Congress for not completing its work on the budget. Meanwhile, the cycle for the FY 1997 budget was already starting, although Clinton delayed submission of the plan by over a month and submitted only the rudiments of a regular budget.

The deadlock over the balanced budget plan was not so much resolved as it was postponed. In late April, both sides agreed to a bill that would fund agencies through the end of the fiscal year. Both sides still had their own versions of a balanced budget plan, and both sides planned to use the failure to reach a compromise in the 1996 presidential and congressional elections. There was no extraordinary resolution of the 1995–1996 budget deadlock. Instead, it was resolved in part by the mixed message of the election. With the reelection of Bill Clinton by a substantial margin and the trimming of Republican majorities in Congress, the 1996 elections set the stage for eventual agreement on a balanced budget plan in 1997.

The disciplined Republican majority in Congress demonstrated its capacity to formulate a budget policy and control the legislative agenda. However, this episode also shows the limits of congressional leadership without the majorities to override a presidential veto. The Republicans were unable to pressure Clinton into accepting their plan, and their tactics backfired politically. In retrospect, many Republicans believed that it had been a mistake to force the government shutdowns in order to pressure the president. President Clinton, who had been reduced to holding a press conference to deny he was "irrelevant" right after the Republicans captured Congress, boosted his leadership ratings by standing up to the Congress. Nonetheless, Republicans succeeded in getting the president to commit to a balanced budget by 2002 and bringing him closer to their position in many areas. The 1996 elections created a different context in 1997, where President Clinton and Republican leaders in Congress, helped by a booming economy, achieved a plan to balance the budget by 2002 after all.

The Clinton Budget Proposals

In 1997, Congress and the Clinton administration engaged in extensive negotiations throughout the year, from the outline of the budget agreement in a budget resolution, to its implementation in two reconciliation bills, to negotiating over the content of the thirteen appropriations bills. Despite the progress made toward a balanced budget, Republicans pursued constitutional approaches to fiscal restraint as well. Congress came within a whisker of passing a balanced budget amendment, and President Clinton became the first (and only) president to employ the line-item veto.

The Political and Economic Environment

Congress and the president had faced a series of deficit crises since 1981. As we have seen, previous efforts had never even come close to reaching a balanced budget or even an agreement to balance the budget. What was different about 1997?

The 1996 elections convinced both parties that either they must compromise with each other or else deadlock would continue. The fact that Clinton had won convincingly but not overwhelmingly in 1996, and the Republicans had won a reduced majority in the House, provided a more realistic message than the message Republicans took from the 1994 results. Congressional Republicans were faced with the choice of compromising and getting something substantively and symbolically important to deliver to constituencies, or continuing to hold out for total victory.

The second factor that made it possible to reach a budget agreement was the strength of the economy and related improvement in long-term deficit forecasts. Just as the deficits had ballooned during the recession of the early 1990s, so did they shrink because of better-than-expected growth in the mid-1990s. This was particularly true during 1997, when between January and May, the Congressional Budget Office revised their deficit forecasts, "finding" $225 billion over five years. This made compromise much easier, allowing bigger tax cuts and elimination of some of the most unpopular and controversial spending cuts.

The experience of the failed negotiations over a balanced budget agreement in 1995 and 1996 provided an important foundation for 1997. Several factors came into play. The Republicans moderated their tactics from two years earlier, although there was still plenty of rhetoric. However, with Gingrich suffering his own problems within the Republican caucus, other, more pragmatic leaders took the lead on the budget negotiations. Many Republicans believed that they had kept control of Congress by moving major legislation, such as welfare reform in late 1996, before the elections.[8] Many wanted a budget deal for the same reasons. In addition, the negotiators knew the areas where the other side was more likely or not to bend. There were substantial areas of agreement in terms of tax cuts, Medicare restraints, and domestic spending limits. Nonetheless, the macrobudgetary choices still represented the fundamental values of both parties, and ground would not be given without a fight.

The President's FY 1998–FY 2002 Budget

Typical of presidential budget messages, Clinton's FY 1998 message extolled the accomplishments of the past, particularly deficit reduction and reductions in the number of federal employees.[9] He noted that the size of the deficit had fallen by 63 percent, from $290 billion in 1992 to $107 billion in 1996. The federal work force had fallen by 250,000 positions to its lowest number in thirty years. But in terms of what the budget promised, far more emphasis was placed on new initiatives and priorities than on budgetary discipline:

> We must not only provide tax relief for average Americans, but also increase access to education and training; expand health insurance to the unemployed and children who lack it; better protect the environment; enhance our investments in biomedical and other research; beef up our law enforcement efforts; and provide the needed funds for a thriving global policy and a strong defense.[10]

Unlike many other presidential budgets proposed to a Congress of the opposite party, President Clinton's FY 1998 budget was *not* pronounced "dead on arrival" by members of Congress.[11] Rather, Congress largely worked from the president's numbers rather than writing competing budgets, an approach that was possible because the administration had moved toward the GOP, to the dismay of many congressional Democrats who felt that their party message was being blurred. Clinton's budget contained tax cuts, including capital gains tax cuts that Democrats had opposed for years, and substantial Medicare cuts. Clinton sent Congress a budget calling for $1.687 trillion in spending and revenues of $1.567 trillion, resulting in an estimated deficit of $76 billion.[12] More important was the five-year plan for balancing the budget. Clinton's plan proposed a net savings over five years of $388 billion that would result in a budget surplus of $17 billion by 2002. The components of the Clinton plan that were highlighted in the budget message included the following over five years:[13]

- Tax cuts of $98 billion targeted on middle-income families and small business.

- Revenue increases of $76 billion extending expired taxes, closing loopholes, and additional taxes for net tax cuts of $22 billion.
- A "trigger" mechanism that would cancel tax cuts and further cut spending if budget projections proved less optimistic.
- A net savings of $137 billion in discretionary spending, but increased spending for education and training, the environment, and law enforcement.
- A reduction in outlays by $22 billion in Medicaid, offset by growth in some areas for a net savings of $9.3 billion.
- A reduction in outlays over projected levels by $109 billion in Medicare, splitting the difference between the last Democratic and Republican proposals.
- An increase in offsetting receipts by $36 billion through broadcast spectrum auction.
- An increase in spending by $18 billion to repeal the welfare reform provisions stripping legal aliens of benefits.

Revenues With caps severely limiting discretionary spending, many of Clinton's budget initiatives were found on the revenue side of the budget. Education was at the top of the list. The FY 1998 budget proposed $38.4 billion in tax preferences through various credits, deductions, and exclusions. First, the Hope Scholarship tax credit would provide a $1,500 tax credit for two years of post-secondary schooling for families with incomes below $80,000. Second, families with incomes below this level could also take up to a $10,000 deduction to offset the cost of post-secondary education. Third, the president proposed to allow people to take penalty-free withdrawals from their individual retirement accounts (IRAs) for college. Fourth, the president proposed that the provisions exempting the value of employer-provided education benefits from taxation be extended.[14]

Other proposals on the revenue side included the $500 tax credit for children under age thirteen for families earning less than $75,000. This initiative, similar to some Republican plans, was estimated to cost $46 billion over five years. Clinton also moved toward the Republicans in proposing a limited capital gains tax reduction. He proposed that profits on the sale of a home of up to $500,000 be exempt from capital gains taxes. If adopted, it would reduce revenues by $1.4 billion. The administration also proposed expanding IRAs to individuals with higher incomes and allowing the money to be withdrawn penalty-free for the purchase of a first home. These proposals reduced revenue by $5.5 billion over five years. Also included were a set of revenue initiatives to help distressed urban areas and tax credits for employers who hired welfare recipients at a cost of $3.2 billion over five years.

In total, Clinton's revenue proposals would reduce receipts from current policy by $98 billion over five years, far less than most Republican alternatives and nowhere near the $550 billion in tax cuts that Bob Dole had promoted during the 1996 presidential campaign. These tax cuts were offset by $76 billion in new revenues, leaving a net tax cut in the president's budget of only $22 billion. New revenues came primarily from eliminating tax breaks for corporations and wealthy taxpayers. Excise taxes were expanded, including restoration of the excise tax on airline tickets that had expired. The proposed trigger mechanism would be employed in 2001, canceling most of the tax cuts if the budget was not on a path to balance by 2002.

Spending Much of the deficit reduction that had been achieved over Clinton's first five years came from restraint in the growth of discretionary spending and larger-than-expected revenues. His five-year plan proposed in the FY 1998 budget continued that approach, although it was heavily back loaded, with most of the reductions coming in 2002. For FY 1998, discretionary spending would actually increase above the rate of inflation. Education, the environment, and law enforcement were at the top of the priority list. Clinton proposed $56.2 billion for education, an increase of $4.9 billion or nearly 10 percent over FY 1997. This would go toward school building programs, particularly school modernization in urban areas. Funding for technology literacy would be doubled from the previous year to help schools connect to the Internet. In terms of higher education, an additional $2.8 billion was requested for student loans. For the environment, the administration asked for significant increases in the budget of the Environmental Protection Agency and the superfund. EPA spending was slated to increase by 17 percent to $7.7 billion, and the superfund would grow to $2.1 billion, an increase of 33 percent. Spending for justice-related activities were also boosted in Clinton's FY 1998 budget, with a total request of $24.2 billion, an increase of 16.6 percent from FY 1997. Much of this was mandated under earlier anti-crime legislation, but several new initiatives were included, such as increased appropriations for the Federal Bureau of Investigation, the Drug Enforcement Administration, and the Bureau of Alcohol, Tobacco, and Firearms.

Much of the proposed savings in the president's budget came from Medicare and Medicaid, despite the Democrats' controversial attacks against Republicans for proposing Medicare cuts during the 1996 campaign. Clinton proposed cuts in Medicare of $109 billion over five years, 43 percent of all spending cuts. Medicare spending in FY 1998 would amount to $207 billion, an increase of 6.6 percent over 1997 but more than 4 percent below previous projections. Cuts would be achieved by reducing payments to doctors, hospitals, and health maintenance organizations (HMOs). Hospital payments would decline $33 billion over five years over earlier baselines, while HMOs would receive $34 billion less. Medicaid would suffer no cuts under the president's budget in FY 1998 but would suffer net cuts of $9.3 billion over five years from previous projections. Proposals to set a per capita limit on payments to states in return for more flexibility in administration would generate nearly $22 billion in savings. This would be offset by proposals to increase health insurance for children and unemployed workers and other initiatives that would cost nearly $13 billion.

Despite strong Republican opposition, one of the president's priorities in his budget proposals was to revise certain provisions of the 1996 welfare reform bill.[15] His requests included changes to increase spending by $3.1 billion on food stamps for families with high housing costs or with vehicles above a certain value. He proposed an additional $300 million to allow disabled children to continue to receive Medicaid benefits that they had lost with welfare reform. An additional $3 billion was requested for states and cities to hire welfare recipients. The largest proposal was an additional $14.6 billion to allow legal immigrants who become disabled to receive SSI and Medicaid and for their children to receive Medicaid. Mayors and governors of both parties around the country were clamoring for this change.

Another issue that would divide Congress and the president in the 105th Congress was the balanced budget amendment to the Constitution. The Clinton budget message contained a strong brief against the amendment. Calling the requirement "potentially dangerous," the administration argued that it would endanger the automatic stabilizers built into federal spending:

> Consider what could happen under a balanced budget amendment. A weak economy would mean fewer tax revenues and more spending on unemployment and other programs. As a result, a balanced budget requirement could force a tax increase or spending cuts—or both—in the middle of a recession. These steps could make a weak economy even weaker. . . . The better practice is to aim for balance, but to adjust budget policy according to circumstances.[16]

Congressional leaders criticized many aspects of the Clinton plan. They were particularly critical of what they saw as a "gimmicky" estimate for $36 billion in revenues from the broadcast spectrum auction, 90 percent of which would come in 2002. Clinton's budget projected a budget surplus of $17 billion in 2002. CBO budget forecasts were much less optimistic than OMB's. Their analysis of the president's budget concluded that it would still leave a deficit of $69 billion in 2002.[17] The competing numbers had profound consequences for reaching an agreement. Accepting CBO's five-year projections necessitated cutting from the president's budget an additional $187 billion from the deficits over five years. Three months later, it would turn out that even OMB's numbers had been too pessimistic.

As the House and Senate Budget Committees began markup of their respective budget resolutions, the main lines of difference between the president and Congress began to clarify. The Republicans wanted more cuts in discretionary spending, more restraint in Medicare and Medicaid, a broad-based capital gains cut indexed for inflation, and substantially greater tax cuts across the full range of incomes.

As the negotiators from the White House and Congress were working on these and other issues, the Republicans returned to what they believed would be permanent solutions to deficits: a constitutional amendment to balance the budget and a constitutional requirement for supermajorities for tax increases. The outcome of the balanced budget amendment vote could affect the ongoing budget negotiations. On one hand, bruising partisan fights over the amendments could endanger bipartisan efforts. On the other hand, the sense that a balanced budget agreement was finally close after nearly two decades of deficit battles could diminish the urgency for a more drastic solution. Either way, it was an important part of the budget politics that would determine the outcome of Clinton's FY 1998 proposals.

Republican Constitutional Proposals

The Balanced Budget Amendment

Not only did congressional Republicans want to balance the federal budget; they also wanted to make it a constitutional requirement to balance the budget as in many of the states. To keep taxes low, they proposed a second amendment that would require supermajorities in both houses to raise taxes. The balanced budget amendment, a proposal that had been around for many decades, has been called by one observer "the constitutional equivalent of the Energizer bunny."[18] The modern effort did not gain political momentum until the mid-1970s after state legislatures, prompted by the National Taxpayers Union, called for a federal constitutional convention to propose such an amendment.[19] Later, the Reagan administration endorsed the balanced budget amendment campaign, and it became an integral part of the Republican Party platform. It is, in general, supported by approximately 75 percent of the public, although support declines when it is linked to cuts in popular programs.

Despite its widespread appeal, the two-thirds majority requirement in both houses of Congress has proven to be an insurmountable barrier to the amendment. In 1982, a proposal was approved by a two-thirds majority in the Senate, but it failed in the House. A 1986 measure passed the House but fell short in the Senate by a single vote. Efforts in 1990 and 1992 were successful in the Senate but not in the House, by seven votes and nine votes respectively. The 1994 version did not obtain the requisite two-thirds majority in either house. Undaunted, Republican leaders pledged to make the balanced budget amendment their highest priority, including it in their "Contract with America." Still, while the 1995 and 1996 proposals comfortably passed the House, they failed each time in the Senate by a handful of votes.

The 1997 version of the balanced budget amendment prohibited outlays for a fiscal year from exceeding total receipts unless authorized by three-fifths vote of the whole number of both houses of Congress, and this version required a three-fifths vote of the whole number of each house to increase the public debt.[20] A simple majority of each house was necessary to increase revenues. The proposal included an exception to these provisions in times of war. The amendment would become effective in 2002, or in the second year following ratification by three-fourths of the states, whichever came later.[21]

The year 1997 appeared to be the best chance ever to pass an amendment because of the 1996 Senate elections. Several balanced budget opponents had been defeated, and a number of new senators had pledged to support the amendment during their campaign. It would be taken up in the Senate first where the margin was seen as closer. While negotiators were haggling over the outline of a balanced budget agreement, debate over the amendment took place over an intense four-week period in February and March. Attention focused on four undeclared freshmen Democratic Senators: Robert Torricelli (NJ), Mary Landrieu (LA), Tim Johnson (SD), and Max Cleland (GA). If they all voted aye, the amendment would pass. Each had supported the amendment in his or her Senate campaigns, and two of the Senators, Toricelli and Johnson, had voted for similar proposals while serving in the House. Once debate over the amendment began, the four freshmen pledged to meet frequently and discuss the measure in order to support one another and avoid any quick decisions which might give the amendment momentum and place increased pressure on the remaining undecided Senators.[22] Despite initial criticisms that he wasn't working hard enough against the amendment, President Clinton and Treasury Secretary Robert Rubin lobbied aggressively against the amendment. Cleland announced that he would support it, but Johnson followed with an announcement that he would oppose it, still leaving the issue in doubt. Landrieu announced her support as the vote approached, leaving proponents only one vote away. But on February 26, Torricelli announced that he would vote against, which would probably kill the amendment.

Torricelli's decision prompted an outcry by Senate Majority Leader Trent Lott, who denounced Torricelli and Johnson, although not by name, from the Senate floor. "This is a question of honesty. It is a question of truth in government. We wonder why people are cynical, why they wonder about us, why they question us. This is Exhibit A."[23] Democrats introduced a dozen amendments to the amendment, including several measures to protect Social Security cuts. All failed, but the linkage had been made to Social Security, and some critical political cover was provided. One commentator noted that by tying the amendment to Social Security, Clinton had found the "political equivalent of a magic bullet."[24] When the vote was finally taken on March 5, all fifty-five Republicans and eleven Democrats voted in favor of the amendment, and thirty-four Democrats opposed the measure, one vote shy of the two-thirds majority requirement.

The Tax Supermajority Amendment

The balanced budget amendment was not the Republicans' only attempt to reform federal budgeting in 1997 by constitutional means. They also made a second attempt to pass an amendment requiring a supermajority to increase federal taxes. The Tax Limitation Amendment of 1997, like its earlier counterpart in 1996, required two-thirds of the House and Senate members present to approve any bill increasing internal revenue laws "by more than a de minimis amount."[25] Under this proposal, members could still enact legislation by a simple majority that raised some taxes but cut others as long as the net effect was zero. The 1997 amendment required a two-thirds majority of the House and Senate members present to enact "any bill to levy a new tax or increase the rate or base of any tax."[26] An exception to this requirement would be made only if the country was at war or in a military conflict that included a threat to national security. Republican leaders scheduled a symbolic floor vote on April 15, the IRS deadline for filing taxes. A majority supported it by a vote of 230–190, but it was far short of the requisite two-thirds majority. The Senate did not vote on the proposed amendment.

The amendment to require a supermajority to increase taxes was strongly opposed by the Clinton administration. However, perceiving it as more of a sideshow than a real threat, the administration's efforts were not as urgent or intense as with the balanced budget amendment. Nonetheless, the fact that the Republicans wanted to debate the tax amendment and highlight partisan differences with the Democrats just as bipartisan negotiations over the balanced budget agreement were reaching a climax is instructive of the political environment surrounding the budget in 1997. It suggests that even as congressional Republicans pressed for a deal, many feared giving away the tax issue and balanced budget issue. It also presaged partisan battles that would continue between the budget resolution and final reconciliation bills, that would hold up appropriations bills until November, and that would characterize President Clinton's use of the line-item veto.

The Balanced Budget Agreement

While Congress was debating and voting on the two constitutional amendments, negotiations over the budget agreement continued. They were marked by the usual public posturing and predictions of failure if the other side did not compromise. In mid-March, Senate Budget Committee Chair Domenici said that the chances of getting a negotiated budget were "finished."[27] House Republicans passed a nonbinding resolution demanding that President Clinton submit a second budget that was more "realistic."[28] But by late April, concessions by both sides had brought them close to the outlines of a deal. With major tax cuts proposed by both sides, negotiators were still having trouble reaching the deficit targets. Trying to find a centrist solution, they continued to be pressured by ideologues of their own parties. House liberals warned the administration that they would not support any more concessions to the Republicans. In the Senate, a group of ten conservative Republicans led by Phil Gramm (TX) warned Majority Leader Trent Lott that their support could not be taken for granted. They set out five key "thresholds" that had to be met in terms of tax cuts and discretionary spending to gain their support.[29] One of their demands was to oppose a change in the way in which federal programs were adjusted for inflation by changing the consumer price index (CPI). Several months earlier, a blue ribbon commission had concluded that the current CPI overestimated inflation by as much as 1 percent, and they recommended adjustments. However, opposition from senior citizen groups made this seemingly innocuous technical adjustment politically dangerous. It would have tremendous budgetary consequences if adopted. CBO estimated that a one-point reduction would shave $141 billion off the deficit in five years.[30]

In late April, negotiators received a windfall from CBO. Its revised estimates of the FY 1997 deficit had dropped dramatically after tax collections surged during the spring. They would now have an extra $225 billion in revenue, requiring much more modest spending cuts and allowing greater tax cuts. This was the final push that the process needed, allowing the most unpopular items to be dropped. Negotiators jettisoned the politically risky CPI revision plan and a cap on Medicaid that was opposed by many Democrats and state governors. On May 2, 1997, the budget pact was announced by effusive Republicans in the rotunda of the Capitol.

In terms of perceived "wins," both parties claimed victory.[31] First and foremost, the agreement promised to balance the budget. In terms of Clinton's FY 1998 proposals, he was able to keep Medicare cuts near to the level he proposed, $115 billion over five years. Tax cuts were increased from a net of $20 billion in the president's requests to $85 billion in the agreement. For Republicans, the agreement contained a total $135 billion in tax cuts, including capital gains, a priority for their party since the Reagan administration. For Clinton and the Democrats, the package included $35 billion in tax preferences for education, $17 billion for health care for poor children, and some $60 billion in additional discretionary spending over five years. His plan to restore welfare benefits for legal aliens was also accepted.

In his news conference on May 2, President Clinton emphasized, in addition to balancing the budget and putting Medicare on a sound financial basis, how many of his key priorities would be achieved:

> This budget meets my goal of making education America's number-one priority on the edge of the 21st century. It will have the largest increase in education funding in 30 years. It will have the largest increase in Pell Grant scholarships in 20 years. . . . It will extend health insurance to uninsured children. . . . It will give businesses incentives and work with mayors to hire people from welfare to work . . . It will protect the environment, providing funds to clean up 500 of our most dangerous toxic waste sites. . . . It includes tax relief for the American people, but . . . the tax relief will be limited, and we'll know the dollar amount not only for the first five years, but for the second five years, so that we will not run the risk of having an explosion in the deficit.[32]

The revenue windfall allowed both sides to deliver benefits to key constituencies while still reaching balance in five years. It also allowed many more difficult issues, such as the CPI adjustment and entitlement growth when baby boomers retire, to be ignored. In fact, with the new numbers, the budget could have been balanced in one or two years rather than five. Most of the painful cuts would not take place until President Clinton was out of office. Congress had reached agreement with the White House on the broad outlines of an agreement that would have to be translated first into a budget resolution and then, more importantly, into specific implementing legislation in which committees would have the opportunity to put their imprimatur on the bill.

Only two weeks after the May 2 announcement, the deal had nearly collapsed because of disputes over what had actually been agreed upon. Direct negotiations between Speaker Gingrich and Majority Leader Trent Lott, and OMB Director Franklin Raines, produced a written agreement that the White House had demanded. The budget resolution passed the House the same day.[33] The most unhappy group was the congressional Democrats. On May 20, Minority Leader Dick Gephardt announced his opposition to the plan, although a majority of Democrats ultimately supported it. The Budget Resolution (H Con Res 84) cleared Congress on June 5 by wide margins, 327–97 in the House and 76–22 in the Senate.[34] A substantial majority of both parties in both chambers supported the resolution, clearly a bipartisan voting pattern that differed significantly from that of most budget resolutions in the preceding twenty years.

Reaching the outlines of a deal was not the same as actually passing and signing a deal. The balanced budget agreement would be implemented through two major reconciliation bills: one to incorporate the spending changes, the other to cover the tax changes. Over the next two months, the balanced budget agreement appeared to be in serious trouble on numerous occasions as Republican-led committees fleshed out the details of the resolution. For example, the only absolute number in the agreement concerning taxes was a net tax cut of at least $85 billion over five years. This left important details about everything from capital gains to credits for college education to be worked out. Bill Archer, Chair of the House Ways and Means Committee, was particularly adamant about shaping the details of the tax cuts. The administration monitored committee action, often accusing Republicans of violating the agreement and, on occasion, threatening a presidential veto. The negotiations between the White House and congressional leaders were continuous throughout the summer, with the negotiations including not only Republican party leaders, with whom the original agreement was struck, but also Budget Committees and tax-writing committees for the reconciliation bills, and finally the Conference Committee.

Jockeying for partisan advantage continued despite the bipartisan agreement in principle. The GOP again showed questionable public relations instincts by holding up an urgent disaster relief bill by trying to attach a budget freeze to it. When they finally passed the bill, it included the provision that agency budgets would be frozen at prior-year levels after October 1 if the regular appropriations bills had not passed. It also included a ban on the use of sampling techniques in the 2000 Census. Clinton vetoed it, and the Republicans were blasted in the media for playing politics while the flood victims in the upper Midwest suffered. Three days later, Congress passed a clean bill without the two amendments, and the president signed it. This seemed to strengthen the president's hand in the ongoing negotiations over the content of the reconciliation bills. Discontent within the Republican Party over this debacle would contribute to an abortive coup attempt in the House to topple Speaker Gingrich. The public tone hardly sounded as if an agreement had been reached. Trent Lott called Clinton a "spoiled brat" at one point, and House Majority Leader Dick Armey was quoted as saying he did not feel bound by the budget agreement.[35]

The appropriations process also began in earnest. On June 18, the House Appropriations Committee approved its 602(b) discretionary spending allocations to the subcommittees, and the Senate Appropriations Committee followed the next day. Both committees would have $517 billion in discretionary funds to appropriate, less than one-third of the total budget, but containing many of the most important federal programs.

The House and Senate were intently trying to put together the two reconciliation bills. In the House, the Budget Committee chaired by John Kasich (R-OH) had to piece together the work of eight house committees into a single spending cut bill. It would provide $137 billion in net budget savings, primarily through Medicare cuts. The administration and House Democrats complained that the bill violated the budget agreement by failing to restore benefits for legal aliens and by reducing the president's children's health initiatives. The tax bill, centered in the Ways and Means Committee, was also the subject of controversy and negotiation. The main objection from the Democrats was the failure to incorporate many of the president's education initiatives and the overall bias of the tax cuts to wealthy taxpayers. The process of assembling the two bills was more bipartisan in the Senate where the Democrats had more input. Downward reestimation of the revenues from the broadcast spectrum auction left members scrambling to make up the difference.

The Clinton administration had serious objections to both reconciliation bills in the House of Representatives. The president chose, however, to get the bills into Conference Committee and take a stand there. In a letter to House Democrats, he urged them to vote for the bill, "to advance—not oppose—this significant achievement." He continued, "We certainly understand that we need to improve the legislation further. We expect and will insist that the final budget resolution be in conformance with the budget agreement."[36] The spending cut bills passed the House and Senate on June 25 by votes of 270–162 and 73–27 respectively.[37] Both of these were party votes using the 50 percent criterion, with Republicans (97 percent voting with party) more unified than Democrats (75 percent voting with party). The tax bills passed the next day by a vote of 253–179 in the House and a vote of 80–18 in the Senate. The House vote was much more partisan, with 99 percent of Republicans and 87 percent of Democrats voting with their parties. The Senate vote, where Democrats had much more input in the legislation, was not a party vote. The negotiations would shift to the Conference Committee after the Independence Day recess. Those negotiations would be completed by the end of July.

Despite facing a Congress controlled by the opposition party, Clinton had a number of political advantages working for him during the final negotiations. His popularity was nearly an all-time high for his administration. He had demonstrated his willingness to use the veto on budget matters and his ability to sustain it. The Republicans were eager to reach a budget deal quickly and deflect attention from the failed attempt to remove Speaker Gingrich. While many Democrats still opposed the budget deal, Clinton's ability to prevail on a number of his top budget priorities in the agreement finally brought a majority of Democrats (although a narrow majority in the House) to his side. Major remaining issues concerned children's health spending, indexing of capital gains taxes, and the president's education tax credits. In the end, Republicans conceded to the president's position on all of these issues.

Final agreement was reached on July 29. The spending portion of the bill passed the House the next day by a vote of 346–85, and the Senate on July 31 by a vote of 85–15.[38] The tax bill passed by similar margins, and on August 5, Republican and Democratic lawmakers gathered at the White House for the signing ceremony.

The Balanced Budget Act and the Taxpayer Relief Act of 1997

The Balanced Budget Act and the Taxpayer Relief Act included the following provisions:[39]

- Net tax cuts of $95 billion over five years, including a middle-class tax credit, $35 billion in higher-education tax breaks, a reduction in the long-term capital gains tax from 28 to 20 percent, and dozens of special-interest tax provisions.

- New taxes on air travel that would add revenues of $33 billion over five years, as well as additional taxes on cigarettes.
- $115 billion reduction in the projected growth in Medicare achieved by reductions in payments to providers and increased premiums; proposal to raise eligibility age to 67 was dropped.
- $24 billion to states to provide health care assistance to children of uninsured, low-income families.
- $10 billion in savings from Medicaid primarily through cuts in payments to providers.
- $18 billion to cover the costs of welfare benefits for legal aliens.

Although a majority of House and Senate Democrats voted for the conference agreement of the major bills, congressional Democrats were divided. How much had the president's compromises preserved key Democratic Party positions? The administration was able to prevail on a number of initiatives: repeal of certain provisions of welfare reform, enactment of most education proposals, and increases in spending on the environment and law enforcement. The final version of the Balanced Budget Act provided for Medicare cuts of $115 billion over five years, only slightly more than his initial proposal of $109 billion and significantly less than the Republican proposals from the previous Congress. Clinton's proposals for health care for children were funded. His main concession to the Republicans was on the size of the tax cut. His budget proposals in February called for a net tax cut of only $20 billion; the final version provided $95 billion. Even so, the administration had significant influence on the content of the tax changes, such as blocking the Republican proposal to index capital gains taxes. The Republicans gained a great deal of their agenda as well, including a balanced budget by 2002, significant tax cuts, and a capital gains tax cut that had been sought since the 1980s. In the end, both sides declared victory.

Would the agreement really result in a balanced budget? Given the economic conditions that prevailed at the end of 1997, CBO concluded that it would.[40] Economic and technical changes contributed as much to bringing the budget into balance as the policy changes enacted in the two bills.[41] Because of greater-than-expected economic growth, the deficit in 2002 was projected to be $89 billion less than under the assumptions used at the start of the year. Technical changes in making estimates of revenues and spending knocked another $36 billion off the deficit projection for 2002. Policy changes would reduce the deficit by $95 billion that year, or about 40 percent of the total reduction. The agreement reached as part of the FY 1998 budget was not nearly as large in real dollars of deficit reduction as the much-maligned budget deals in 1990 under

Figure 7–1
Comparison of deficit reduction agreements, 1990, 1993, and 1997 (in constant 1997 dollars): deficit reduction over five years.

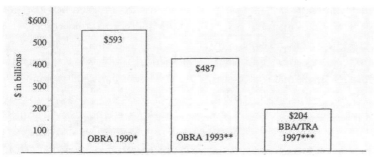

Source: CBO, Senate Budget Committee, reported in Lance T. LeLoup et al., "President Clinton's FY 1998 Budget: Political and Constitutional Paths to Balance," *Public Budgeting and Finance* 18 (Spring 1998): 18.
*Omnibus Budget Reconciliation Act of 1990; bipartisan agreement under Bush.
**Omnibus Budget Reconciliation Act of 1993; Clinton Democratic deficit reduction package.
***Balanced Budget Act and Taxpayer Relief Act of 1997; bipartisan agreement to balance the budget by 2002.

Bush and in 1993 under Clinton. Figure 7–1 compares the net five-year deficit reduction in all three plans in constant 1997 dollars.

By a margin of 41 percent to 32 percent, the public gave the Congress more credit than the president for the agreement, and by 39 percent to 33 percent, they believed that the Republicans got more of what they wanted than the president did.[42] For the first time in twenty-three years, public approval of Congress was higher than disapproval: 45 percent to 39 percent. The numbers had been nearly reversed a few months earlier. Despite the political gains for the Republicans, Clinton had helped himself as well. His popularity ratings moved above 60 percent, a level comparable to that of Reagan and Eisenhower at similar points in their second term. Nearly 70 percent of the people believed that things in the country were going well. Reaching a plan to balance the budget proved to be good politics for everyone involved.

Conclusion

The bipartisan budget agreement in 1997 was historic. For the first time in a generation, Congress and the president had put revenues and expenditures on a realistic path to reach balance. Driven by the booming economy, the budget would actually be balanced in two years instead of five. The 1996 elections settled the division of power in a way that the 1994 elections had not. If a balanced budget was to be agreed on, congressional Republicans would have to work with the Democratic president. An agreement was achieved because both parties were able to take out the most unpalatable items and still protect issues important to their core constituencies.

Once again, congressional budget rules helped facilitate the enactment of a balanced budget by packaging complex tax and spending measures in two reconciliation bills, subject to a final up or down vote and protected on the floor from amendment and dilatory tactics. The 1997 balanced budget agreement reflected the enhanced capacity of Congress in macrobudgeting. Congress had come a long way from the era of subcommittee-based scrutiny and incremental adjustment of agency appropriations described by Richard Fenno in 1965.[43] What emerged is a multistage bargaining process involving both branches, first negotiating the broad outlines and then filling in the details at increasing levels of specificity. No major changes in budget rules were part of the balanced budget agreement. However, the failed balanced budget amendment and the tax increase supermajority amendment were two Republican attempts to adopt constitutional rules that would both institutionalize their policy positions and enhance their reputation with voters.

The Omnibus Budget Reconciliation Act of 1990 (OBRA-90) and the Budget Enforcement Act (BEA) helped make the balanced budget agreement possible in several ways. OBRA-90 produced savings of $593 billion in 1997 dollars. Second, the enactment of the BEA and the scrapping of GRH deficit targets ushered in a more "realistic" era of congressional budgeting, with PAYGO and discretionary caps where Congress concentrated on factors within its control rather than economic and technical factors driving the deficits. Third, the initial failure of the 1990 budget agreement held important lessons for leaders in 1997. Top-level negotiators avoided excessive detail, instead setting broad parameters and letting the committees fill in the details. They also avoided a "summit" and were careful not to get too far out in front of the rank and file in terms of major policy issues.

Although making relatively few changes in budget rules, the Omnibus Budget Reconciliation Act of 1993 (OBRA-93) also helped make possible a budget agreement in 1997. It extended the appropriations caps and many of the key provisions of the Budget Enforcement Act. Although the economic recovery was already underway, the 1993 deficit reduction package instilled confidence in Wall Street and helped stimulate robust growth and lower interest rates. The result was significant progress in deficit reduction under Clinton, from a deficit of $290 billion in his first year in office, to only $22 billion in 1997.

Does the bipartisanship in enacting the 1997 balanced budget agreement weaken partisan explanations of congressional budgeting or the importance of divided government? Republican leadership in Congress was less centralized in 1997 than it had been in 1995, Gingrich's first year leading a majority. Committees were regaining some autonomy, and there was dissatisfaction with the speaker's leadership after only two and a half years. He would be forced out after the 1998 elections. More committee chairs played key roles in negotiating the budget agreement, but the Republicans remained highly cohesive. In the Senate, minority Democrats had some participation in the process. Engaging in what was called "triangulation," the Democratic administration negotiated primarily with congressional Republican leaders, leaving minority Democrats on the sidelines for the most part. This undermined Democratic cohesion in Congress, as we saw in the voting patterns. Because of the realistic possibility of actually balancing the budget for the first time in thirty years, the Clinton administration and congressional Republicans made important concessions to each other. The compromise was greatly facilitated by the improved deficit forecasts and the "windfall" in May that reduced the total amount of deficit reduction that had to be achieved. Although a notable achievement, the balanced budget agreement was not comparable in scope to either OBRA-90 or OBRA-93 as Figure 7–1 indicates.

Despite the contrast between the 1997 balanced budget agreement and the 1993 Democratic budget package, there is still evidence of fundamental underlying partisan divisions in budgeting and the importance of party leaders and strong budget rules. It was reflected in the continued efforts of Republicans to push budget-related constitutional amendments. It was reflected in the level of rhetoric and rancor in implementing the outline of the budget agreement in May. It was reflected in some party votes along the way. Comparisons between the 1993 and 1997 reconciliation bills reflect the significant impact of divided government in the content of deficit reduction agreements. Unlike Bush in 1993, Clinton often used the veto and the threat of a veto in 1997 to increase his leverage in bargaining with Congress. The veto of the supplemental appropriation act in June seemed to be particularly efficacious for the president. Republicans knew that the veto threat was credible and that since they could not override, they had to deal. Subsequently, Democratic positions were protected in education, Medicare, and the environment.

Partisanship in Congress would reach new heights in 1998 and 1999 with the impeachment proceedings against President Clinton. After a balanced budget was achieved in 2000, it would become clear that partisanship was not limited to budgeting under deficits. As we will see in the next chapter, Republicans and Democrats would remain polarized over what to do with the surplus for several years. Budget issues would remain at the forefront after the 2000 elections which produced a return to unified government, the first unified Republican government since 1953.

CHAPTER 8

Bush, Congress, and Tax Cuts, 2001 and 2003

When the 107th Congress convened in January 2001, the Budget and Impoundment Control Act of 1974 had been in place for more than a quarter-century. Congressional budgeting had evolved, surviving challenges and criticisms and emerging as a core element of the legislative process and a key tool of party leaders. Over the next three years, it would again be a critical element in determining the results of major budget initiatives but in a political and economic environment that had dramatically changed. With Republican George W. Bush in the White House, and unified Republican government for the first time since 1953, tax cuts would be at the center of the policy agenda. Despite a recession and a return to deficits, a midsession change in party control of the Senate in 2001, the tragedy of September 11, and wars in Afghanistan and Iraq, major tax-cutting legislation would pass in 2001and 2003. These legislative enactments present the latest cases and a final opportunity to assess the impact of rules and institutions, the role of parties, and the consequences of party control of government on congressional budget decisions.

Tax Cuts and the Budget, 2001

The Political and Economic Environment

The context for national budgeting would be shaped by the 2000 elections. Bush would assume the presidency having lost the popular vote in one of the most controversial elections in history which only enhanced partisan animosity in the Congress and the country. The 2000 elections returned a Republican House of Representatives but produced a 50–50 tie in the Senate. After weeks of negotiations, Republican and Democratic leaders in the Senate

worked out a unique power-sharing agreement which kept Senator Trent Lott
(R-MS) as majority leader and maintained an equal number of Republicans
and Democrats on each committee but with a Republican chairing each
panel. Tom Daschle (D-SD) remained as minority leader. With Vice President
Cheney producing the 51st vote in the Senate, Bush began his term with the
narrowest imaginable unified party control of government. In the House,
Dennis Hastert (R-IL), who had assumed the speakership after Newt
Gingrich resigned from Congress after the 1998 elections, remained in that
position. Representative Jim Nussel (R-IA) took over as Chair of the House
Budget Committee. Senator Peter Domenici (R-NM) remained as Chair of
the Senate Budget Committee.

Congressional Republicans, who had maintained majority status for the
fourth consecutive election, faced a very different political situation with a
Republican president. For the last six years of Clinton's presidency,
Republicans had used the budget resolutions to shape the negotiations with
the president. Even though Clinton and the Republican Congress had successfully balanced the budget, Clinton had effectively used the veto and the
veto threat to check Republican budget priorities and to promote Democratic
programs such as Medicare and education.[1] According to spatial models of
the legislative process, change in party control of the presidency would
change the "veto pivot," shifting the area of policy agreement between president and Congress and changing the dynamics of interbranch negotiations.[2]

Bush and the 107th Congress would begin shaping the broad outlines of
the federal budget in an economic environment far different from that of
their recent predecessors. In January 2001, budget projections showed huge
surpluses as far as the eye could see. The Congressional Budget Office forecast a budget surplus of $5.6 trillion over the next ten years.[3] Nearly half of
these projected surpluses were in the general funds portion of the budget
rather than in the Social Security and Medicare trust funds, meaning that the
funds were available for tax cuts, spending increases, or debt reduction. As
we have seen in prior years, projections can change quickly. The rapid change
from surpluses to deficits between 2001 and 2003 was one of the most dramatic reversals in the history of U.S. national budgeting.

Dealing with surpluses was certainly a much more pleasant task than dealing with deficits, but the emergence of the surpluses appeared to have little
impact on the budget process in Congress, except for the fact that congressional spending discipline relaxed considerably. The budget resolutions in
1999 and 2000 appeared to be less consequential than in prior years, as
appropriators and program advocates pushed discretionary spending

upwards. The period after the 1997 balanced budget agreement was not characterized by significant changes in budget rules and institutions as had occurred in prior years. Some provisions of the Budget Enforcement Act were allowed to expire. Reconciliation and the protections it provides from amendment and obstruction would prove critical in budgeting in 2001 and 2003 as it had in earlier major budget packages.

Having the budget in surplus did not appear to diminish the perceived political stakes for the parties. Despite the surpluses, bipartisan agreement could not be reached on shoring up entitlements: projections still showed both Medicare and Social Security trending toward insolvency in the coming decades. Republicans and Democrats battled over what to do with the surpluses, how much to cut taxes, how much public debt to retire, and whether to spend additional monies on defense or domestic programs. From the perspective of President Bush and congressional Republicans, however, unified Republican control of the White House and the Congress appeared to be a favorable situation for delivering the largest tax cut in history.

The Bush Tax Cut Plan

The tax cut package had its genesis long before Bush's inauguration as the 43rd President of the United States. Along with education reform, tax cuts were at the center of the Bush campaign and a favorite theme among Republicans and conservatives. The projection of large surpluses gave Bush the luxury of pushing for a politically popular tax cut rather than a tax increase as his father and Clinton had done. Even Democrats acknowledged that some tax cuts were appropriate, but they wanted much smaller cuts targeted toward lower-income groups. There was a sense of urgency among Republicans, however, because signs of economic weakening and a possible recession were already on the horizon. Democrats warned that excessive tax cuts could lead to a return to deficits.

The administration started a lobbying campaign for the tax cuts shortly after the inauguration.[4] The first week of February, Treasury Secretary Paul O'Neill came to Capitol Hill to outline the administration's proposed tax cuts while the president mixed public events with private meetings to promote his agenda. "I want the members of Congress and the American people to hear loud and clear," the president said. "This is the right-size plan, it is the right approach, and I'm going to defend it mightily."[5] Bush had chosen a total reduction for the tax cut of $1.62 trillion over ten years. Some of the main proposals included the following:[6]

- *Reduce income tax rates.* Create a new 10 percent bracket and lower the rates on all other brackets, moving the maximum rate of 39 percent to 33 percent. The estimated cost was approximately $724 billion.
- *Phase out estate taxes.* Eliminate what Republicans call "death taxes" and gift taxes. The total cost was approximately $236 billion.
- *Child credits.* Increase tax credits for taxpayers with children at a cost of $162 billion.
- *Eliminate the "marriage penalty."* Provide tax relief to two-income married couples who pay more tax than one-income couples at the same income level. The approximate cost was estimated to be $88 billion.
- *Charitable contributions.* Increase the number of taxpayers who are allowed to deduct contributions to charities. The cost was estimated to be $80 billion.
- *Research and development tax credit.* Give large corporations a benefit for spending on R&D at a cost of $24 billion.

Bush formally presented the outline of his budget proposals in a televised speech to Congress February 27.

House Action

The House of Representatives wanted to move the tax cut package quickly, even before the budget resolution was adopted. Republican Party leaders wanted to take up a number of tax cut bills immediately, some that went well beyond what the president was asking. This move was criticized by Democratic leaders and others who felt that it undermined the comprehensiveness of the budget process. Many of the more conservative House Republicans did not believe that Bush's proposals went far enough and had aspirations of expanding the scope of the tax cuts. They wanted the $1.6 trillion to be a floor for tax cuts, with some of the most enthusiastic tax-cutters talking about cuts as high as $2.2 trillion over ten years.[7]

Democrats, lacking a president of their own party in the White House for the first time in eight years, were having difficulty in agreeing on a position that would be an alternative to the Republican plan. With the size of the surplus, most Democrats felt that some tax cuts were appropriate but that the $1.6 trillion number was dangerous and irresponsible. A consensus began to emerge for a figure of around $700 billion in tax cuts over ten years, focusing more of the cuts on lower- and middle-income groups. This figure was later expanded to $900 billion. In the twenty years since Reagan's major tax cut, the number of conservative southern Democrats had steadily been reduced. Some, like Phil Gramm, had switched to the Republican Party; others were defeated and replaced by conservative Republicans. The successor to the "Boll Weevils" of the 1980s was the so-called Blue Dog Democrats. Formed in 1995, by 2001 the group counted thirty-three House Democrats as members, including founder Charles Stenholm (D-TX) who had earlier been one of the Boll Weevils who helped pass Reagan's economic and budget plan.[8] With a slim eleven-vote Republican majority in the House, many believed that the Blue Dogs would play a key role in ensuring the passage of Bush's tax cuts. This would prove not to be the case because of the degree of party unity among House Republicans and the control of the budget process by Republican leaders.

As a result, when markup of tax legislation began in the Ways and Means Committee, input from the Blue Dog Democrats was neither sought nor listened to when it came. The committee took up and expanded the largest of the president's proposals—the across-the-board rate cuts that would reduce revenue by $958 billion. After just two days, the Ways and Means Committee reported out the rate-cut bill (HR 3) by a straight party line vote of 23–15.[9] Democrats, including Blue Dogs, were critical of the bill because it was enacted before the budget resolution and because they were completely excluded from the process. The bill was moved quickly to the floor for debate and passed on March 8 by a vote of 230–198. Ten Democrats joined unanimous Republicans in approving the bill. The Ways and Means Committee announced plans to move four other tax bills before the spring recess on April 5, before the budget resolution would be approved.

On March 21, markup of the FY 2002 budget resolution began in the House Budget Committee. In February, the House had passed "lockbox" legislation to reserve surpluses in the Medicare and Social Security trust funds for debt reduction only. This largely symbolic effort to reassure voters that these two programs would not be touched received overwhelming bipartisan support in a 407–2 vote. It would be encompassed in the House version of the budget resolution. The resolution, drafted by HBC Chair Jim Nussle, would essentially be rubber-stamped by the committee majority. The major Republican deviation from the Bush proposals was to increase the size of the tax cuts. Because of problems with the size of the tax cut in the Senate, this was as much as anything a negotiating strategy for the House-Senate conference to follow. Another issue of concern was the target for discretionary spending. Conservative Republicans hoped to ratchet back on the rapid growth of discretionary spending that had occurred at the end of the Clinton administration, but appropriators were pushing for significant growth above inflation. The House version of the budget resolution limited growth in FY 2002 to 3.9 percent.[10] After one day of markup, the House Budget Committee reported the budget resolution by a straight party line vote of 23–19.

The House took up the budget resolution on the floor March 28. Under strict rules for debate and amendment, the outcome was close but never in doubt. The resolution was adopted by a nearly party line vote of 222–205. Only three Democrats and two Republicans crossed the aisle and voted with the other party. That translates into Democratic Party unity of 98.5 percent and Republican unity of 99 percent.

Senate Action

With the Senate tied 50–50, the political dynamic in the Senate was much different than in the House. Only one Democrat, Zell Miller (D-GA), announced support for the president's tax cuts proposals at the level of $1.6 trillion. That meant that Majority Leader Lott and the White House could only lose one of the fifty Republican votes in order to allow Vice President Cheney to cast the tie-breaking vote. However, several Republicans had expressed reservations about the size of the proposed tax cuts and, despite intense lobbying, did not seem willing to budge. These reluctant Republican moderates included Lincoln Chaffee (R-RI), Arlen Specter (R-PA), and James Jeffords (R-VT). Some members suggested adding a "trigger" or "circuit-breaker" provision to the tax cuts that would repeal them in future years if the surplus projections fell short. The administration and Republican leaders opposed any such provisions. Senate Finance Committee Chair Charles Grassley (R-IA) opted against moving tax legislation before the budget resolution. He recognized that the Senate would need to consider the tax cuts under the protection of the budget rules (see below). He also made a much more bipartisan appeal than his House counterparts, saying that he hoped to have a tax package that could include Democratic support.[11] His efforts were hampered by anger among Senate Democrats about how their counterparts had been treated in the House process.

There was little bipartisanship on the Senate Budget Committee either. Still, SBC Chair Domenici drafted a resolution that attempted to gather support from pivotal moderate members. Rather than follow the House model of using the president's proposed $1.6 trillion in tax cuts as a floor, the Senate resolution would make it a ceiling. The Senate resolution would also encompass a trigger mechanism to be specified later by the Finance Committee. The resolution kept the president's figure for growth of discretionary spending similar to the House version. These gestures were not enough to sway a single Democrat on the Senate Budget Committee. With the panel evenly divided (eleven Republicans and eleven Democrats), the result was that no resolution could pass out of committee. However, under the rules of the budget process, party leaders could bypass the committee altogether and bring the resolution directly to the Senate floor. Its success there would depend on whether the budget resolution could be used to provide protection to the tax cut bill through its reconciliation instructions.

Reconciliation Controversy

Reconciliation had been a critical part of congressional budgeting for twenty years but still remained controversial. As we have seen in earlier chapters, it had turned out to be a critical institution in the deficit reduction efforts of the 1980s and 1990s. Once the budget headed toward balance, however, a new controversy emerged: whether reconciliation could apply to tax cuts as well as deficit reduction. In 1996, Senate Parliamentarian Robert Dove made a crucial ruling allowing reconciliation legislation to be used for tax cuts. Democrats argued that reconciliation could be used only for legislation that would reduce the deficit. The ruling was appealed by Minority Leader Tom Daschle (D-SD), but the Republicans prevailed in a straight party line floor vote, establishing a precedent.[12] Dove restricted his ruling, however, saying that any tax cuts that were moved under reconciliation could not extend past the time frame of the budget resolution.[13] Republicans noted that the 1997 balanced budget agreement, implemented in the form of two reconciliation bills, included tax cuts. In 2000, Republican leaders had enacted a tax cut eliminating the so-called marriage penalty as a reconciliation bill. To allow the tax cut under reconciliation rules, they added provisions that it would expire (or "sunset") in five years, the time frame covered by the budget resolution. Clinton vetoed the bill.

In 2001, the controversy over the use of reconciliation arose again with regard to the Bush tax cut package. Leading the Democrats' opposition to allowing reconciliation to be used for the tax cuts was Senator Robert Byrd (D-WV), one the original architects of the 1974 Budget Act and author of the Byrd rule which restricts amendments to reconciliation bills. Making matters more difficult for Republicans, Parliamentarian Dove was beginning to have doubts about his original 1996 ruling. Domenici and Majority Leader Lott were ultimately successful in getting reconciliation protection for the tax cut bill in the Senate. Even if Dove had ruled against them, his ruling could have been overturned by a simple majority vote. Recognizing that the Democrats would lose in a party line vote, Byrd and Daschle declined to force the issue to a vote, recognizing that if they lost the vote, the precedent would be strengthened further. To allow larger tax cuts, Republican leaders expanded the time horizon of the budget resolution from five years to ten. In the Senate, to keep reconciliation protection, all of the tax cut proposals would expire after ten years. Most felt, though, that ten years down the road, it would be politically unpopular to let them expire.

The Senate took up the budget resolution, and intense negotiation and bargaining took place behind the scenes among Republicans. Despite pressure from the White House and Republican leaders, Specter, Jeffords, and Chaffee refused to support tax cuts as large as $1.6 trillion. The key vote was taken on April 4 when the three joined the Democrats in approving an amendment to reduce the tax cuts figure by $448 billion and use half the money for education.[14] After making some of the tax cuts retroactive, the total in the budget resolution for tax cuts became $1.27 trillion over ten years. With that compromise reached, the budget resolution passed the Senate by a more comfortable margin, 65–35. Fifteen Democrats voted with the unanimous Republicans. The Senate version also called for a discretionary spending target that was $28 billion higher than the House version, an 8 percent versus a 4 percent increase. This would also be a major dispute in conference.

Conference Committee Action

Congress returned to Washington after a two-week Easter recess, and the Conference Committee on the FY 2002 budget resolution convened April 25. The partisan tone of the conference was reflected in the comments of Senator Domenici who told the Democrats, "We don't expect you to sign it [the conference agreement] so we don't expect you to be needed."[15] Except for a handful of centrist Democrats invited to the White House, the administration was also largely ignoring Democratic leaders in their legislative lobbying. The main negotiations were between administration representatives and Republican congressional leaders who reached an agreement on April 30. It provided for a tax cut of $1.35 trillion, around 82 percent of what Bush had proposed, and also accepted the House and administration number for growth in discretionary spending. Most expected, however, that spending would exceed the target.

Another problem with the budget rules arose May 3 concerning the placement of a $5.6 billion contingency fund in the budget resolution. Senate

Parliamentarian Dove ruled that inclusion of that item in the resolution would make it subject to a sixty-vote point of order on the Senate floor. Eventually, the fund was removed from the resolution, but, frustrated with the Parliamentarian's rulings, Majority Leader Lott relieved Dove of his duties.[16]

The House voted 221–207 to approve the conference report on the budget resolution on May 9. At a meeting of the Blue Dog Democrats the day before, a vote was taken to officially oppose the resolution. As a result, only six Democrats joined the majority while three Republicans voted against it. The Senate approved the resolution the next day by a vote of 53–47. Unhappy with the lower discretionary spending target, only five Democrats voted for the resolution while two Republicans (Chaffee and Jeffords) voted against. This measure, not needing the president's signature but binding only on subsequent action, paved the way for the adoption of the tax cuts.

Passage of the Tax Cuts

Both the House Ways and Means Committee and the Senate Finance Committee moved into high gear on the reconciliation tax bills after the passage of the budget resolution. The House had already passed its third tax cut bill of the session which would have to be revised in the new comprehensive bill. Although the resolution specified the total amount of the tax cuts, many critical decisions remained on the details, particularly differential treatment of lower-, middle-, and upper-income taxpayers. The House passed its version on May 16 by a vote of 230–197, picking up a few additional Democratic votes. The House bill reaffirmed the centerpiece of the president's proposals, the across-the-board income tax rate cuts.

In the Senate, Finance Committee Chair Grassley and the ranking minority member, Max Baucus (D-MT), attempted to work out a bipartisan compromise that could pass by a larger margin. Grassley was at odds, however, with Majority Leader Lott who threatened to take the bill away from the committee and take the legislation directly to the floor. The administration was still lobbying hard to get as many of its desired provisions included in the $1.35 trillion total.[17] Led by Minority Leader Daschle, the Democrats continued to oppose the bill, keeping the Senate in session for four days and two nights. Two sudden changes in the political and economic environment changed the strategy of the administration—they decided to compromise on the best deal they could get and declare victory. The Senate passed its version of the Tax Cut Reconciliation Bill on May 23 by a vote of 62–38.

Why had the administration quickly settled? The first change involved new and troubling budget projections showing that the economy was slowing and that the surpluses would not be as large as expected. Second, Senator James Jeffords announced May 22 that he was leaving the Republican Party and would become an Independent, caucusing with the Democrats. Jeffords had been frustrated with his treatment by the administration and unhappy with Republican leaders in the Senate on a number of issues, particularly funding for education. That meant that the country's return to unified Republican control of the presidency and both houses of Congress would be short-lived. The Democrats would take over the Senate 50–49–1, Daschle would become majority leader, and committees would be reorganized, giving the Democrats the majority and the chairmanship on all of them. Divided government would return for the remainder of the 107th Congress. This was a distressing shock to the administration and congressional Republicans. Under the power-sharing agreement worked out earlier in the year, a contingency had been arranged if one of the two parties took control. Jeffords decided that his switch would become official on the day the tax bill reached the president's desk.

After learning of Jeffords's switch, the administration and Republican leaders struck the best deal they could get. President Bush urged the Congress to finish its work on the tax bill immediately, noting that "our economy cannot afford any further delays."[18] House-Senate conferees tied up loose ends and sent the compromise package back to their respective houses. The compromises broadened the support for the bill among Democrats. The House passed the final bill 240–154, with twenty-eight Democrats voting for the bill and twenty-nine abstaining. No Republicans voted against the bill. In the Senate, twelve Democrats supported the compromise and seven abstained in a final vote of 58–33. Republicans Chaffee and John McCain (R-AZ) voted against final passage. In a rush to recess for Memorial Day weekend and with Senator Paul Wellstone (D-MN) needing to go to the hospital immediately for back pain, the Senate cut short its final debate and sent the bill to the president's desk.

The Tax Cut Reconciliation Act was signed by President Bush June 7 and was hailed as a great victory for the administration. Many Republicans were dissatisfied, however, and promised to seek additional cuts that had been deleted. The final bill lowered top rates but not to the 33 percent that the administration wanted. The rate cuts reduced revenues by $875 billion over ten years. Estate and gift taxes were reduced by $138 billion, the marriage penalty by $63 billion, and child tax credits by $172 billion; and retirement provisions lowered revenues by $29 billion. As required under reconciliation rules, most of the cuts would sunset in 2011, requiring further action by

Congress down the road if they were to be made permanent. Two years later, after the tragedy of September 11 and in an economy having difficulty recovering from recession, President Bush would revisit the issue of tax cuts.

Tax Cuts, 2003

The war on terrorism had created a very different budgetary environment. At least in the early stages, President Bush was likely to get whatever he said was necessary to protect homeland security and to pursue the war on terror. So despite the worsening budgetary situation in terms of deficits, other policy objectives were deemed more important. Economic stimulus was one of those objectives, as the economy had languished for over two years. While the recession had ended in 2001, economic growth was tepid, and unemployment continued to increase. Despite a record loss of jobs during the first two years of his administration, Bush had campaigned hard for Republican congressional candidates in the fall of 2002. With his record after 9/11, a war in Afghanistan, and a looming war in Iraq, Bush helped Republicans recapture Congress in the 2002 midterm elections.

Republicans picked up several seats in the House and also picked up two critical seats in the Senate to give them a 51–49 majority. Although the narrow margin meant that a handful of moderates would continue to have significant bargaining position in the 108th Senate, the Republicans would organize the chamber and chair all the committees after eighteen months of Democratic control under Majority Leader Tom Daschle. The Republicans would have a new Majority Leader in the Senate. Former leader Trent Lott became ensnared in a controversy over ill-considered public comments at Senator Strom Thurmond's birthday party and was forced to step down. The Republican senator from Tennessee, Dr. Bill Frist, was selected as majority leader despite his inexperience. Daschle would remain as minority leader. In the House, Speaker Hastert was selected for a fourth term. Senator Don Nichols (R-OK) took over as the new Senate Budget Committee Chair, and the committee itself had become much more conservative in the 108th Congress than in the 107th. The seven new Republicans on SBC had an average rating by the American Conservative Union (ACU) of 93.8 percent compared to an average ACU rating of 79.8 among the six Republicans who had left the committee.[19] The ranking Democrat on the committee, Kent Conrad (D-ND), charged that moderates had been "purged" from the Budget Committee.

In the two years since the first package of tax cuts passed, budget forecasts had made one of the fastest (and unfortunate) turnarounds in history. From projections of a decade of trillion dollar surpluses, by 2003, estimates showed deficits growing in size and duration. The budget process had suffered in 2002 under divided government. For the first time since its inception, no budget resolution passed the Congress. This played havoc with the appropriations process, and by the start of the 108th Congress, eleven of the thirteen spending bills from the previous Congress were still not enacted. One of the most positive aspects of having budget surpluses for members of Congress was that they no longer had to vote for an extension of the public debt ceiling. No extension of government borrowing authority was needed between 1997 and 2002. In 2002, however, as the surpluses turned into deficits, Congress was forced to increase the debt limit. It would need to be extended again in 2003 as well. Several other key budgetary changes had occurred in 2002 largely below the radar, such as abandoning spending caps and removing the lockbox provisions to protect entitlements that had been so prominent in the days of surpluses.

A new rule for assessing, or scoring, tax bills would be introduced in 2003 under unified Republican control. For years, tax cut proponents argued that traditional static estimates of the costs of tax cuts overestimated the loss of revenue by not including the revenue gains caused by economic growth. They proposed instead a method called "dynamic scoring" which factors in the projected revenue gains in the future.[20] Democrats argued that dynamic scoring was a bogus system designed by Republicans to hide the real costs of tax cuts. In January 2003, the House adopted a new rule for the 108th Congress requiring dynamic scoring for all bills moving through the Ways and Means Committee. This system would be supported by the new head of CBO, Douglas Holtz-Eakin, a tax cut advocate who came to Capitol Hill from the White House.

Another issue concerning the budget rules in 2003 was the question of the duration of the budget resolution. Over the past twenty-eight years, budget resolutions covered more and more years as they became more comprehensive.[21] For the first five years in the 1970s, resolutions covered only one year, allowing gimmicks such as moving the date of a pay raise by one day to the next fiscal year to create an apparent "savings." In the 1980s, resolutions were extended to cover three years, and by the 1990s, five years was the norm. The 1997 balanced budget agreement was implemented through a seven-year plan. The first ten-year budget resolution was passed in 1999 and again in 2001, in the latter case, to incorporate as large a tax cut as possible. But this issue divided Republicans in 2003. Many felt that the ten-year time horizon was impossibly unrealistic and that with rising deficits, resolutions should be limited to five years. On the other side, the administration was pushing for a ten-year duration to allow as large a package of tax cuts as possible. The president's own budget, however, presented Congress with only a five-year time horizon. SBC Chair Don Nichols announced that he favored returning to a five-year budget resolution. These and other rules changes would help shape the tax cut package in 2003.

The President's Proposals

Buoyed by the 2002 election results, the Bush administration wanted to press for another major tax cut package in 2003. Given the continued sluggish economic growth, the Bush tax cuts would be promoted more as a "growth and jobs" package than had the 2001 plan. On January 6, the president unveiled the outlines of his plan which would cost $674 billion over ten years:

- Eliminate taxation on stock dividends paid to individuals at a cost of $364 billion.
- Reduce rates on personal income taxes at an estimated cost of $64 billion.
- Further eliminate the marriage penalty at a cost of $58 billion.
- Expand the income limit to qualify for the lowest tax rate at an estimated cost of $48 billion.
- Provide incentives for small business, aid to the states, and other provisions estimated to cost $49 billion.

Reaction to the plan was predictable. Democrats immediately attacked the idea on the basis that the country could not afford any more tax cuts because of the costs of war and recession. Some Republicans felt that the proposals did not go far enough, and House Majority Leader Tom Delay (R-TX) complained about the lack of a capital gains cut. The growth and jobs package was the administration's centerpiece and highest priority, but it was only the beginning of other tax cuts they would propose in 2003. In his budget proposal released in February, Bush added to his list of desired tax cuts:[22]

- Accelerate the effective date of the 2001 tax cuts at a cost of $262 billion over ten years.
- Extend some of the other tax cuts adopted in 2001 to the year 2013 at a cost of $601 billion.
- Provide tax incentives for health insurance purchases, charitable contributions, education expenses, and other purposes at a cost of $190 billion.

All together, the Bush administration was proposing $1.49 trillion in new tax cuts, nearly as much as he had asked for in 2001. With no immediate need to extend the tax cuts that would not expire until 2011, and with Democrats arguing that some of the upcoming tax cuts should be suspended rather than accelerated, most of the focus remained on the growth and jobs package. The administration undertook an extensive lobbying campaign. Newly appointed Secretary of the Treasury John Snow led the administration effort on the Hill.

House and Senate Budget Resolutions

From the start of congressional action, it became apparent that the full scope of Bush's tax proposals, now grown to $1.57 trillion over eleven years, would not be incorporated in the concurrent resolution on the budget for FY 2004. Given the alarming growth in deficit projections, the cost was simply too high for many congressional Republicans. Republican leaders did concede to the administration, however, in agreeing to a duration of ten years in the resolution so that a larger amount of tax legislation could be encompassed under reconciliation. Once again, the procedural protection of reconciliation would be necessary to get a tax cut package through the Senate with its narrow Republican majority. The majority leadership also agreed to put two other controversial measures in the reconciliation bill: the debt limit and drilling in the Alaskan National Wildlife Refuge (ANWR). The Bush stimulus package was calculated by Congress to cost $726 billion over a period of eleven years.

The growing deficit projections were causing serious strains within the Republican majorities. By March, the OMB was predicting a deficit of $304 billion for 2003, with a larger deficit in 2004. The House and Senate Budget Committees proceeded to mark up companion versions of the budget resolution, but they moved in different directions. The House committee, concerned about the deficits, tried to offset the costs of tax cuts by making significant cuts in spending. The Senate committee followed more closely along the lines of the president's proposals, but several prominent moderates (not on the committee) expressed a desire to reduce the tax cut package to $350 billion. On March 13, both budget committees reported the budget resolution by straight party line votes, 24–19 in the House and 12–11 in the Senate.[23] The Senate committee projected deficits through 2013. As war in Iraq appeared imminent, however, public attention shifted away from the budget.

Democrats were having difficulty finding any coherent policy alternative to the president and congressional Republicans. Most of the half-dozen plans put forward by various Democratic members focused strictly on short-term stimulus, providing immediate tax relief for one year only at a cost of $100 billion to $150 billion. They remained unified in opposing Bush's proposed cut in the taxation of stock dividends, arguing that it was another example of administration policies favoring the rich.

Concerns with the costs of the war in Iraq added to deficit worries. A number of House Republicans were also concerned about the politically damaging $200 billion cuts in Medicare that were included in the HBC's proposed budget resolution and other spending cuts. These cuts were eventually removed from the resolution in order to gain support within the party. Even so, the vote was unusually close in the House, which adopted the budget resolution on March 21 by a vote of 215–212. The Speaker pleaded with reluctant Republicans not to allow an embarrassing defeat during the first week of the war, and Vice President Cheney made a number of calls to wavering members. House leaders kept the vote open after Democrats edged ahead. Finally, two Republicans switched their votes to provide the needed margin, and the vote was closed. Twelve Republicans and 199 of 200 Democrats voted against the resolution.[24]

Shrinking the Tax Cuts

In the Senate, Democrats tried to shrink the size of tax cuts that would be allowed in the resolution. They succeeded in passing an amendment on the floor of the Senate 52–47 reducing the tax cut from $726 billion to $626 billion and using the other $100 billion to create a reserve fund for war costs. The administration remained silent on the projected costs of the war, to the chagrin of members of both parties. Democrats were also successful in stripping ANWR drilling provisions from reconciliation protection, 52–48, when they were joined by eight Republicans. The most significant threat to the Republican plan, however, was a motion by Senator John Breaux (D-LA)—a moderate—to reduce the size of the overall tax cuts to $350 billion. After a week of debate over the resolution, Breaux's amendment was defeated 38–62. Despite the margin of defeat, Breaux was actually much closer to victory than he appeared to be.[25] When over the weekend of March 21 the Bush administration announced that the initial cost of the Iraq war would $74.7 billion, Breaux reorganized and revised the amendment. This time he was able to attract three Republican votes and united the Democrats. As a result, the amendment was adopted on a second try by a vote of 51–48. The Senate would go to conference with the House with a resolution that called for half the tax cuts.

The return to deficits was leading the House and Senate to once again have to deal with the debt limit and reconsider rules to enforce spending discipline. The deficits were causing government borrowing to bump up against the statutory ceiling that had been passed the year before. In the House, the Republicans had revived the old "Gephardt rule" which provides that once a House budget resolution is passed, a comparable debt limit extension is deemed to have been passed. This avoided a politically sensitive separate vote on the debt limit. Since the Senate had no such rule, it would have to pass a free-standing bill. Both House and Senate also considered some additional budget rules that would help slow the growth of spending. The fiscal discipline shown by Congress after the Budget Enforcement Act of 1990 had slipped during the surplus years, and many provisions of the BEA were allowed to expire. The pay-as-you-go rules were still in force, and Senate budget writers wanted to revive rules that would subject any legislation that violates budget limits to a sixty-vote point of order. A subcommittee of the House Judiciary Committee also revived the balanced budget amendment.

The Conference Committee negotiation was marked by complex bargaining and a critical side agreement that threatened to sharply divide Republicans. In the conference itself, the familiar strategy of splitting the difference was used to come up with a figure of $550 billion for tax cuts that could be included under the protection of reconciliation. The budget resolution was taken up in the House which met into the night, finally approving the 2004 budget resolution by a vote of 216–211 at 3 A.M. Every one of the 203 Democrats voting voted against the resolution, and they were joined by 7 Republicans.[26]

The task would be even more difficult in the Senate where Democrats and three or four moderate Republicans held fiercely to the belief that $350 billion was the largest amount of tax cuts the nation could afford given the war and the deficits.[27] The only way that the Senate leadership could pass the conference version of the budget resolution was to make a promise to Republican Senators Olympia Snowe (R-ME) and George Voinovich (R-OH) that nothing would come out of the Senate Finance Committee with more than $350 billion in revenue losses. Even with this promise, the budget resolution vote ended up tied, and Vice President Cheney cast the decisive vote to give the Republicans a 51–50 victory. Democrat Zell Miller, as he had in 2001, voted with the Republicans, while McCain and Chaffee voted with the Democrats.

House Republican leaders were incensed when they learned the next day about the side agreement that Majority Leader Frist had made with moderates to get the crucial votes to pass the budget resolution.[28] He was accused of double dealing and of making "rookie" mistakes. Speaker Hastert had understood that he and the leader of the Senate had a definite deal on $550 billion as the size of the tax cuts. Frist went to the House to meet with leaders and apologize, but reportedly his apology was not accepted.[29] Furthermore, there was no solution in sight as Snowe and Voinovich refused to support any tax cuts greater than $350 billion. Congress was left with a budget resolution that would allow $550 billion in tax cuts but a promise in the Senate that nothing more than $350 would be allowed to reach the floor.

Enacting the Tax Cuts

With the passage of the budget resolution, attention turned to the House Ways and Means Committee and the Senate Finance Committees who would draft the specifics of the tax reductions. With the White House focused primarily on the war in Iraq, and urging Congress to do what was "right for the soldiers," congressional leaders more than the administration were shaping the tax bills.[30] Bush was critical of the Senate version, noting that he wanted more than a "little bitty" tax cut.[31] At the same time, Republican interest groups, including the Club for Growth, began trying to pressure Senators Voinovich and Snowe by launching a series of television ads in their home states of Ohio and Maine. The White House's hopes for a larger tax cut lay in getting two more senators to support the $550 billion number.

The most controversial element of the president's proposals remained the elimination of taxation on dividends. Despite Bush's wartime popularity, Ways and Means Chair Bill Thomas (R-CA) announced that the dividend tax elimination had been taken out of the House bill. Instead, the bill would reduce the rate of taxation on dividends and on capital gains, not part of the president's plan.[32] The committee version also included an acceleration of the 2001 tax cuts for individuals and business tax breaks. On the Senate side, Finance Committee Chair Grassley was trying to find offsets to allow the tax cut to grow beyond $350 billion. Critics argued that it made no sense to raise taxes to allow a bigger tax cut. Grassley also attempted to insert earlier sunset provisions in the bill to make the officially scored version of the bill look lower. This too was not accepted.

The House Ways and Means Committee reported its tax cut bill on May 6 by a 24–15 party line vote, and it was taken up on the floor. There the leadership had little trouble gathering enough support among Republicans to pass the bill 222–203. Only three Republicans and four Democrats voted with the other party. In the Senate, in addition to limiting the overall size of the tax cut, leaders had been forced to add $20 billion in aid to the states to secure final passage of their version. Having lost the dividend taxation provisions in the

House, the administration had more success in the Senate.[33] In the substitute bill, 50 percent of dividends would be exempted from taxation in 2003, and all dividends would be exempt from 2004 to 2006. This key element of the president's original proposal would be on the table for the Conference Committee. The Senate tax bill again was narrowly passed, 51–49 on May 15, with three Democrats and three Republicans voting with the other party.[34]

Under pressure to come up with a bill as soon as possible, conferees reached an agreement on the economic stimulus/tax cut package the week of May 19.[35] Fearing a divisive conference, the administration intervened to urge the House to accept the lower Senate figure on tax cuts. However, the administration and House Republicans had the last laugh. By manipulating the dates that tax cuts were phased in and the dates when they were supposed to expire, Republicans were actually able to encompass most of the House tax cuts but have it officially scored as within the $350 billion ceiling.[36] The rate on taxation of dividends was reduced to a top rate of 15 percent but not eliminated. Income tax cuts approved two years earlier to take effect in 2006 were accelerated. Child tax credits were increased to $1,000, and a number of tax breaks for business were included.

Votes in the House and Senate reflected familiar patterns and the razor-thin Republican majority in the Senate. The House passed the bill 231–200. Only one Republican voted against and seven Democrats voted for the package. In the Senate, a 50–50 tie was again broken by the vice president to give the Republicans a one-vote victory.[37] Three Republicans and two Democrats defected. The administration, retreating from Bush's earlier characterization of $350 billion as a "little bitty" cut, declared victory. Although the final number in the compromise was only 48 percent of what Bush had originally requested, if Congress did not allow the provisions to sunset in later years, the bill would actually produce tax cuts of almost double that amount over eleven years.[38] The administration touted the tax cut, adjusting for inflation, as second only to the 2001 tax cut in the twenty-two years since the Reagan plan in 1981.

The political glow of the Republican-proclaimed success on the tax cut stimulus was dimmed by a little-noticed provision in the new law. In the week after the passage of the tax bill, Democrats seized on a study of its impact that revealed that in trying to keep the total amount of the cut under $350 billion, conferees had excluded 12 million poor children and their families from the expanded child tax credit.[39] Because of the barrage of unfavorable publicity, Republicans quickly prepared legislation to extend the benefits to most low-income families. The Senate passed the legislation by voice vote, and the House eventually went along. Public support for the tax cut remained lukewarm at best. A CNN/Gallup Poll revealed that only 47 percent of the public felt that the tax cuts were a good idea, while 43 percent thought they were a bad idea.[40]

Conclusion

Cutting taxes had been one of the top Republican priorities since Reagan. With Congress and the presidency under unified Republican control for the first time since 1953 and 1954, they were able to enact significant tax cuts in 2001 and 2003. In the latter case, although the overall size of the cut was substantially less than the administration wanted, it was achieved despite huge deficit projections and staggering costs associated with the war in Iraq.

The votes on budget resolutions and tax bills in 2001 and 2003 revealed two parties sharply divided. In some cases, party unity was as great in the Senate as in the House, but because of the slimmer majorities in the Senate, building a party coalition was significantly more difficult there. House leaders had more resources at their disposal to maintain party discipline, in one case holding a vote open long enough to get two wavering members to switch their votes. One Senate Democrat, Zell Miller, consistently voted with the Republicans, but three or four moderate Republican senators enjoyed disproportionate leverage on the outcome because of the narrow majority. In both 2001 and 2003, much of the bargaining focused on this handful of Republican moderates and resulted in a number of compromises on the part of the administration and congressional leaders. Overall, however, the voting alignments were consistent with high degrees of unity displayed by both parties.

By 2003, the congressional budget process had evolved into a critical tool for enacting major legislation. Budget rules were instrumental in facilitating the policy accomplishments of the Republican majority. Protection under reconciliation rules was virtually the only means by which tax cuts could be enacted in the Senate because of the narrow majorities. By limiting debate, restricting amendments, and preventing a filibuster, Republicans were able to enact nearly $2 trillion in tax cuts in the first three years of the Bush administration.

The 2001–2003 period provided a unique opportunity to compare unified and divided control of government. When the Democrats regained narrow control of the Senate in May 2001 and retained it until the start of the 108th Congress in 2003, the Bush administration and congressional Republicans were much more constrained in enacting tax cuts and shaping budget policy.

In 2002, under divided government, Congress was unable to pass a budget resolution for the first time since 1975, and eleven of the thirteen appropriations bills were not enacted until the new Republican Congress was sworn in the next year. Differences in divided and unified government were not as pronounced in terms of bargaining within the Senate. In all three years, the small group of pivotal moderate Republicans and Democrats in the Senate were the focal point of negotiations.

Party control of the presidency was crucial in determining the direction of budgetary policy in the early 2000s. It is apparent that had Democrat Al Gore won the Electoral College vote as well as the popular vote in the close 2000 election, policy outcomes would have been far different. Tax cuts of the magnitude that were enacted would not have occurred under a Democratic president and a Republican-controlled or a split party–controlled Congress. The change in party control of the presidency would have likely led to the same kind of veto bargaining that took place between Clinton and the Republican Congresses in the late 1990s.

What conclusions can we draw about the evolution of congressional budgeting over the past three decades? What can we conclude about the development of congressional institutions and specialized budget rules in terms of majority party control of macrobudgeting? What are the prospects for Congress to tackle the large deficits projected to 2012 and beyond in future years? How will the election results of 2004 and beyond help determine future deficits and budget policy? These and other questions are examined in the final chapter.

CHAPTER 9

Conclusion

One of the main challenges facing national policy makers in the next decade is the return of chronic budget deficits. The recession of 2001, the September 11 attacks, the costs of the wars in Afghanistan and Iraq, and the Bush tax cuts have all combined to turn huge budget surpluses into a sea of red ink. Will Congress and the president be able to return to a balanced budget or even shrink the deficits? What have we learned from thirty years' experience of congressional budgeting? The previous chapters have examined and analyzed the most important budget legislation of recent years, tracing the recent evolution of congressional budgeting. Chapter 1 posed a number of research questions about macrobudgeting and changes in congressional budget rules, the role of parties in budgeting, and the consequences of divided government. This final chapter takes an overview of congressional budgeting by summarizing the impact of budget rules, looking at trends in party cohesion and their significance, examining outcomes associated with divided government, and concluding with implications for the future.

Congressional Institutions and Budget Rules

The congressional institutions and rules resulting in the development of macrobudgeting have profoundly changed the way Congress makes public policy and works with the president. Congressional budget rules facilitate the ability of leaders to steer sweeping taxing and spending legislation through Congress. The most important rules to emerge in the budget process concern reconciliation. It is particularly potent in the Senate where it provides protection from the filibuster. The Byrd rule protects reconciliation bills from nongermane amendments and provides the Senate with certain bargaining leverage in conference with the House. Congressional Budget Act points of order have been used to enforce budget procedures and substantive provisions of budget resolutions.

Reconciliation is an optional two-step process that has become the means for party leaders to assure compliance with decisions made in the budget resolution.[1] Reconciliation instructions are instructions to committees to change spending and revenue statutes, usually by a stated amount. Committees are bound by the dollar amounts in the instructions. The Budget Committees are responsible for assembling the committee actions into a single omnibus bill. The most important aspects of reconciliation are the special rules for floor consideration which protect the bills from dilatory tactics, extraneous materials, or amendments that would increase the deficit. For more than twenty years, reconciliation bills have had special status. In the Senate, all debate on reconciliation bills is limited to twenty hours. After the twenty-hour limit has been reached, amendments may be considered without debate. The House does not have the same limits but does not need them given the strength of their own Rules Committee. Reconciliation bills are usually considered in the House under a special rule that limits debate and restricts amendments to a few major substitutes. Reconciliation was originally used principally for deficit reduction but, since the mid-1990s, can be used for tax cuts as well.

The Byrd rule has also been an important part of congressional budgeting since 1985. It was made permanent in 1990, amending the Congressional Budget Act.[2] It allows a point of order to be raised against extraneous matter included in a reconciliation bill and can be waived only by a three-fifths vote of the Senate. A matter can be determined to be extraneous if it does not change spending or revenues, if a provision is not in compliance with reconciliation instructions, if a provision is outside a committee's jurisdiction, if it increases the deficit, or if it changes Social Security. As we have seen, the Byrd rule also provides the Senate with certain advantages in Conference Committee since matter included in conference that was not in the Senate bill will be subject to a point of order when it returns to the Senate floor.

Points of order have also become an important part of congressional budgeting that enforce budget rules and protect substantive decisions.[3] They may be raised against legislation that violates a provision of the budget resolution or against spending or tax legislation before a budget resolution is passed. Of course, these procedures can be waived and have been in numerous cases. As we saw in 2003, for example, the House Republican leadership wanted to pass several tax bills for strategic purposes before the budget resolution was enacted. It is largely the party leaders who determine when the rules will be used as written to enforce the process and when they will be waived for some other reason.

Congressional budget rules help leaders solve a difficult collective action problem in a way that enhances the incentives for party cohesion and voting.

Budget rules have weakened anti-majoritarian institutions.[4] They provide the capacity for Congress to challenge a president of the opposite party or facilitate the program of a president of the same party. They help party leaders overcome the fragmentation and lack of coordination that previously weakened Congress in its negotiations with the presidency. They provide the means for adopting more coherent budget policy—to take actions to increase or decrease the deficit without getting bogged down procedurally. Certainly, rules have been sidestepped, and the list of tricks and gimmicks used to circumvent budget discipline over three decades is long. But the bottom line is that the budget process and budget rules have measurably strengthened congressional majorities, and since 1981 and 1982, those have been predominantly party majorities.

Macrobudgeting has become the much more dominant process in Congress than microbudgeting. Appropriations remain essential for making more detailed decisions on what to spend and the specifics of tax changes, but it is not the dominant process that it was for much of the twentieth century until the 1970s. Fundamental differences between the two levels of budgeting are still apparent in terms of the nature of voting alignments, as we will see in the next section. Although the appropriations process too has become more partisan, appropriation bills are still primarily adopted by bipartisan majorities. They continue to follow the distributive and universal patterns that were more predominant in the 1960s and 1970s with weaker parties.

The increased utilization of omnibus appropriations is also an important institutional development. Although rank-and-file members dislike such bills, the bills can help overcome gridlock and empower the leadership. As one observer noted:

> An omnibus immediately shifts the burden of finishing the budget from appropriators to party leaders, and the act of assembling such a bill gives those leaders an opportunity to decide what stays and what goes. They can exclude provisions that a majority, including members of their own party, voted for once before on the floor, or include provisions that a majority rejected.[5]

Congressional budgeting is characterized by a complex set of rules and procedures that have revolutionized the way taxing and spending decisions are made. Although the process has been frequently criticized for its messiness, its improvisational nature, and the "blue smoke and mirrors" that have been used, looking at the big picture, it has given Congress a remarkable capacity to budget.

Not all changes in rules have been consistent or effective. On several occasions, rules were adopted to produce certain budgetary outcomes and to symbolize legislative commitment to certain budget goals. As record budget deficits grew in the early 1980s, these rules were designed primarily to reduce the deficits. The most extreme example of this is the Balanced Budget Act (Gramm-Rudman-Hollings) in 1985 and its revised version in 1987. Its failure to force a balanced budget through mandatory across-the-board cuts is documented in chapter 4. However, despite the failure to achieve its policy objectives, it achieved certain electoral objectives for both parties in sending the message of Congress's determination to deal with deficits. John Kerry in the 2004 presidential campaign even touted his support of GRH during the debates as evidence of his resolve to reduce deficits. Other budget rules, such as the Budget Enforcement Act of 1990, were more successful with appropriation caps, pay-as-you-go rules, and enforcement provisions. Reconciliation, as adapted in the early 1980s, became oriented toward deficit reduction. After the Republican takeover of Congress in 1994, however, it became more neutral in its application and could be used for cutting taxes as well as cutting deficits. The budget resolution itself has not always proven effective as a check on spending. Even in recent years under Republican majorities, spending has often exceeded totals passed earlier in the budget resolution.

The Role of Parties in Congressional Budgeting

As discussed in chapter 1, a number of congressional scholars have theorized about the role of political parties in the legislative process. Cox and McCubbins suggested that strong party leaders serve members' interest in protecting a party's reputation with the voters. Rohde's theory of conditional party government suggests that strong majority party leadership occurs when the parties are unified and polarized, characterized by intraparty cohesion and interparty conflict.[6] Under these conditions, members will be willing to cede more power to majority party leaders, and leaders themselves will be willing to act more assertively. On the other hand, Krehbiel and others theorize a spatial model of voting based on member preferences where party plays no independent role in determining outcomes. What do the cases of major budget legislation suggest in terms of the role of political parties in budgeting?

Partisanship or Preferences?

Krehbiel's "pivotal politics" theory suggests that whether a change in the status quo occurs depends on the ideological position of the pivotal median House or Senate member, regardless of majority size, party, or divided government.[7] Partisanship, he suggests, may simply be an artifact of policy preferences bringing "no marginal predictive power to the table."[8] As he notes, there is no way to determine whether it is simply preferences or whether party exerts an independent effect as suggested by party theorists. Seeking other means to determine a possible effect of party, he posits that party change should result in abrupt and large policy shifts "directionally consistent with the majority party in Congress."[9] Additionally, to test the partisan electoral connection, he argues that there should be some evidence of loyal party members using the party brand name in subsequent elections.

Krehbiel examined the adoption of the Clinton deficit reduction plan in 1993 as a "particularly tough test" of the pivotal politics theory. He concluded that the pivotal politics theory performs reasonably well. Acknowledging that party theories fit well in terms of partisan rhetoric and voting behavior, he suggests that they perform poorly in terms of explaining budget outcomes and the electoral connection.[10] His conclusion about policy shifts after party change is based on examining changes in discretionary defense and domestic appropriations following the Democrats' capture of the Congress and the White House in 1992. The results, he finds, are incremental, showing little change over the deficit reduction package produced in 1990. As far as using the party brand name in subsequent elections, he finds instead that many Democrats ran away from Clinton in the 1994 elections.

Some problems exist with this analysis. Krehbiel looks at appropriations as well as budget resolutions and reconciliation, not distinguishing between macrobudgeting and microbudgeting. As we have seen, macrobudgetary decisions such as budget resolutions and reconciliation evoke a significantly more partisan response in Congress than individual appropriation bills. Second, except for noting the removal of the filibuster pivot in the Senate, his analysis does not account for budget rules and institutions that allow party leaders to control the agenda and protect budget packages during floor consideration. Third, it has long been recognized that incrementalism in outcomes may be in the eye of the beholder and depends on the time frame.[11] Over a period of five years, for example, the policy changes wrought in 1993 are more dramatic and in the expected direction. In addition, the content of the deficit reduction package under Democratic government was significantly different from the 1990 deficit reduction package under divided government. In particular, OBRA-93 contained higher tax increases and smaller domestic spending cuts than OBRA-90. Fourth, timing could also be a factor in using the party brand name in elections, and many other issues intervene

Figure 9–1
Party cohesion in votes on budget resolutions in the House, 1975–2003.

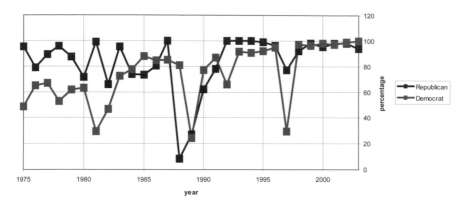

Source: Rice Index: House party cohesion.
Note: 100 represents complete unity, and 0 represents equally divided party, by fiscal year.

in campaigns. In years after 1994, when the budget was moving rapidly toward balance, Democrats were much more likely to trumpet the achievement of OBRA-93 in election campaigns. In 1994, Clinton and the Democratic Party label were tarnished by the health care issue.

Party Cohesion in Approving the Congressional Budget

Although measures of party cohesion or party defection may not in themselves prove that partisanship is the underlying causal factor, a wealth of other evidence points to partisanship as an explanatory factor and suggests that party cohesion is a meaningful empirical measure to consider. In the previous chapters, we have examined a number of budget votes in the House and Senate. Systematically compared over time, the overall trend of increased party cohesion is striking. Figures 9–1 and 9–2 examine intraparty cohesion for Republicans and Democrats in the House and Senate between 1975 and

Figure 9–2
Party cohesion in votes on budget resolutions in the Senate, 1975–2003.

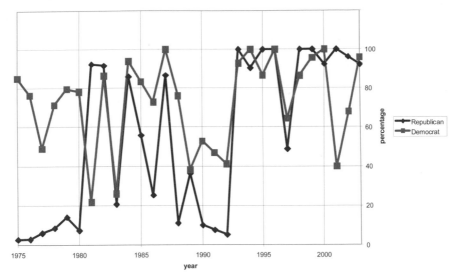

Source: Rice Index: House party cohesion.
Note: 100 represents complete unity, and 0 represents equally divided party, by fiscal year.

2003 in votes on the congressional budget resolution.[12] The Rice index of cohesion, a measure developed in the 1920s, is used to measure intraparty unity.[13]

In the House, Republicans have been the more cohesive of the two parties over time, but since 1992, both parties have had cohesion scores close to 100 with the exception of 1997 (FY 1998 on figure 9–1), the year of the bipartisan balanced budget agreement. From 1975 to 1990, House Republicans were consistently more cohesive than the Democrats with the exception of the period surrounding Gramm-Rudman-Hollings in the mid-1980s. Over the full twenty-eight-year period, House Democrats have gradually become more cohesive as a voting bloc. Consistent with other evidence of the increased partisanship in the House, with the progressive realignment of the South, there has been a steady reduction of conservative Democrats who vote with Republicans on the congressional budget. Consideration of the outliers is instructive as well. In 1981, as we saw in chapter 3, a number of House

Democrats were willing to split with their party in approving a budget resolution in May 1981 along the lines proposed by President Reagan. Recall that on the vote on the crucial reconciliation bill in June 1981, the Democrats were more cohesive than on previous votes but because of election losses in 1980 suffered too many defections to defeat the Republicans. The other low cohesion scores for House Democrats were in 1988 and 1989 and in 1997. The budget resolutions in 1988 and 1989 represented a compromise with the administration in Reagan's last year and a bipartisan agreement with President Bush in his first year in 1989 that did not make significant policy changes. That period represents the only major exception to Republican Party unity as well. During the rest of the time, average Republicans scores were above 80.

Figure 9–2 confirms the fact that party unity has been less pronounced in the Senate than in the House, but that it has trended upwards. Perhaps most significantly, since 1992, both parties have been consistently more cohesive, and the patterns look very much like those in the House. Unlike in the House, in the period 1975–1992, the Republicans were less cohesive than Senate Democrats. Recall from chapter 2 that during the first five years, a more bipartisan atmosphere surrounded the budget process, with Senators Muskie and Bellmon trying to build bipartisan support. The Senate Republican caucus split nearly evenly over whether to support the budget resolution. That pattern changed after 1980 when the Republicans became the majority party in the Senate for six years. While more cohesive as a party, the patterns were inconsistent. After Republicans lost control of the Senate in the 1986 elections, the party returned to the pre-1980 pattern of dividing over support of the budget resolutions. Senate Democratic cohesion scores from 1975 to 1992 averaged around 60. Once Bill Clinton became president in 1993, however, the two parties in the Senate became more sharply divided and cohesive. The exceptions were again the bipartisan 1997 balanced budget agreement, and for the Democrats, the first budget resolution under George W. Bush in 2001. As they had in 1981, many Senate Democrats chose to support the budget resolution with the popular tax cuts proposed by the Republican president.

The patterns of party cohesion in Congress since 1992 suggest that something similar to Rohde's conditional party government has evolved in congressional macrobudgeting. House-Senate differences have been reduced in this period in terms of budget resolution votes. The partisan pattern goes back even further for House Republicans and, as we saw in chapter 2, predated 1975 in terms of using debt limit votes to criticize the budget policy of the majority party.

Figure 9–3

Party voting on individual appropriations bills in the House and Senate, 1975–2003.

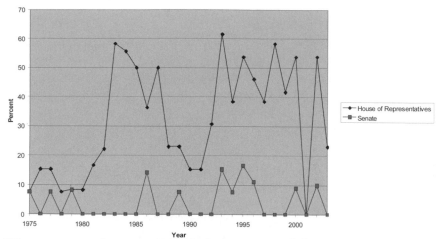

*The percentage of votes on individual appropriation bills where a majority of one party voted against a majority of the other party.

The analysis of voting patterns also provides evidence of differences in congressional voting patterns in macrobudgeting and microbudgeting in Congress. Since the implementation of the congressional budget process in 1975, votes on individual appropriation bills have remained less partisan than votes on budget resolutions and less partisan than votes on all measures. Figure 9–3 looks at the percentage of individual appropriation bills throughout the period that met the minimum criteria as a party vote (a majority of one party against a majority of the other party) between 1975 and 2003. All omnibus bills involving two or more appropriation bills are excluded. In the Senate, a party split on appropriations bills has remained a rarity; at the most, one or two bills may find a majority of Republicans facing a majority of Democrats. In the House, partisanship on appropriations bills has increased since 1982, but, on average, fewer than half of the votes meet the minimum qualification of a party vote.

Impact on Party Leadership

Party leaders have been more assertive and more powerful in the congressional budget process since the 1980s. In the House, the Budget and Rules Committees have become important tools of majority party leaders. Leaders influence the selection of members to these key committees. House leaders dominate the budget process, manipulating the floor agenda and the rules to their advantage. Even in the more decentralized, egalitarian Senate, leaders have become much more powerful in budgeting. Although they consult extensively with rank-and-file members, it is leaders or their designees, not committees, shaping the budget resolutions, reconciliation bills, and omnibus budget legislation. Majority Leader Trent Lott fired the Senate parliamentarian in 2001 because his interpretation of reconciliation was unfavorable to Republicans. He and other majority leaders have brought bills directly to the floor of the Senate, bypassing the Finance Committee or other panels. While Republicans complained about their treatment at the hands of the Democrats during the long period they held the majority, since 1994, Republicans have run the House and Senate with a strong hand. Although Senate leaders have made periodic attempts to reach out to minority Democrats, a partisan strategy remains dominant.

The nature of conference committees and the role of majority and minority party members have changed as well. Facing united Republican opposition in 1993, Democratic leaders in Congress held one-party-only conference negotiations over the deficit reduction plan. Since 1995, under the Republican majorities, Democrats have been largely excluded from meaningful participation on major budget conference committees. More House-Senate differences are resolved at the leadership level or are "pre-conferenced" by selected participants.[14] In the 2003 conference on the Medicare reform/prescription drug bill, only two sympathetic Democrats were invited to participate in the negotiations.

Looking at major macrobudgeting legislation since 1975, qualitative and quantitative evidence suggests that the insights of party theorists provide a more satisfactory basis for explanation than the spatial preference models. This is not to say that party government in a parliamentary sense exists or that budgeting fits the responsible parties model. We have seen evidence that median members are important in shaping outcomes, particularly in a closely divided Senate. Recall the influence of moderate Senate Republicans John Chaffee, John McCain, and Olympia Snowe in reducing the Bush tax cuts in 2001 and 2003. The cases we have examined suggest, in general, that party leaders are instrumental in creating stable policy alliances in budgeting *and* play a role in convincing wavering party members to support the party position, even if it is somewhat at odds with their preferences. We have seen instances, such as with the Clinton deficit reduction plan in 1993, where party leaders in the House have been able to convince a few members to change a vote already cast to provide the winning margin. Another example occurred with the House passage of Medicare reform in November 2003 in the House of Representatives. The bill contained the most significant changes in Medicare since it was first enacted in 1965, including a prescription drug benefit for seniors that was estimated at the time to cost $400 billion over ten years.[15] This was a Republican bill, pushed by the Republican leadership in the House, with the assistance of the Bush White House. Democrats opposed the bill because provisions requiring competition from private health care providers were seen as a threat to the program. But Republican leaders had to struggle for votes because a dozen or so conservatives were concerned about the cost of such a program expansion at a time when deficits were reaching record levels. At 4:00 A.M. when the final House vote was taken, Speaker Dennis Hastert and Majority Leader Tom Delay could see from the totals on the electronic scoreboard that they were losing 216–218 and the normal fifteen minutes allowed for voting in the House had expired. This result would be a serious setback for the president and the Republican Party.

The Speaker kept the vote open past the deadline while he and Majority Leader Delay sought to get several Republican members to change their vote. Hastert found Representative Nick Smith (R-MI), who was retiring from Congress, put his arm around his shoulder, and said, "I need your help."[16] Smith stayed firm despite a call on his cell phone from the president at 5:30 A.M. and despite a promise from Delay that he would endorse Smith's son in an upcoming election if he would support the bill. But a handful of others did succumb to the pressure. Hastert and Delay kept the vote open for a record 2 hours and 51 minutes and finally found enough members to switch their votes to manage a final vote total of 220–215 for the Medicare bill. Democrats were outraged by what they saw as a gross abuse of legislative rules. In the fall of 2004, the bipartisan House Ethics Committee admonished Majority Leader Delay for his actions toward Smith and for linking "support for the personal interests of another member as a part of a quid pro quo to achieve a legislative goal."[17]

Although policy concessions were made to create a winning party majority on the Medicare bill and tax cut bills, the Republican administration was still able to get the vast proportion of its proposals adopted through the work of the party leaders in Congress. Even in 2003, when the size of the Bush tax cuts appeared to be cut in half, by manipulating the expiration and effective dates of the provisions, the total amount of the tax cuts are likely to be close to what was originally requested.

Partisanship without Responsible Parties?

As parties have become more ideologically cohesive and congressional leaders have been more adept at using public relations and media strategies, message politics has become more important in legislative policy making.[18]
Partisan message politics depends on the cohesiveness of member preferences
and the degree of issue ownership with the public.[19] That is to say, highly
polarized congressional parties do not necessarily act like responsible parties
staking out clear and distinctive positions unless their position is favored by
the public. If it is not, parties act like rational parties and try to reframe or
spin issues where they are disadvantaged. Certainly, the Medicare reform in
2003 was about the high cost of prescription drugs and their impact on seniors. But it was also about majority Republicans hoping to reshape their
party image on health care and reduce the Democrats' historical advantage
on this issue.

As sincere reflections of policy preferences, certain party positions have
changed over the past generation as the composition of Congress and members' electoral bases have changed. Since 1981 and the Reagan administration, Republicans have "owned" the tax issue (for cutting taxes or not raising taxes). Although Reagan agreed to several tax increases as president, the
main exception to the Republican stance on taxes was George H. W. Bush in
1990. Although his acceptance of tax increases in OBRA-90 allowed a significant deficit reduction package to pass, it splintered the Republican Party
in Congress, including the leadership, and reduced Republican cohesion in
voting. George W. Bush has featured tax cuts as a dominant theme of his
administration. Democrats have adopted a defensive position on this issue,
not opposing tax cuts per se, just tax cuts for the rich and tax cuts that make
the deficit worse.

For several generations, Democrats have generally been seen by the public
as the party with more favorable positions on Social Security and Medicare.
The only major stumble by the Reagan administration in 1981 was the ill-fated
trial balloon about the possibility of cutting Social Security. Congressional
Republicans, sensing the danger to their party, joined with Democrats in passing a resolution against any cuts in Social Security. In the two major deficit
reduction packages in 1990 and 1993, Medicare cuts were an important part
of the total, but Democrats protected their party reputation by supporting the
smallest cuts possible. In the brief surplus years, both parties competed to protect Medicare and Social Security trust funds with largely symbolic plans for
"lockboxes," firewalls, and the like. It is instructive that despite budget surpluses, the two parties remained just as polarized as they had with deficits.

How the 2003 Medicare reform will affect the reputation of the Republicans and Democrats remains to be seen. George W. Bush and the Republicans kept a campaign promise by providing a prescription drug benefit, but anger by seniors over the significant gaps in the coverage and prohibitions against buying "medigap" policies could foil the Republican strategy.

Deficits are the quintessential macrobudgetary issue, but one that has not distinguished the parties in recent years as clearly as taxes and entitlements. The balance between revenues and spending has generated political conflict over the years going back to the nineteenth century.[20] Beginning in the 1930s, with Franklin D. Roosevelt's acceptance of Keynesian principles of discretionary fiscal policies sanctioning deficits to stimulate the economy, the Democratic Party was identified with favoring deficits when necessary. Deficit spending allowed Democrats to protect benefits to their traditional constituencies and support higher levels of domestic spending. Traditional Republican "fiscal orthodoxy," on the other hand, advocated a balanced budget and decried deficit spending, at least through the end of the 1970s. The Democrats' position on deficits was much more one of cautious tolerance than advocacy because, other things equal, Americans favor a balanced budget and dislike deficits. Yet voters generally do not get very concerned about deficits, and the economics of deficits and debt are rather obscure. Americans' attention to deficits has usually followed actions by political elites and media coverage. The only time deficits were mentioned by more than 15 percent of respondents in the Gallup Poll open-ended question, "What is the most important problem facing the nation?" was while Congress considered Gramm-Rudman-Hollings in 1985 (17 percent), during the 1990 budget summit (21 percent), after the passage of the 1993 deficit reduction plan (15 percent), and during the government shutdown in January 1996 (28 percent).[21]

The major change in the Republican position on deficits came indirectly as a result of Ronald Reagan's emphasis on tax cuts as the top domestic priority. The shift caused some discomfort to traditional Republicans, but by the election of George W. Bush in 2000, tax cuts were entrenched as the cornerstone of Republican philosophy. The centrality of tax cutting for Republican has two philosophical sources: "supply-side economics" and "starving the beast," a phrase attributed to David Stockman, Reagan's first budget director.[22] Supply-side economics argues that by cutting taxes, the economy will be stimulated and will produce additional revenues to compensate for the cuts. The starve-the-beast philosophy suggests that by cutting off the source of revenues, government will have to stop expanding and possibly shrink. Ronald Reagan seemed to endorse this view when he spoke of "putting government on a diet."

George W. Bush indicated sympathy for this view when he commented in August 2001 that the disappearance of the budget surplus was "incredibly positive news" because it would put the government in a "fiscal straitjacket."[23]

The Democratic Party position on deficits changed in response to the deficits of the Reagan administration. The record-level budget deficits in the early 1980s seemed to be one of Reagan's only potential weaknesses but also constrained Democrats from using government programs to solve societal problems.[24] Democrats became hawkish on deficits because, in the words of the Director of the House Democratic Study Group, "there's no way you can talk about liberal social programs—there's no way you can talk about anything—until you talk about deficits."[25] The result was that both parties publicly opposed budget deficits but blamed them on different causes: Democrats blamed them on the tax cuts while the Republicans blamed them on excessive domestic spending and big government. The actual solutions to the deficits were potentially dangerous to both parties. Raising taxes and cutting defense could be perilous positions for Democrats, and cutting entitlements and certain popular domestic spending programs could be damaging to Republicans. The positions of the two parties against deficits include not just political calculations and economic concerns but fundamental moral values as well. According to White and Wildavsky:

> The whole complex of moral notions surrounding the deficit—household management, trusteeship, care for future generations, good government—spoke to the self-worth of . . . [members of Congress] . . . rather than to that of the public. The politics of responsibility was self-imposed by many of our leaders upon their visions of themselves.[26]

Although sharp partisanship in budgeting has not produced the consistently clear positions of the responsible party model, party differences are distinct on many issues. The positions of the two parties on major budget issues facing the United States have emerged both from electoral calculations and from sincere policy preferences. They are also shaped by the political and economic environment at the time and by party control of Congress and the presidency. It is to that question that we turn in the next section.

The Impact of Divided Government on Congressional Budgeting

In terms of presidential-congressional relations, partisanship in congressional budgeting has made divided or unified control of government exceptionally important. Divided government manifests itself not in terms of traditional deadlock, but rather in terms of delay and other manifestations of procedural breakdown, in extra-legislative means of resolution such as summits and bipartisan commissions, and in the policy content of budget packages. In pursuing major budgetary changes, unified government allows a president, after bargaining primarily with members of his own party, to enact budget packages that will normally command cohesive party support (and opposition) in the House and Senate.

Delay, Shutdowns, and Omnibus Appropriations

Divided government makes it more difficult to pass the congressional budget resolution in a timely fashion than under unified government. Sarah Binder found that divided government was associated with delay in enacting the budget resolution.[27] According to the congressional budget timetable, the budget resolution is supposed to be passed by both houses by April 15. Although there is no penalty for not making the deadline, delays cause problems with the authorization and appropriations processes and make it less likely that Congress will be able to enact spending bills on time. Using updated data through FY 2004, table 9-1 looks at the number of days past the deadline that the concurrent resolution on the budget passed. Because failure to pass any budget resolution is a symptom of deadlock, in the two years when no budget resolution passed (1998/FY 1999 and 2002/FY 2003), the number of days remaining in the calendar year were included. Table 9-1 shows greater delays under divided government (an average of 70.9 days late) compared to under unified government (an average of 8.5 days late). Excluding the two years when no budget resolution was passed (both occurred under divided government), the budget resolution still was an average of 50.9 days late.

Divided government is also associated with failure to pass continuing appropriations when needed and the resulting government shutdowns. Since 1980, all appropriation funding gaps and the sending home of nonessential government employees have occurred under divided government.[28] Table 9-2 looks at the dates and duration of funding gaps. Gaps occurred under Ronald Reagan eight times for a total of fourteen days. Under George H. W. Bush, the government shut down once for three days after the original version of OBRA-90 was defeated in the House. The most prolonged government shutdown occurred under Bill Clinton in 1995, his first year to confront the new Republican Congress. The government was shut down for a total of twenty-six full days. The negative political repercussions from that episode seemed

Table 9–1

Consequences of divided government: number of days past deadline for passage of budget resolution

Under Unified Government		Under Divided Government	
Fiscal Year		Fiscal Year	
1978	2	1976	1
1979	2	1977	0
1980	9	1982	6
1981	28	1983	39
1994	0	1984	39
1995	27	1985	139
2002	0[a]	1986	78
2004	0	1987	73
		1988	70
		1989	52
		1990	33
		1991	176
		1992	37
		1993	36
		1996	75
		1997	59
		1998	51
		1999	260[b]
		2000	0
		2001	0
		2003	260[b]
Average	8.5 days		70.9 days
Average excluding 1999 and 2002			50.9 days

Source: Updated from data reported in Allen Schick with Felix LoStracco, *The Federal Budget: Politics, Policy, Process* (Brookings Institution, 2000): 109.
[a]Republicans maintained control of the Senate until June 2001, making it unified government when FY 2002 budget resolution passed.
[b]No budget resolution passed; number of days remaining in calendar year reported.

to have discouraged both branches from such showdowns, and to date, the last appropriation gap and government shutdown occurred during the period 1995–1996.

In addition to delays and government shutdowns, divided government is also associated with the failure to pass regular appropriations bills by the

Table 9–2

Divided government and government shutdowns: appropriation funding gaps, FY 1981–2000

Fiscal Year	Date Begun	Full Days(s) of Gap	Date Ended
1982	11/20/81	2	11/23/81
1983	9/30/82	1	10/02/82
	12/17/82	3	12/21/82
1984	11/10/83	3	11/14/83
1985	9/30/84	2	10/02/82
	10/03/84	1	10/05/84
1987	10/16/86	1	10/18/86
1988	12/18/87	1	12/20/87
1991	10/05/90	3	10/09/90
1996	11/13/95	5	11/19/95
	12/15/95	21	1/06/96

Source: U.S. Library of Congress, Congressional Research Service, *Preventing Federal Government Shutdown: Proposals for an Automatic Continuing Resolution,* by Robert Keith, CRS Report RL30339 (PDF), November 8, 1999.

start of the fiscal year and the resulting need to rely on omnibus appropriations bills. Table 9–3 compares the number of appropriations bills included and the relative size of omnibus appropriations under divided and unified party control of government since 1993.

Extraordinary Means of Resolution

Another consequence of divided government is the increased probability of using extraordinary means to resolve presidential-congressional disputes.[29] Three main types of extraordinary resolution have occurred under divided government since 1980. First, we have seen many examples of interbranch budget summits—ad hoc negotiating groups of varying size and composition—outside of the normal legislative process. This was particularly true during the twelve-year span of divided government of the Reagan and Bush administrations, 1981–1993. Some sort of budget summit was held in all but a few of those years, including the memorable 1990 budget summit which included a second, smaller group of negotiators who met in secret at Andrews Air Force Base. Summits have the effect of centralizing power in

Table 9–3
Divided government and omnibus appropriations, 1993–2003

Divided Government			Unified Government		
Year	No. of Bills	% of Discretionary Spending	Year	No. of Bills	% of Discretionary Spending
			1993	0	0%
			1994	0	0%
1995	5	32.5%			
1996	6	74.7%			
1997	0	0%			
1998	8	88.6%			
1999	5	65.9%			
2000	3	19.7%			
			2001*	0	0%
2002	11	51.6%			
			2003	7	48%
Average	5.4	47.5%		1.75	12%

Source: Compiled by research assistant James Dukesherer.
*Unified until Democrats took control of the Senate in June 2001.

Congress and strengthening party leaders as a smaller and smaller subset of legislators decide the overall shape of the budget for years to come. Summits do not usually occur during periods of unified government, although informal discussions between majority party leaders and the White House regularly take place.

A second form of extraordinary resolution is the creation of a bipartisan commission to study and recommend solutions to difficult or deadlocked problems. Again, the history of these commissions dealing with budget issues over the past twenty-five years suggests that it predominantly occurs under conditions of divided government. We have seen several examples of these commissions in earlier chapters where some members are appointed by the president and some by congressional leaders. One of the most effective was the Greenspan Commission on Social Security in 1982. It primarily provided political cover for a very difficult compromise agreed to between President Reagan and Speaker O'Neill. More typical is the example of the National Economic Commission which failed to break the deadlock over what to do about the long-term financial viability of Medicare and Social Security. The pattern of bipartisan commissions under divided government may have changed under President George W. Bush. In 2001, he created a presidential commission to reform Social Security, and in 2005 a bipartisan commission to examine tax reform. Both occurred under unified Republican control.

A third form of extraordinary resolution is the attempt to use rules to structure certain budget outcomes. This most prominently took the form of the Balanced Budget Act of 1985, which attempted to create an "automatic device" to reduce the deficit. As we saw in chapter 4, Gramm-Rudman-Hollings created deficit targets and required mandatory across-the-board spending cuts if targets were missed. Two years later, Congress revised the deficit targets and repaired the constitutional flaw. The experiment proved unworkable and was essentially abandoned after five years. The number of cases of automatic devices such as this is small, but both cases (1985 and 1987) occurred under divided government. Other use of the rules to shape budget outcomes include the Budget Enforcement Act of 1990 which was amended in 1997, again both under divided government. These changes did not try to force a balanced budget but rather attempted to enforce earlier agreements and set limits on discretionary spending. The ultimate rule change is to amend the Constitution. It also appears that constitutional amendments dealing with the budget are more likely to be proposed under divided government than under unified government. Examples of the amendments proposed during divided government over the past quarter-century include proposals to restrict taxation, to limit outlays to a fixed percentage of GDP, and to require a balanced budget. Such measures are more likely to be proposed during times of deficits and are much more popular with Republicans than Democrats. Thus, if deficits expand significantly through 2012 as projected, congressional Republicans may resuscitate some of the constitutional proposals even if unified Republican control remains in place. In 2004, some Republicans began talking about reviving the balanced budget amendment.

The Content of Policy

With the predominance of partisanship in budgeting, a significant consequence of divided government is in the content of budget packages that are enacted. The contents of major budget packages enacted since 1981 are difficult to compare because of the deficit situation. The major tax cuts of 1981 and 2001 were achieved by Republican administrations with the deficit not yet a problem (1981) or with the budget in surplus (2001). These two major reductions in taxes (which were both accompanied by increases in defense spending) share many similarities, although Reagan's plan was achieved under divided government and Bush's under unified government. However, with a Republican Senate and the defection of three dozen conservative Democrats, for two years, Reagan enjoyed a working cross-partisan majority in budgeting that resembled a president with unified party control.

The existence of large deficits, the case for most of the period of this study, allows budget packages to be compared more directly since their purpose was deficit reduction. Although the number of cases is small, the differences are apparent in the expected direction. Under divided party control, deficit reduction packages in 1982, 1987, 1990, and 1997 include fewer tax increases than in the major deficit reduction package under unified Democratic control in 1993. One would imagine that a future deficit reduction package under unified Republican control would overwhelmingly emphasize spending cuts. Deficit reduction packages under divided control are more likely to strike a balance between additional revenues, entitlement cuts, discretionary domestic cuts, and defense reductions. None of the deficit reductions packages in 1982, 1987, 1990, or 1997 included more than one-third of the total reductions in the form of additional revenues. In 1997, with a booming economy, there were actually tax cuts. In 1993, the Democrats were able to narrowly adopt a plan where half of the deficit reduction over five years came in the form of tax increases. This could not have been passed under divided government. These conclusions are important in analyzing the prospects for returning the budget to balance in the coming decade.

Budget Prospects for the Coming Decade

Macrobudgetary trends in the United States are heavily dependent on the performance of the economy. Differences between multiyear budget projections and the actual numbers are a result of changes in the economy and technical errors in estimating revenues and outlays; only one-third of the variation comes from policy changes. That third is critical, however, as it is what Congress and the president have the ability to change for policy purposes. What those policy purposes are will depend on election results—which party wins and whether divided government results.

Projections in 2005 showed that deficits over the ensuing decade could add $2 trillion to the national debt. These estimates did not include the cost of the war in Iraq and Afghanistan or the potential cost of reforming Social Security, possibly adding another $2 trillion in costs. How might the two parties address the issue of the federal budget and high deficits over the next decade? Will macrobudgeting be increasingly partisan? Is the budget more likely to be balanced under unified government or under divided government?

George W. Bush's victory over John Kerry in 2004 renewed unified Republican control of national government as Republicans extended the size of their majorities in the House and Senate. Given the trend of redistricting to protect incumbents of both parties, fewer and fewer districts are competitive, so prospects for continued Republican majorities look promising for the moment. Does this mean that because of stronger rules and greater partisanship, Congress will increasingly do the president's bidding? No. Greater partisanship in the American system of separation of powers is still far from a parliamentary system. It does mean that under unified Republican control, negotiations over budget totals in Congress and interbranch bargaining over major budget decisions will be done overwhelmingly within the Republican Party, excluding Democrats. Those negotiations could prove increasingly difficult, however. Several factors could threaten party cohesion and weaken the president's influence, including the fact that while congressional Republicans faced reelection in the future, President Bush did not.

If members' incentives for supporting party leaders and the president of their party change, or if party positions pose perceived electoral risks rather than rewards, party unity could disintegrate. Party members might be unwilling to act alone even if they have the votes. An example is the Bush administration proposal to allow younger workers to invest a portion of their Social Security taxes into private or personal accounts. Social Security as an issue has proven politically "dangerous" for Republicans for decades. As a result, many Republicans in Congress believed that Social Security reform could proceed only with some bipartisan support. Even under unified government, certain issues require a sharing of political risks. Restructuring the federal tax code (as opposed to tax cuts) is likely another such issue.

Budget deficits have the potential to chip away at the unity of congressional Republicans in coming years. The division between orthodox fiscal conservatives (deficit hawks) and supply-siders (deficit doves) could cause friction within the party. Even Republican unity over tax cuts could be challenged as efforts are made to make the 2001 and 2003 tax cuts permanent. Perhaps sensing unease among his own party, George W. Bush more explicitly addressed the deficit situation in 2005, promising to cut the deficit in half by the end of his second term. Based on how congressional budgeting has evolved since the 1970s, the Republican path to deficit reduction will certainly emphasize spending cuts over revenue increases.

Democrats, if they return to power, would be more likely to pursue a deficit reduction strategy that was based on revenue increases and spending cuts. Taxes would likely be shifted toward upper-income groups along the lines of Clinton's tax changes in 1993. But Clinton's experience with deficit reduction through new taxes provides a cautionary tale for Democrats. Although OBRA-93 was critical in leading the budget toward balance, the Democrats suffered an overwhelming political defeat in the congressional elections of 1994.What might happen with unified Democratic control concerning entitlement growth and the question of the financial solvency of Medicare and Social Security when the baby boomers begin to retire after 2010? Democrats may be more willing to risk tax increases than to threaten their advantages with entitlements. Domestic spending would also be difficult to cut because of party constituencies. It would be just as difficult for a unified Democratic government to return to a balanced budget as it would be for Republicans.

What if there is a return to divided government in the next decade? Some have suggested that in the 1980s, divided government caused budget deficits. That probably was not the case then and will not be in the future. Under divided government, because of the strength of partisanship in Congress and the capacity to develop and pass a budget, the process might reflect delay and shutdown, omnibus legislation, and a return to budget summits. However, experiences of the past thirty years show that divided government does not preclude serious efforts at deficit reduction. Split control can provide some political cover for unpopular positions on taxes and entitlements and shifting of blame to the other party if deficit reduction is a real priority for both parties. Whatever the future party alignment, congressional budgeting has evolved into a system that allows party majorities to formulate macrobudgetary policies that can support a president's program or formulate a coherent alternative.

NOTES

Notes to Chapter 1

1. Paul Pierson, "Increasing Returns, Path Dependence, and the Study of Politics," *American Political Science Review* 94 (June 2000): 251–67.

2. David W. Rohde, *Parties and Leaders in the Post Reform House* (Chicago: University of Chicago Press, 1991); Gary W. Cox and Mathew D. McCubbins, *Legislative Leviathan* (Berkeley: University of California Press, 1993).

3. David W. Brady and Craig Volden, *Revolving Gridlock* (Boulder: Westview, 1998).

4. Charles M. Cameron, *Veto Bargaining* (Cambridge: Cambridge University Press, 2000).

5. Congressional Budget Office, *The Budget and Economic Outlook: An Update* (August 2003): 1. The figure reported is the sum of projected deficits for FY 2003–2010.

6. Kenneth Shepsle, "Institutional Arrangements and Equilibrium in Multidimensional Voting Models," *American Journal of Political Science* 23 (1979): 27–59.

7. Keith Krehbiel, *Pivotal Politics* (Chicago: University of Chicago Press, 1998); Brady and Volden 1998.

8. Rohde 1991.

9. Cox and McCubbins 1993.

10. Donald P. Green and Ian Shapiro, *Pathologies of Rational Choice Theory* (New Haven: Yale University Press, 1994), in particular, chapter 6 on congressional research.

11. Barbara Sinclair, *Unorthodox Lawmaking,* 2nd ed. (Washington, DC: CQ Press, 2000).

12. See James March and Johan P. Olsen, *Rediscovering Institutions* (New York: Free Press, 1989); Karen Orren and Stephen Skowronek, "Beyond the Iconography of Order: Notes for a 'New' Institutionalism," in Lawrence Dodd and Calvin Jillson, eds., *The Dynamics of American Politics: Approaches and Interpretations* (Boulder: Westview, 1994), and "Policy Forum: Institutions and Institutionalism," *Polity* 28 (1995): 84–147.

13. Richard C. Fenno, *Congressmen in Committees* (Boston: Little Brown, 1973).

14. Richard C. Fenno, *The Power of the Purse* (Boston: Little Brown, 1965).

15. Aaron Wildavsky, *The Politics of the Budgetary Process* (Boston: Little Brown, 1964).

16. Louis Fisher, *Presidential Spending Power* (Princeton: Princeton University Press, 1975).

17. Allen Schick, *The Capacity to Budget* (Washington, DC: Urban Institute Press, 1990), 52.

18. Lance T. LeLoup, *The Fiscal Congress: Legislative Control of the Budget* (Westport, CT: Greenwood Press, 1980), 20.

19. Lance T. LeLoup, "From Microbudgeting to Macrobudgeting: Transition in Theory and Practice," in Irene Rubin, ed., *New Directions in Budget Theory* (Albany: SUNY Press, 1988), 19–42.

20. Ibid., 153–55.

21. The passage of the Medicare Act in 1965 had profound budgetary implications, including expansion of the program in the 1970s to include the disabled and other beneficiaries; and the rapid increases in health care costs made it one of the fastest-growing elements of the federal budget. Social Security, the largest entitlement program, also expanded rapidly in the 1970s through several huge election-year increases in benefits, and later by indexing benefits to inflation during a period of high inflation. Entitlements increased from $65 billion in 1970 to $267 billion in 1980, an increase of over 400 percent. Entitlements' budget share expanded from 33 percent of outlays to 47 percent in that decade.

22. Roy Meyers, *Strategic Budgeting* (Ann Arbor: University of Michigan Press, 1995).

23. Public Law 93–344, Budget and Impoundment Control Act of 1974.

24. Sinclair 2000, 80. The data cover 1987–1990 and 1993–1998.

25. Cox and McCubbins 1993, 164.

26. Leroy Reiselbach, *Congressional Reform* (Washington, DC: CQ Press, 1986), 41–78.

27. Norman J. Ornstein, "Causes and Consequences of Congressional Change: Subcommittee Reforms in the House of Representatives," in Norman J. Ornstein, ed., *Congress in Change* (New York: Praeger, 1975), 88–114.

28. Reiselbach 1986, 82.

29. Lawrence C. Dodd and Bruce I. Oppenheimer, "The House in Transition: Partisanship and Opposition," in Lawrence C. Dodd and Bruce I. Oppenheimer, eds., *Congress Reconsidered,* 3rd ed. (Washington, DC: CQ Press, 1985), 47.

30. Lance T. LeLoup and Steven A. Shull, *Congress and the President: The Policy Connection* (Belmont, CA: Wadsworth, 1993), 105–6.

31. Rohde 1991, 17–33.

32. Gary Cox and Mathew D. McCubbins, "Toward a Theory of Legislative Rules Changes: Assessing Schickler and Rich's Evidence," *American Journal of Political Science* 41 (Oct. 1997): 1376–86.

33. Eric Schickler, "Institutional Change in the House of Representatives, 1867–1998: A Test of Partisan and Ideological Power Balance Models," *American Political Science Review* 94 (June 2000): 269–88.

34. Woodrow Wilson, *Congressional Government* (1881).

35. Austin Ranney, *Curing the Mischiefs of Faction: Party Reform in America* (Berkeley: University of California Press, 1975), 43.

36. APSA Committee on Political Parties, "A Report of the Committee on Political Parties," *American Political Science Review* 44 (Sept. 1950).

37. V. O. Key, *Parties, Politics, and Pressure Groups* (New York: Crowell, 1964).

38. David Mayhew, *The Electoral Connection* (New Haven: Yale University Press, 1974), 27.

39. David W. Brady and Charles S. Bulloch III, "Coalition Politics in the House of Representatives," in Lawrence C. Dodd and Bruce I. Oppenheimer, eds., *Congress Reconsidered,* 2nd ed. (Washington, DC: CQ Press, 1981): 381–407.

40. Rohde 1991, 45–58.

41. Roger H. Davidson and Walter J. Oleszek, *Congress and Its Members* (Washington, DC: CQ Press, 2004), 273.

42. Keith Pool and Howard Rosenthal, *Congress: A Political-Economic History of Roll Call Voting* (New York: Oxford University Press, 1997).

43. Sean M. Theriault, "The Case of the Vanishing Moderates: Party Polarization and the Modern Congress." Paper presented at the Western Political Science Association, Denver, CO, March 2003.

44. John H. Aldrich and David W. Rohde, "The Logic of Conditional Party Government," in Lawrence Dodd and Bruce Oppenheimer, eds., *Congress Reconsidered,* 7th ed. (Washington, DC: CQ Press, 2001), 282.

45. Robert S. Erikson and Gerald C. Wright, "Voters, Candidates, and Issues in Congressional Elections," in Dodd and Oppenheimer, eds. (2001), 74–75.

46. Cox and McCubbins 1993.

47. Rohde 1991.

48. Joseph Cooper and David W. Brady, "Institutional Context and Leadership Style: The House from Cannon to Rayburn," *American Political Science Review* 75 (1981): 411–25.

49. Aldrich and Rohde 2001, 275.

50. Barry Weingast, "A Rational Choice Perspective on Congressional Norms," *American Journal of Political Science* 23 (1979): 245–62.

51. Kenneth Shepsle, *The Giant Jigsaw Puzzle: Democratic Committee Assignments in the Modern House* (Chicago: University of Chicago Press, 1978).

52. Herbert S. Weisberg et al., "The Study of Congress: Methodologies and the Pursuit of Theory," in Weisberg et al., eds., *Classics in Congressional Politics* (New York: Longman, 1999), 15.

53. Cox and McCubbins 1993, 2.

54. Ibid., 73.

55. Ibid., 110.

56. C. Lawrence Evans, "Committees, Leaders, and Message Politics," in Dodd and Oppenheimer, eds. (2001), 222.

57. Krehbiel 1998.

58. Krehbiel 1998, 202.

59. Krehbiel 1998, 199 (italics his).

60. Krehbiel 1998, 220–23.

61. Krehbiel 1998, 187–88.

62. LeLoup 1980, 26.

63. Lloyd Cutler, "Now Is the Time for All Good Men," *William and Mary Law Review* 30 (1989): 391.

64. Mathew McCubbins, "Party Governance and U.S. Budget Deficits: Divided Control and Fiscal Stalemate," in Alberto Alesina and Geoffrey Carliner, eds., National Bureau of Economic Research, *Politics and Economics in the Eighties* (Chicago: University of Chicago Press, 1991), 83–111.

65. Brady and Volden 1998, 33.

66. Mayhew 1991.

67. Sean Q. Kelly, "Divided We Govern: A Reassessment," *Polity* 25 (Spring 1993): 475–84.

68. George C. Edwards III, Andrew Barrett, and Jeffrey Peake, "The Legislative Impact of Divided Government," *American Journal of Political Science* 21 (April 1997): 545–63.

69. Morris Fiorina, *Divided Government*, 2nd ed. (Boston: Allyn and Bacon, 1996), 89

70. Sarah A. Binder, "The Dynamics of Legislative Gridlock, 1947–96," *American Political Science Review* 93 (Sept. 1999): 519–33; Sarah A. Binder, *Stalemate* (Washington, DC: Brookings Institution, 2003): 34–56.

71. John Coleman, "Unified Government, Divided Government, and Party Responsiveness," *American Political Science Review* 93, no. 4 (Dec. 1999): 821–35.

72. Ibid., 821.

73. Keith Krehbiel, "Institutional and Partisan Sources of Gridlock: A Theory of Divided and Unified Government," *Journal of Theoretical Politics* 8 (Jan. 1996): 7–40; Keith Krehbiel, *Pivotal Politics: A Theory of U.S. Lawmaking*, (Chicago: University of Chicago Press, 1998).

74. Brady and Volden 1998.

75. Ibid., 3.

76. Ibid., 34.

77. Ibid., 37–38.

78. Binder 2003, 75–79.

79. Cameron 2000.

Notes to Chapter 2

1. Linda K. Kowalcky and Lance T. LeLoup, "Congress and the Politics of Statutory Debt Limitation," *Public Administration Review* 53, no. 1 (Jan./Feb. 1993): 14–28.

2. Lovis Fisher, *Presidential Spending Power* (Princeton: Princeton University Press, 1975).

3. Robert A. Wallace, *Congressional Control of Federal Spending* (Detroit: Wayne State University Press, 1960), 10.

4. Barry Weingast, "A Rational Choice Perspective on Congressional

Norms,"*American Journal of Political Science* 23 (1979): 245–62.

5. Wallace 1960, 8.

6. David Brady and Mark A. Morgan, "Reforming the Structure of the House Appropriations Process: The Effects of the 1885 and 1919–20 Reforms on Money Decisions," in Matthew D. McCubbins and Terry Sullivan, eds., *Congress: Structure and Policy* (Cambridge: Cambridge University Press, 1987), 207–34.

7. Larry Berman, *The Office of Management and Budget and the Presidency, 1921–1979* (Princeton: Princeton University Press, 1979).

8. Brady and Morgan 1987, 229–33.

9. Brady and Morgan 1987, 229.

10. See an earlier review of these changes in Lance T. LeLoup, *The Fiscal Congress: Legislative Control of the Budget* (Westport, CT: Greenwood Press, 1980), 4–6.

11. Lance T. LeLoup, *Budgetary Politics,* 4th ed. (Brunswick, OH: Kings Court, 1988), chapter 7.

12. Brady and Morgan 1987, 229–33.

13. Jesse Burkhead, "Federal Budgetary Developments 1947–48," *Public Administration Review* 8 (Autumn 1948): 267–74.

14. Louis Fisher, "Experience with a Legislative Budget," in Committee on Government Operations, U.S. Senate, *Improving Congressional Control over the Budget: A Compendium of Materials* (March 27, 1973), 37.

15. Aaron Wildavsky, *The Politics of the Budgetary Process* (Boston: Little Brown, 1964).

16. Richard F. Fenno, *The Power of the Purse: Appropriations Politics in Congress* (Boston: Little Brown, 1966).

17. Ibid., 143.

18. Ibid., 499.

19. Ibid., 141.

20. Allen Schick, *Congress and Money* (Washington, DC: Urban Institute Press, 1980), 418.

21. Fenno 1966, 499.

22. Ibid.

23. Schick 1980, chapter 10.

24. Joint Study Committee on Budget Control, *Recommendations for Improving Congressional Control over Budgetary Outlay and Receipt Totals,* April 18, 1973, 93rd Congress, 1st sess.: 8.

25. Leroy Reiselbach, *Congressional Reform* (Washington, DC: CQ Press, 1986).

26. Lance T. LeLoup, "Appropriations Politics in Congress," *Public Budgeting and Finance* 4, no. 4 (Winter 1984): 78–81.

27. Schick 1980, 434.

28. Ibid., 429.

29. Ibid., 438.

30. LeLoup 1980, 8–9.

31. Allen Schick, "Congressional Control of Expenditures," U.S. House of Representatives, Committee on the Budget, 95th Cong., 2nd sess. (Jan. 1977): 49–59.

32. Schick 1980, 37.

33. *Weekly Compilation of Presidential Documents* 8, no. 31 (July 26, 1972): 1176.

34. *Congressional Quarterly Weekly Report* (Nov. 4, 1972): 2907–10.

35. LeLoup 1980, 19.

36. HR 10961, 93rd Cong., 1st sess.

37. *Congressional Quarterly Weekly Report* (Feb. 23, 1973): 514.

38. Schick 1980, 72–74.

39. Ibid., 73.

40. LeLoup 1980, 24.

41. Joint Economic Committee, *The 1976 Joint Economic Report*, 94th Cong., 2nd sess.: 78.

42. *Congressional Record,* H3404–5, April 29, 1975.

43. *Congressional Record,* H3552–3591, May 1, 1975.

44. Aage Clausen and Richard Cheney, "Comparative Analysis of Senate and House Voting on Economic and Welfare Policy: 1953–1964," *American Political Science Review* 64 (March 1970): 151.

45. This conclusion is based on comparing ratings by Americans for Democratic Action (ADA) and Americans for Constitutional Action (ACA) for Budget Committee members by party to the mean ratings for the Republican/Democratic caucuses. Ratings are as published in *Congressional Quarterly Weekly Reports,* 1975–1980.

46. Data are compiled from committee roll-call voting records, House Budget Committee, 1975–1980.

47. From personal interviews with members of the House Budget Committees; see LeLoup 1980.

48. The votes on conference reports and second resolutions generally produced very similar partisan divisions.

49. Quoted in *Congressional Quarterly Weekly Report* (April 30, 1977): 776.

50. Michael B. Berkman, *The State Roots of National Politics* (Pittsburgh: University of Pittsburgh Press, 1993).

51. *Congressional Quarterly Weekly Report* (Aug. 4, 1979): 1582.

52. Joseph White and Aaron Wildavsky, *The Deficit and the Public Interest* (Berkeley: University of California Press, 1989), 44–49.

53. Budget and Impoundment Control Act of 1974, section 301(b)(2).

54. For data on the numbers and reasons for waivers, see LeLoup 1980, 139–140.

55. LeLoup 1980, 136–57.

56. James L. Blum, *Congressional Budget Office Testimony,* Statement before the Subcommittee on Taxation and Debt Management, Committee on Finance, U.S. Senate, July 31, 1990.

57. For a brief history, see the *Congressional Record,* Sept. 24, 1917: A991–993. Also see Jeffrey A. Cantor and Donald R. Stabile, *A History of the Bureau of the Public Debt: 1940–1990* (Washington, DC: U.S. Government Printing Office, 1990).

58. *Budget of the United States FY 1992,* Part 7: 74–77.

59. Rep. Daniel Reed (R-NY), *Congressional Record,* July 31, 1953: 10705.

60. *Congressional Record,* June 28, 1962: 12163.

61. See Kowalcky and LeLoup 1993, 22, for a more complete listing of Treasury actions.

62. *Congressional Record,* Sept. 26, 1979: H26342.

63. Ibid., H26343.

64. HR 5369, H. Rept. 96–472.

65. *Congressional Record,* Sept. 26, 1979: H26349.

66. Kowalcky and LeLoup 1993, 20.

67. See Kowalcky and LeLoup 1980, 24–25, for a more complete list of amendments.

Notes to Chapter 3

1. A cross-partisan majority is defined as the situation in which voting divisions largely follow party lines, but enough members of one party vote with the other party to make a majority. See Charles Jones, *The Presidency in a Separated System* (Washington, DC: Brookings Institution, 1994), 30.

2. February 5, 1981, quoted in Joseph White and Aaron Wildavsky, *The Deficit and the Public Interest* (Berkeley: University of California Press, 1989), 73.

3. See Paul R. Abramson, John H. Aldrich, and David W. Rohde, *Change and Continuity in the 1980 Elections* (Washington, DC: CQ Press, 1982).

4. Lawrence I. Barrett, *Gambling with History* (Garden City, NY: Doubleday, 1983), 48.

5. White and Wildvasky 1989, 75.

6. Lance T. LeLoup, *Budgetary Politics,* 4th ed. (Brunswick, OH: Kings Court Inc., 1988), 111.

7. White and Wildavsky 1989, 89.

8. Richard A. Stubbing, "The Defense Budget," in Gregory B. Mills and John L. Palmer, eds., *Federal Budget Policy in the 1980s* (Washington, DC: Urban Institute Press, 1984), 101.

9. See a discussion of this incident in White and Wildavsky 1989, 108–10.

10. Text is reprinted in *Congressional Quarterly Weekly Report* (Feb. 7, 1981): 286–87.

11. Barrett 1983, 141.

12. White and Wildavsky 1989, 110.

13. William Grieder, *The Education of David Stockman and Other Americans* (New York: Dutton, 1982), 36.

14. Gail Gregg, "'Let Us Act Together,' Reagan Exhorts Congress," *Congressional Quarterly Weekly Report* (Feb. 21, 1981): 331–35.

15. Office of Management and Budget, *Fiscal Year 1982 Budget Revisions* (March 10, 1981).

16. Gail Gregg, "Reagan Plan Clears First Hurdle," *Congressional Quarterly Weekly Report* (March 21, 1981): 499–500.

17. David Stockman, *The Triumph of Politics* (New York: Harper and Row, 1986), 161–62.

18. Dale Tate, "Senate Committee Rejects Reagan Budget," *Congressional Quarterly Weekly Report* (April 11, 1981): 621.

19. Gail Gregg, "Democrats Score on Budget," *Congressional Quarterly Weekly Report* (April 11, 1981): 619.

20. Steven V. Roberts, "Some Democrats in House Accuse O'Neill of a Lack of Strong Leadership," *New York Times* (April 30, 1981): A26.

21. See Steven J. Wayne, "Congressional Liaison in the Reagan White House: A Preliminary Assessment of the First Year," in Norman J. Ornstein, ed., *President and Congress: Assessing Reagan's First Year* (Washington, DC: American Enterprise Institute, 1982), 44–65.

22. Ronald Reagan, *An American Life* (New York: Simon and Schuster, 1990), 216.

23. White and Wildavsky 1989, 127.

24. Dale Tate, "House Provides President a Victory on the 1982 Budget," *Congressional Quarterly Weekly Report* (May 9, 1981): 783–85.

25. Former CBO Director Rudolf Penner once recounted an episode when he was explaining the congressional budget process to a visiting delegation from the Peoples Republic of China. When asked what happens when the House and Senate disagree over economic assumptions, Penner replied that conferees vote on which ones to accept. When the translator relayed the answer, he was instructed to ask again by the perplexed Chinese. When the reply was the same, another translator was brought in and asked the question for a third time. When the reply was again the same, the delegation shrugged their shoulders and walked out of the room.

26. White and Wildavsky 1989, 134.

27. Pamela Fessler, "Reagan Faces Fight on Social Security," *Congressional Quarterly Weekly Report* (May 16, 1981): 842–43.

28. Ibid.

29. White and Wildavsky 1989, 141.

30. *Congressional Record,* June 24, 1981.

31. Ibid., June 25, 1981.

32. White and Wildavsky 1989, 137.

33. Dale Tate, "Reagan and Rostenkowski Modify Tax Cut Proposals," *Congressional Quarterly Weekly Report* (June 6, 1981): 979–80.

34. William Greider 1981, 27–54.

35. White and Wildavsky 1989, 174.

36. Lou Cannon and Thomas B. Edsall, "Reagan Makes Appeal to Voters for Tax Bill," *Washington Post* (July 26, 1981), A1, A6.

37. CBS/New York Times poll, January 1981.

38. Sam Kernell, *Going Public: New Strategies of Presidential Leadership* (Washington, DC: CQ Press, 1993), 130–31.

39. William W. Lammers. "Policy Achievements in the First Year: Carter, Reagan and Clinton," paper delivered at the American Political Association Annual Meeting, New York, September 1–4, 1994.

40. Grieder 1981.

41. Harrison Donnelly, "Stopgap Funds Bill Cleared," *Congressional Quarterly Weekly Report* (Dec. 12, 1981): 2428–29.

42. Congressional Budget Office, *The Economic and Budget Outlook FY 1983–88.*

43. C. Eugene Steuerle, *The Tax Decade* (Washington, DC: Urban Institute Press, 1992).

44. Ibid., 42.

45. Ibid., 43.

46. Sung Deuk Hahm, Mark S. Kamlet, and David C. Mowery, "Postwar Deficit Spending in the United States." Paper presented at the Annual Meeting of the American Political Science Association, New York, Sept. 1–4, 1994.

47. Barrett 1984, 178.

48. Stockman 1986, 353.

49. White and Wildavsky 1989, 249.

50. Rich Thomas, "Why Reagan Switched," *Newsweek* (Aug. 23, 1982): 27.

51. Allen Schick, "The Budget as an Instrument of Presidential Policy," in Lester Salamon and Michael Lund, eds., *The Reagan Presidency and the Governing of America* (Washington, DC: Urban Institute Press, 1985), 108–9.

52. For a detailed analysis of the Social Security bailout, see Paul Light, *Artful Work: The Politics of Social Security Reform* (New York: Random House, 1985).

53. Pamela Fessler and Harrison Donnelly, "Congress Seeking to Assure Retirement Income Security," *Congressional Quarterly Weekly Report* (Nov. 28, 1981): 2333–36.

54. See an analysis of commission membership in Tyler Fitch and Lance T. LeLoup, "Extraordinary Resolution of Policy Deadlock: Bipartisan Summits and Commissions." Paper presented at the Annual Meeting of the Southern Political Science Association, New Orleans, March 18–20, 1993.

55. David Brady and Craig Volden, *Revolving Gridlock* (Boulder: Westview Press, 1998), 60–62.

56. Ibid., 61.

57. White and Wildavsky 1989, 621n53.

58. Quoted in White and Wildavsky 1989, 131.

59. Brady and Volden 1998, 63.

60. LeLoup 1988, 210.

61. Final votes on House and Senate passage of appropriation bills in 1981 were compiled from *Congressional Quarterly Weekly Reports*. Three of the Senate votes were on conference reports because initial passage was by voice vote.

62. PL 94–344.

63. See John Gilmour, *Reconcilable Differences?* (Berkeley: University of California Press, 1990).

64. Lance T. LeLoup and John Hancock, "Congress and the Reagan Budgets: An Assessment," *Public Budgeting and Finance* 8, no. 3 (Autumn 1988): 30–54.

65. Steven Gettinger and Diane Granat, "A Weary 98th Congress Finally Calls It Quits," *Congressional Quarterly Weekly Report* (Oct. 13, 1984): 2615.

66. Dale Tate, "Politics Prods Congress to Clear Money Bill," *Congressional Quarterly Weekly Report* (Oct. 13, 1984): 2616.

67. Lawrence C. Dodd and Bruce I Oppenheimer, "Consolidating Power in the House," in Lawrence C. Dodd and Bruce I. Oppenheimer, eds., *Congress Reconsidered,* 3rd ed. (Washington, DC: CQ Press, 1985), 48.

68. U.S. House of Representatives, Committee on Rules, *Report on the Congressional Budget Act Amendments of 1984* (98th Cong., 2nd sess.).

Notes to Chapter 4

1. *Los Angeles Times* exit polls, Nov. 6, 1984. Reported in *National Journal*, Nov. 10, 1984.

2. Elizabeth Wehr, "Reagan, Senate GOP Reach '86 Budget Accord," *Congressional Quarterly Weekly Report* (April 6, 1985): 627–30.

3. Ibid.

4. Lance T. LeLoup, *Budgetary Politics*, 4th ed. (Brunswick, OH: Kings Court, 1988), 172.

5. Andy Plattner, "Congress Adopts a Budget and Goes Home," *Congressional Quarterly Weekly Report* (Aug. 3, 1985): 1519–24.

6. The following section relies in part on Lance T. LeLoup, Barbara Luck Graham, and Stacey Barwick, "Deficit Politics and Constitutional Government: The Impact of Gramm-Rudman-Hollings," *Public Budgeting and Finance* 7, no. 1 (Spring 1987): 83–103.

7. Steven B. Roberts, "Phil Gramm's Crusade against the Deficit," *New York Times Magazine* (March 30, 1986): 20–23, 40, 57, 60.

8. Joseph White and Aaron Wildavsky, *The Deficit and the Public Interest* (Berkeley: University of California Press, 1989), 443–44.

9. Elizabeth Wehr, "Senate Passes Plan to Balance Federal Budget," *Congressional Quarterly Weekly Report* (Oct. 12, 1985): 2035–38.

10. Jonathan Fuerbringer, "Plan to Balance U.S. Budget by '91 Delayed in Senate," *New York Times* (Oct. 5, 1985): A1, A3.

11. *Congressional Record* (Oct. 5, 1985): S12730–32.

12. *Congressional Quarterly Weekly Report* (Oct. 12, 1985): 2073.

13. Elizabeth Wehr, "Conferees Strive to Fathom Budget-Balancing Plan," *Congressional Quarterly Weekly Report* (Oct. 19, 1985): 2093.

14. Elizabeth Wehr, "Difficult Questions Unresolved in Budget Measure Conference," *Congressional Quarterly Weekly Report* (Oct. 26, 1985): 2148.

15. White and Wildavsky 1989, 448.

16. *Congressional Record* (Nov. 1, 1985): H9615. Only one Republican and two Democrats crossed party lines.

17. This account is taken in part from an interview by the author with Representative Richard Gephardt, June 1986.

18. Quoted in White and Wildavsky 1989, 431–32.

19. *Congressional Record* (Dec. 11, 1985): S17444.

20. *Congressional Record* (Dec. 11, 1985): H11903.

21. Elizabeth Wehr, "Congress Enacts Far-Reaching Budget Measure," *Congressional Quarterly Weekly Report* (Dec. 14, 1985): 2604.

22. Ibid.

23. Interview with the author, June 1986.

24. This section is based on the Balanced Budget and Emergency Deficit Reduction

Act of 1985 (Public Law 99–177).

25. Robert Keith and Edward Davis, "The Senate's 'Byrd Rule' against Extraneous Matter in Reconciliation Bills," *Congressional Research Service* (July 9, 1993).

26. *Congressional Record* (Oct. 24, 1985): S14032.

27. Interview with the author, June 1986.

28. Allen Schick, "Explanation of the Balanced Budget and Emergency Deficit Control Act of 1985," prepared for Congressional Research Service (Dec. 1985): 9–13.

29. *Federal Register*, vol. 51, no. 10, book 2 (Jan. 15, 1986).

30. For a more detailed examination of the calculation and allocation of the cuts, see Harry Havens, "Gramm-Rudman-Hollings: Origins and Implementation," *Public Budgeting and Finance* 6 (Autumn 1986): 4–24.

31. Congressional Budget Office, *The Economic and Budget Outlook: Fiscal Years 1987–1991* (Feb. 1986).

32. *Synar v. United States,* 626 Supp. 1374 (D.D.C. 1986).

33. *Congressional Quarterly Weekly Report* (March 15, 1986): 315.

34. Steven Gettinger, "Spending Panels Confront Life after Gramm-Rudman," *Congressional Quarterly Weekly Report* (June 7, 1986): 1258–61.

35. See Jeffrey H. Birnbaum and Alan S. Murray, *Showdown at Gucci Gulch* (New York: Random House, 1988), and Timothy J. Conlan et al., *Taxing Choices: The Politics of Tax Reform* (Washington, DC: CQ Press, 1990).

36. For example, *United States v. Nixon* 418 S.Ct. 683 (1974) and *Buckley v. Valeo* 424 S.Ct. 612 (1976).

37. *Charles A. Bowsher, Comptroller General of the United States v. Mike Synar, Member of Congress et al.,* 106 S.Ct. 3181 (1986).

38. For example, the Congressional Research Service prepared a constitutional analysis of four of the most questionable provisions. See *Congressional Record* (Oct. 24, 1985): E4793–95.

39. The District Court provided its views on this issue so that the Supreme Court could take them into account during review and so that delay would not result if it were necessary to remand the case.

40. *Bowsher v. Synar* at 10 (slip opinion).

41. Stephen Gettinger, "Deficit-Cutting Proposals Seek to Avoid Cuts," *Congressional Quarterly Weekly Report* (Sept. 20, 1986): 2180.

42. The text of the economic bill of rights was reprinted in *Congressional Quarterly Weekly Report,* (July 11 1987): 1531–33.

43. Elizabeth Wehr, "A Weary Congress Clears Bill to Raise Taxes, Cut Spending," *Congressional Quarterly Weekly Report* (Dec. 26, 1987): 3187–92.

44. Jacqueline Calmes, "Reagan Wins Concessions in Final Funding Bill," *Congressional Quarterly Weekly Report* (Dec. 26, 1987): 3185–86.

45. Author interviews with Senate parliamentarian Robert Dove, June 1986, and assistant Gail Culper, June 1987.

46. Gallup Poll, September 1985.

47. Elizabeth Wehr, "Gramm-Rudman Both Disappoints and Succeeds," *Congressional Quarterly Weekly Reports* (Nov. 15, 1986): 2879–82.

Notes to Chapter 5

1. Inaugural address of George Herbert Walker Bush, January 20, 1989, reprinted in *Congressional Quarterly Weekly Report* (Jan. 21, 1989): 142–43.

2. Cable News Network—Los Angeles Times exit polls, November 8, 1988; reported in *National Journal* (Nov. 12, 1988).

3. Paul Abramson, John Aldrich, and David Rohde, *Change and Continuity in the 1988 Elections* (Washington, DC: CQ Press, 1990): 193–94.

4. David Rapp, "Budget-Making to Be an Insider's Art This Year," *Congressional Quarterly Weekly Report* (Jan. 14, 1989): 63–65.

5. A look at interest group ratings (ADA, ACA) of NEC members who served in Congress reveals that there were significant ideological differences between the Republican and Democratic members.

6. Rapp, Jan. 14, 1989, 63.

7. "Deficit Commission Issues Split Report," *Congressional Quarterly Weekly Report* (March 4, 1989): 435.

8. David Rapp, "Negotiators Agree on Outlines of Fiscal 1990 Plan," *Congressional Quarterly Weekly Report* (April 15, 1989): 804–5.

9. Ibid.

10. Jackie Calmes, "It Was Supposed to Be Easy: Where Did the Good Will Go?," *Congressional Quarterly Weekly Report* (Dec. 2, 1989): 3309–10.

11. Office of Management and Budget, *Budget of the United States Fiscal Year 1991* (Jan. 29, 1990).

12. Congressional Budget Office, *The Economic and Budget Outlook: Fiscal Years 1991–1995* (Feb. 1990).

13. Office of Management and Budget, *Budget of the United States, Fiscal Year 1991*.

14. "Moynihan Plan Debated," *Congressional Quarterly Weekly Report* (Feb. 3, 1990): 306.

15. *Congressional Quarterly Almanac 1990* (Washington, DC: CQ Press), 128.

16. Ibid., 129.

17. Lance T. LeLoup and Steven A. Shull, *Congress and the President: The Policy Connection* (Belmont, CA: Wadsworth, 1993), 194–98.

18. *Congressional Quarterly Almanac 1990*, 130.

19. Presidential statement reprinted in ibid., 131.

20. Ibid., 132.

21. LeLoup and Shull 1993, 195.

22. House Budget Committee, outline of budget agreement, released September 30, 1990.

23. Janet Hook, "Anatomy of a Budget Showdown," *Congressional Quarterly Weekly Report* (Oct. 6, 1990): 3189.

24. LeLoup and Shull 1993, 196.

25. *Congressional Quarterly Almanac 1990*, 137.

26. Text of presidential veto message reprinted in ibid., 137.

27. LeLoup and Shull 1993, 197.

28. *Congressional Quarterly Weekly Report* (Nov. 3, 1990): 3764, 3769.

29. Congressional Budget Office, *The 1990 Budget Agreement: An Interim Assessment* (Dec. 1990): 2.

30. Congressional Budget Office, *The Economic and Budget Outlook: FY 1992–FY1996* (Feb. 1991): 45.

31. The Bush administration sought contributions from Middle East allies such as Kuwait, Saudi Arabia, and others to defray the cost of the buildup and, eventually, the Gulf War. In the end, nearly $50 billion was raised, enough to cover the costs of the war.

32. Omnibus Budget Reconciliation Act of 1990, section 253.

33. Ibid., section 13133.

34. Congressional Budget Office (Feb. 1991): 49.

35. See Edward M. Gramlich, "U.S. Federal Budget Deficits and Gramm-Rudman-Hollings," *American Economic Review, Papers and Proceedings*, vol. 80, no. 2 (May 1990), 75–80.

36. OMB estimated the increase at $22 billion, CBO at $27 billion; see Reischauer 1990, 232.

37. Congressional Budget Office, *The Economic and Budget Outlook FY 94–FY98* (Jan.1993): 124.

38. Reischauer 1990, 225–26.

39. Calculated from data contained in Congressional Budget Office, *An Analysis of the President's Budgetary Proposals for Fiscal Year 1983* (1982), and subsequent volumes through 1991.

40. Reischauer 1990, 227.

41. Ibid., 229.

42. Peter J. Wallison, "Bush's Reagan Moment," *New York Times* (Oct. 26, 2003, section 4): 11.

43. Barbara Sinclair, *Unorthodox Lawmaking*, 2nd ed. (Washington, DC: CQ Press, 2000).

44. Lance T. LeLoup, "The Fiscal Straitjacket: Budgetary Constraints on Congressional Foreign and Defense Policymaking," in Randall B. Ripley and James M. Lindsay, eds., *Congress Resurgent: Foreign and Defense Policy on Capitol Hill* (Ann Arbor: University of Michigan Press, 1993).

45. Richard Doyle and Jerry McCaffery, "The Budget Enforcement Act in 1991: Isometric Budgeting," *Public Budgeting and Finance* (Spring 1992).

46. *Congressional Quarterly Weekly Report* (Nov. 17, 1990): 3888.

47. Richard Doyle and Jerry McCaffery, "The Budget Enforcement Act in 1992: Necessary But Not Sufficient," *Public Budgeting and Finance* 13, no. 2 (Summer 1993): 21.

48. Ibid., 22.

49. Ibid., 34.

Notes to Chapter 6

1. CBO, The Economic and Budget Outlook FY1994–1998 (Jan. 1993): 1–28.

2. House Budget Committee, Press Release of Aug. 4, 1993 citing testimony of Alan Greenspan and CBO scorekeeping.

3. Karl O'Lessker, "The Clinton Budget for FY 1994: Taking Aim at the Deficit," *Public Budgeting and Finance* 13, no. 2 (Summer 1993): 7.

4. George Hager, "Time Bombs for Clinton Seen in Bush's Final Budget," *Congressional Quarterly Weekly Report* (Jan. 9, 1993): 68–70.

5. CBO, *The Economic and Budget Outlook FY1994–1998* (Jan. 1993): 38.

6. George Hager, "GOP Ready to Fight Clinton over Economic Policy," *Congressional Quarterly Weekly Report* (Jan. 23, 1993): 170–71.

7. An outline of the president's proposals was printed in *A Vision of Change for America,* Feb.17, 1993.

8. George Hager, "Both Parties Struggle for Unity as First Votes Draw Near," *Congressional Quarterly Weekly Report* (March 6, 1993): 505.

9. David E. Rosenbaum, "Senators Put Up a New Obstacle in Budget Fight," *New York Times* (May 21, 1993): A1.

10. David Wessel, "Entitlement-Cap Proposals Resurface ahead of Vote on Deficit Reduction," *Wall Street Journal* (May 24, 1993): A15.

11. George Hager and David S. Cloud, "Democrats Pull Off Squeaker in Approving Clinton Plan," *Congressional Quarterly Weekly Report* (May 29, 1993): 1340–47.

12. Jackie Calmes, "Democrats Draft New Tax Plan in Senate," *Wall Street Journal* (June 17, 1993): A3.

13. George Hager and David S. Cloud, "Test for Divided Democrats: Forge a Budget Deal," *Congressional Quarterly Weekly Report* (June 26, 1993): 1633.

14. Ibid., 1634.

15. See table in *New York Times* (June 18, 1993): A11.

16. Janet Hook, "Conference without Walls," *Congressional Quarterly Weekly Report* (Aug. 7, 1993): 2128.

17. Transcript of presidential address, *New York Times* (Aug. 4, 1993): A10.

18. Robert Reinhold, "For DeConcini, The Vote Is a Gamble," *New York Times* (Aug. 5, 1993): A11.

19. George Hager and David S. Cloud, "Democrats Tie Their Fate to Clinton's Budget Bill," *Congressional Quarterly Weekly Report* (Aug. 7, 1993): 2122–29.

20. Ibid., 2127.

21. Ibid., 2122.

22. These were the figures used by Democrats during the floor debate and generally the figures reported by major news outlets such as *Congressional Quarterly, New York Times,* and *Wall Street Journal.*

23. Office of Management and Budget, *Mid-Session Review of the 1994 Budget* (Sept. 1993): 19–26.

24. Congressional Budget Office, *The Economic and Budget Outlook: An Update* (Sept. 1993): 29–34.

25. Congressional Budget Office, *The Economic and Budget Outlook: Fiscal Years 1995–1999* (Jan. 1994): 56.

26. Robert Keith and Edward Davis, "Budget Process Changes in the House-

Passed Reconciliation Act of 1993," *Congressional Research Service* (June 14, 1993).

27. Ibid., 16–17.

28. Ibid., 18–23.

29. Edward Davis and Robert Keith, "Budget Process Changes Considered by the Senate: The Reconciliation Act of 1993," *Congressional Research Service* (June 30, 1993).

30. Ibid., 15.

31. See Robert Keith and Edward Davis, "The Senate's 'Byrd Rule' against Extraneous Matter in Reconciliation Measures," *Congressional Research Service* (July 9, 1993).

32. *Congressional Record* (Oct. 24, 1985): S 14032.

33. Senate Budget Committee, Report to Accompany S. Con Res 18, Concurrent Resolution on the Budget, FY 1994 (S.Rept. 103–19, March 12, 1993): 49.

34. Keith and Davis 1993, 6.

35. Office of Management and Budget, *Budget of the United States Government, Fiscal Year 1995* (Feb. 7, 1994): 79.

36. Ibid., 80.

37. OBRA-93, Conference Report to Accompany HR 2264 (Aug. 4, 1993): 936–66.

Notes to Chapter 7

1. "Clinton's Budget: No Cover for GOP," *Congressional Quarterly Almanac 1995* (Washington, DC: CQ Inc., 1996), 2–5.

2. "GOP Throws Down Budget Gauntlet," ibid., 2–30.

3. See Linda Kowalcky and Lance T. LeLoup, "Congress and the Politics of Statutory Debt Limitation," *Public Administration Review* 53, no. 1 (Jan./Feb. 1993): 14–27.

4. Richard L. Berke, "Clinton's Ratings over 50% in Poll as G.O.P. Declines," *New York Times* (Dec. 14, 1995): A1.

5. *Congressional Quarterly Weekly Reports* (Jan. 6, 1996): 53.

6. Ibid., 53–55.

7. *Congressional Quarterly Weekly Report* (Jan. 27, 1996): 213.

8. George Hager, "New Twist for Clinton Budget: A Cordial GOP Reception?," *Congressional Quarterly Weekly Report* (Feb. 1, 1997): 275–77.

9. Office of Management and Budget, *Budget of the United States Fiscal Year 1998,* 3.

10. Ibid.

11. George Hager, "Clinton Budget 'Alive on Arrival' But GOP Wary of Fine Print," *Congressional Quarterly Weekly Report* (Feb. 6, 1997): 327–31.

12. Office of Management and Budget, *Budget of the United States Fiscal Year 1998,* 2.

13. Ibid., 15.

14. Alissa J. Rubin, "Education Taxes Debated," *Congressional Quarterly Weekly*

Report (Feb. 8, 1997): 333.

15. Jeffrey L. Katz, "GOP Balks at Reopening Welfare," *Congressiional Quarterly Weekly Report* (Feb. 8, 1997): 329.

16. OMB, *Budget of the United States Fiscal Year 1998*, 29.

17. Congressional Budget Office, *An Analysis of the President's Budgetary Proposals for Fiscal Year 1998* (March 1997), 2.

18. David E. Kyvig, "Redefining or Resisting Modern Government? The Balanced Budget Amendment to the U.S. Constitution," *Akron Law Review* 28, no. 2 (Fall/Winter 1995): 99.

19. Kvyng, 114–18. By March 1983, thirty-two states had requested a convention, two states short of the required total mandated under Article V of the U.S. Constitution. Later, several states withdrew their request for a convention, and the effort stalled.

20. S.J. Res. 1, 1997. See also "Legislative Background, Consideration of the Balanced Budget Amendment," *Congressional Digest* (March 1997): 73.

21. S.J. Res. 1, 105th Cong. (1997).

22. "Supporters Burned by the 'Torch,'" *Congressional Quarterly Weekly Report* (March 1, 1997): 524.

23. "Senate Again One Vote Short; GOP Says House Will Act," *Congressional Quarterly Weekly Report* (March 9, 1997): 578.

24. Clay Chandler, "Playing the Social Security Card; Clinton Using Fear to Bury the Balanced Budget Amendment, Critics Say," *The Washington Post* (Feb. 24, 1997): A8. In an effort to illustrate their concern about the balancing the budget, and knowing that the measure would undoubtedly fail, Senate Democrats introduced a balanced budget amendment that exempted the Social Security Trust Fund from budget calculations.

25. H.J. Res. 159.

26. H.J. Res. 62.

27. Richard W. Stevenson, "Talks on Budget Reach an Impasse, Leaders Declare," *New York Times* (March 14, 1997): A1.

28. Jerry Gray, "Republicans Demand: A Realistic Budget," *New York Times* (March 13, 1997): A13.

29. Jerry Gray, "Conservative Senators Pressure G.O.P. Leaders in Budget Talks," *New York Times* (April 23, 1997): A1.

30. Reported in *Congressional Quarterly Weekly Report* (Feb. 8, 1997): 328.

31. George Hager, "Clinton, GOP Congress Strike Historic Budget Agreement," *Congressional Quarterly Weekly Report* (May 3, 1997): 993–97.

32. Quoted in *Congressional Quarterly Weekly Report* (May 10, 1997): 1091.

33. AllPolitics—Balancing the Budget—the Latest Developments, http://allpolitics.com/1997/gen/resources/infocus/budget/developments.html, 1–4.

34. George Hager, "Hill OKs Fiscal '98 Resolution, But Trouble Spots Abound," *Congressional Quarterly Weekly Report* (June 7, 1997): 1304.

35. Ibid., 1305.

36. Andrew Taylor, "Tax and Spending Bills Passed," *Congressional Quarterly Weekly Report* (June 28, 1997): 1492.

37. *Congressional Quarterly Weekly Report* (June 28, 1997): 1545, 1552.

38. *Congressional Quarterly Weekly Report* (Aug. 2, 1997): 1832.

39. House and Senate Committees on the Budget, Majority Staff, *Summary of Provisions, The Conference Agreement on the Balanced Budget Act of 1997* (July 30, 1997): 1–11.

40. Congressional Budget Office, *An Economic and Budget Outlook Update* (Sept. 1997): 27–34.

41. Ibid., x–xi.

42. *Congressional Quarterly Weekly Report* (Aug. 2, 1997): 1833.

43. Richard C. Fenno, *The Power of the Purse* (Boston: Little, Brown, 1965).

Notes to Chapter 8

1. Charles M. Cameron, *Veto Bargaining* (Cambridge: Cambridge University Press, 2000).

2. David W. Brady and Craig Volden, *Revolving Gridlock* (Boulder: Westview Press, 1998).

3. Congressional Budget Office, *The Economic and Budget Outlook FY 2002–FY 2011* (Jan. 2001).

4. David Sanger, "Bush Tax Plan Sent to Congress, Starting the Jostling for Position," *New York Times* (Feb. 9, 2001): A1.

5. Quoted in Daniel J. Parks with Andrew Taylor, "The Republican Challenge: Roping the Fiscal Strays," *Congressional Quarterly Weekly Report* (Feb. 17, 2001): 318.

6. Congressional Budget Office, *An Analysis of the President's Budget Proposals for Fiscal Year 2002* (April 2001).

7. Daniel J Parks, "House Panel's Budget Resolution Will Include Flexibility for Larger Tax Cut," *Congressional Quarterly Weekly Report* (March 17, 2001): 597–99.

8. Karen Foerstel, "'Blue Dog' Democrats Get Hackles Up at GOP and Business' Tax Bill Tactics," *Congressional Quarterly Weekly Report* (March 10, 2001): 530–31.

9. Lori Nitschke, "The Elusive Middle Ground," *Congressional Quarterly Weekly Report* (March 3, 2001): 467–69.

10. Daniel J. Parks, "House Budget Resolution Provides Leeway . . ." *Congressional Quarterly Weekly Report* (March 24, 2001): 655–56.

11. Lori Nitschke, "Tax-Cut Bipartisanship Down to One Chamber," *Congressional Quarterly Weekly Report* (March 10, 2001): 529–32.

12. Andrew Taylor," Law Designed for Curbing Deficits Becomes GOP Tool for Cutting Taxes," *Congressional Quarterly Weekly Report* (April 7, 2001): 7870–71.

13. Daniel J. Parks, "Byrd Seeks a Way to Stop Tax Bill from Passing by Simple Majority Vote," *Congressional Quarterly Weekly Report* (March 10, 2001): 533.

14. Daniel J. Parks, "It's the Day of the Centrist as Bush Tax Cut Takes a Hit," *Congressional Quarterly Weekly Report* (April 7, 2001): 768

15. Quoted in Daniel J. Parks, "Bush Starts to Deal on Budget . . . ," *Congressional Quarterly Weekly Report* (April 28, 2001): 903.

16. Andrew Taylor, "Senate's Agenda to Rest on Rulings of Referee Schooled by Democrats," *Congressional Quarterly Weekly Report* (May 12, 2001): 1063–65.

17. Glenn Kessler, "Senate Clears Budget Plan," *Washington Post* (May 11, 2001): A1.

18. Lori Nitschke, "Tax Cut Deal Reached Quickly as Appetite for Battle Fades," *Congressional Quarterly Weekly Report* (May 26, 2001): 1251.

19. Joseph J. Schatz, "Right-Leaning Senate Budget Panel Seeking Strategy to Sell Bush Plan," *Congressional Quarterly Weekly Report* (March 8, 2003): 552. The ACU rankings range from 0 (least conservative) to 100 (most conservative).

20. Jill Barshay, "Can Tax Cuts Pay Their Way?" *Congressional Quarterly Weekly Report* (Jan. 11, 2003): 67–70.

21. Congressional Research Service, cited in *Congressional Quarterly Weekly Report* (March 1, 2003): 503.

22. Alan K. Ota, "Congressional Fine Tuning Ahead for Bush Economic Stimulus Plan," *Congressional Quarterly Weekly Report* (Feb. 8, 2003): 337.

23. Andrew Taylor, "Budget Panels' Disparate Plans Threaten United GOP Front," *Congressional Quarterly Weekly Report* (March 15, 2003): 608–11.

24. Alan K. Ota and Jill Barshay, "Bush's Dividend Plan at Center Stage as Tax Cut Negotiations Begin," *Congressional Quarterly Weekly Report* (March 22, 2003): 688–90.

25. Joseph J. Schatz, "High-Stakes Conference Awaits Senate-Pared Budget Resolution," *Congressional Quarterly Weekly Report* (March 29, 2003): 753–56.

26. *Congressional Quarterly Weekly Report* (April 12, 2003), vote #141: 906.

27. David Firestone, "How the President's $726 Billion Plan Was Cut in Half," *New York Times* (March 26, 2003): A19.

28. Allison Stevens and Andrew Taylor, "Frist Faced with Deep Party Rift after Charge of Double Dealing," *Congressional Quarterly Weekly Report* (April 19, 2003): 931–34.

29. Ibid., 932

30. Bob Kemper, "New Tax-Cut Argument: It's for the Soldiers," *Chicago Tribune* (April 2, 2003): 15

31. Alan K. Ota, "Deadlocked Tax Cut Proposals Expose Rift in GOP Ideology," *Congressional Quarterly Weekly Report* (May 3, 2003): 1029–33.

32. Karen DeYoung and Jonathan Weisman, "Bush Urges Passage of Tax Plan," *Washington Post* (May 3, 2003): A12.

33. Jonathan Weisman, "White House Eases Stand on Dividend Tax," *Washington Post* (April 21, 2003): E1.

34. David E. Rosenbaum, "Senate Adopts a Tax Cut Plan of $350 Billion," *New York Times* (May 26, 2003): A1.

35. Alan K. Ota, "Tax Cut Package Clears amid Bicameral Rancor," *Congressional Quarterly Weekly Report* (May 24, 2003): 1245–49.

36. John D. McKinnon, "The 2003 Tax Package: Tax Cut Embodies Political Agenda," *Wall Street Journal* (May 27, 2003): A2.

37. Jonathan Weisman, "Congress Passes $350 Billion Tax Cut Bill: Cheney Vote Breaks Tie," *Washington Post* (May 21, 2003): A1.

38. McKinnon 2003, A2.

39. Jill Barshay and Alan K. Ota, "GOP Scrambles to Limit Damage of Child Tax Credit Controversy," *Congressional Quarterly Weekly Report* (June 7, 2003): L1371–73.

40. CNN/Gallup Poll of 1,019 adults with a margin of error of +/- 3 percent; cited in ibid.

Notes to Chapter 9

1. Bill Heniff, Jr., "Budget Reconciliation Legislation: Development and Consideration," *CRS Report for Congress,* CRS Report 98–814 (March 5, 2001).

2. Robert Keith, "The Senate's Byrd Rule against Extraneous Matter in Reconciliation Measures," *CRS Report for Congress,* CRS Report 97–695 (Sept. 9, 1998).

3. Bill Heniff, Jr., "Congressional Budget Act Points of Order," *CRS Report for Congress,* CRS Report 98–876 (March 5, 2001).

4. John B. Gilmour, *Reconcilable Differences?* (Berkeley: University of California Press, 1990), 224.

5. Joseph J. Schatz, "Congress Weighs Pros, Cons of the 'Omnibus' Approach," *Congressional Quarterly Weekly Report* (Nov. 3, 2003): 2688–93.

6. David W. Rohde, *Parties and Leaders in the Post Reform House* (Chicago: University of Chicago Press, 1991).

7. Keith Krehbiel, *Pivotal Politics: A Theory of U.S. Lawmaking* (Chicago: University of Chicago Press, 1998).

8. Ibid., 202.

9. Ibid., 198.

10. Ibid., 224.

11. Lance T. LeLoup, "The Myth of Incrementalism," *Polity* X, no. 4 (Summer 1978): 488–509.

12. Votes on the Concurrent Resolution on the Budget, final passage in the House and Senate. In the years when there was a first and second resolution before 1982, the first resolution is used. When there was a voice vote in the Senate, the roll-call vote on the conference report is used. In years when no budget resolution was passed, such as 2002, the data point represents the mean value of the prior and subsequent year.

13. See Meredith Watts et al., *Legislative Roll-Call Analysis.* The Rice index is the absolute value of yea votes minus nay votes for a party divided by the absolute value of yea votes plus nay votes for the party. It varies between 100 (unanimity) and 0 (party members equally divided).

14. Jonathan Allen and John Cochran, "The Might of the Right," *Congressional Quarterly Weekly Report* (Nov. 8, 2003): 2761–62.

15. Jackie Koszczuk and Jonathan Allen, "Late-Night Medicare Vote Drama Triggers Some Unexpected Alliances," *Congressional Quarterly Weekly Report* (Nov.

29, 2003): 2958–59. It was subsequently learned that the Bush administration prevented higher cost estimates from being revealed to Congress or the public.

16. Quoted in ibid.

17. Susan Ferrechio, "Complaint against DeLay Is Once Again the Lead Item in Ethics Panel's Docket," *Congressional Quarterly Weekly Report* (Oct. 2, 2004): 2323.

18. C. Lawrence Evans, "Committees, Leaders, and Message Politics," in Lawrence Dodd and Bruce Oppenheimer, eds., *Congress Reconsidered,* 7th ed. (Washington DC: CQ Press, 2001), 222.

19. Patrick J. Sellers, "Winning Media Coverage in the U.S. Congress," paper delivered at the Norman Thomas Conference on Senate Exceptionalism, Vanderbilt University, Nashville, Oct. 21–23, 1999 (cited in Evans, 2001).

20. For much of the nineteenth century, budget surpluses were actually seen as more dangerous economically than deficits. See Robert A. Wallace, *Congressional Control of Federal Spending* (Detroit: Wayne State University Press, 1960).

21. Gallup Polls taken from 6/25/84 to 9/15/98 on the question, "What is the greatest problem facing the country?" Gallup Organization, Princeton, NJ, <http://198.175.140.8/gallup%5Fpoll%5Fdata/mood/problem.htm>.

22. Paul Krugman, "The Tax-Cut Con," *New York Times Magazine* (Sept. 14, 2003): 54–61.

23. Ibid., 57.

24. Joseph White and Aaron Wildavsky, *The Deficit and the Public Interest* (Berekely: University of California Press, 1989), 412

25. Richard Conlon, quoted in White and Wildavsky 1989, 413.

26. White and Wildavsky 1989, 427.

27. Sarah A. Binder, *Stalemate: Causes and Consequences of Legislative Gridlock* (Washington, DC: Brookings Institution, 2003), 75–78.

28. Sharon S. Gressle, *Shutdown of the Federal Government: Causes, Effects, and Process* (Washington, DC: Congressional Research Service, Nov. 8, 1999), CRS Report 98–844, 1–5.

29. Lance T. LeLoup and Steven A. Shull, *The President and Congress: Collaboration and Combat in National Policymaking,* 2nd ed. (New York: Longman, 2003), 17–18.

INDEX

Adams, Brock, 38
ad hoc budget negotiations (extraordinary resolution), 73, 107–8, 109, 117–26. *See also* budget summits, bipartisan commissions
Alaska National Wildlife Refuge (ANWR), 194, 195
Albert, Carl, 53
Aldrich, John H., 13
American Automobile Association, 114
Amtrak, 118
appropriation caps, 116, 126, 134, 149, 151, 178, 192
Appropriations Committees, 26, 33, 34, 73, 127, 129; 302(b) allocations, 100, 120
appropriations process, 5, 23, 24–26, 30, 32, 160, 192, 200, 203, 205; decline of, 29, 32–33, 169–74; partisan voting patterns, 209; recommittal votes, 28
Archer, Bill, 173
Armey, Dick, 174
authorizing committees, 26, 33, 63
authorization process, 26, 32, 80

backdoor spending, 30, 33
Balanced Budget Act and Taxpayers Relief Act of 1997, 175–77
balanced budget agreement (1997), 3, 159–80, 208
balanced budget amendment, 42, 51, 167, 168–70, 219

Balanced Budget and Emergency Deficit Reduction Act (1985). *See* Gramm-Rudman-Hollings
Balanced Budget and Emergency Deficit Control Reaffirmation Act (1987). *See* Gramm-Rudman-Hollings II
Baker, Howard, 57, 74, 84
Baker, James, 57, 64, 84
Barrett, Andrew, 18
Baucus, Max, 189
Beilensen, Anthony, 81, 91, 96
Bellmon, Henry, 39, 208
Bentsen, Lloyd, 113, 140
Binder, Sarah, 18, 20
bipartisan commissions, 73–75, 114–15, 133, 218–19
Black Caucus, 41, 148
Blackmun, Harry, 102
"Blue Dog" Democrats, 185, 189
"Boll Weevil" Democrats, 57, 66, 73, 185
Boren, David, 143, 146, 147
Bowsher v. Synar (1986), 101
Brady, David, 13, 19, 25, 77
Brady, Nicholas, 113, 115, 118, 122
Breaux, John, 195
Brooks, Jack, 102
budget advocacy and guardianship, 27
budget agreement 1989, 115–16
Budget and Accounting Act (1921), 23, 25
Budget and Impoundment Control Act (1974), 3, 5, 17, 33–37, 83, 181, 201–4; "elastic" clause, 8, 44

Budget Committees, 10, 33, 96, 100,
128, 202. *See also* House Budget
Committee; Senate Budget
Committee
budget deficits, 3, 41, 70–74, 83–86,
98–99, 116, 120, 138–40, 194, 212;
and divided government, 18, 222;
and gridlock, 20
Budget Enforcement Act (1990), 8, 112,
126–30, 138, 151, 152, 178, 183,
196, 204, 219
budget resolutions, 6, 20, 34, 141, 173,
186, 192, 194, 201; components of,
36; duration of, 192–93; functional
subtotals, 37
budget rules, 7–9, 35–37, 77–78, 83,
100–101, 108, 132–33, 199, 201–4.
See also congressional budget process
budget summits, 9, 20, 106, 107–9,
113, 117–22, 132–33, 217–19
budget surpluses, 167, 182, 192, 201,
212
budgetary tricks and gimmicks, 62, 73,
94, 103, 106, 118, 131, 203
Bureau of Alcohol, Tobacco, and
Firearms, 166
Bureau of the Budget, 25
Burger, Warren, 102
Bush, George H. W., 17, 49, 110,
111–36, 137, 207, 212
Bush, George W., 17, 181, 208, 211,
213, 214, 215, 221; 2001 tax cuts,
181–91; 2003 tax cuts, 191–99
Bush tax cuts (2001, 2003), 3, 181–99,
210
Byrd, Robert, 34, 63, 87, 95, 113, 126,
153, 187, 188
Byrd rule, 8, 95, 106, 108, 146, 148,
152–53, 156, 187, 201, 202

Cameron, Charles, M., 20
capital gains tax cut, 117, 121, 164,
193
Carter, Jimmy, 18, 40, 41, 43, 44, 49,
53, 55, 58, 59, 60, 74

census, 174
Chaffee, Lincoln, 186, 188, 190, 196,
210
Cheney, Richard, 182, 186, 195
child tax credit, 198
Chiles, Lawton, 87
civil rights, 146
Cleland, Max, 169
Clinton, William, 17, 135, 182, 183,
185, 187, 200, 205, 208, 210, 215,
222; 1993 deficit reduction plan,
137–57; 1995–96 battles with
Republicans, 159–62; 1997 balanced
budget agreement, 161–78; 1998
budget proposals, 164–67; stimulus
plan, 139–41; televised appeal,
147–48
Coehlo, Tony, 113, 116
Coleman, John, 19
Comptroller General, 90, 96, 97, 102
Conable, Barber, 67
concurrent resolution on the budget. *See*
budget resolutions
conditional party government theory
(CPG), 13–14
conference committees, 202, 210
Congressional Budget Office (CBO), 33,
37, 44, 61, 84, 87, 90, 92, 96, 97,
98, 99, 101, 103, 105, 118, 120,
129, 137, 141, 149, 163, 168, 171,
182
congressional budget process, 33–37,
199, 201–4; delays in, 215–17;
implementation in 1975–76, 38–42;
in 1983–85, 78–80; House-Senate
differences, 39–40; limited impact
1975–80, 45; original timetable, 36;
revised rules and timetable, 93–95
congressional reforms; of 1960s and
1970s, 9–11; attempts at a congressional budget 1946–49, 26–27
Conrad, Kent, 191
conservative coalition, 12
consumer price index (CPI), 171, 172
Conte, Silvio, 80

Contract with America, 158, 169
continuing resolutions (CR), 6, 70, 160
Cooper, Joseph, 13
corporate taxes, 149
cost-of-living-adjustments (COLAs), 58, 61, 63, 64, 75, 85, 98, 150
Council of Economic Advisors, 139
Cox, Gary W., 4, 11, 14, 204
credit budget, 129
cross-partisan majority, 54, 78
crosswalking, 36
Cutler, Lloyd, 18

Darman, Richard, 64, 113, 115, 117, 122, 134, 138, 139; 1990 budget message, 118
Daschle, Tom, 182, 188, 189, 191
Deaver, Michael, 57, 84
DeConcini, Dennis, 147, 148
defense spending, 38, 58, 116, 125, 135, 140, 149; Reagan plan, 59; effect of Gramm-Rudman-Hollings, 88, 105
deficits, 26, 29, 38, 41–44, 54, 63, 72, 84, 138, 220; attempts to limit 1967–74, 31; rapid increase in 1981–82, 70–72; 1993 reduction package, 149–51; 1997 agreement, 159–80
deficit reduction trust fund, 147, 152, 154
Delay, Tom, 193, 211
Democratic Party, 12, 84, 118, 184, 205–9, 213–14, 221–22; liberal wing, 38, 41, 44. See also party leadership
Democratic Policy and Steering Committee, 10
Democratic Study Group, 214
Desert Shield, Desert Storm, 126
discretionary spending, 58, 87, 125, 140, 149, 150, 164, 166
divided government. 17, 40, 137, 158, 190, 200; and congressional budgeting, 214–20; and future deficits, 222;

consequences, 18–20, 214–20
Dodd, Lawrence C., 10
Dole, Robert, 68, 69, 84, 87, 117, 122, 141, 145, 147, 161, 166
Domenici, Pete, 57, 61, 84, 91, 115, 159, 171, 182, 186, 188
Dove, Robert, 187, 189
Drug Enforcement Administration (DEA), 166
Dukakis, Michael, 112
dynamic scoring, 192

Earned Income Tax Credit (EITC), 140, 145, 147
Economic Development Corporation, 118
economic growth in 1990s, 163
Economic Recovery Tax Act of 1981 (ERTA), 67–69; revenue loss from, 71
education, 166
Edwards, George C. III, 18
Eisenhower, Dwight D., 48
elections: of 1978, 55; of 1980, 55; of 1982, 73, 79; of 1984, 82, 83–84; of 1986, 104, 208; of 1988, 112–13; of 1992, 138, 154, 205; of 1994, 158, 205; of 1996, 162, 178; of 2000, 181–82; of 2002, 191; of 2004, 221
Employment Act (1946), 26
empowerment zones, 145
energy taxes, 140, 143, 146, 149, 155
entitlements, 6, 20, 58, 85, 87, 125
Environmental Protection Agency (EPA), 166
Erikson, Robert S., 13
estate taxes, 184, 190
executive orders on deficit reduction, 154
extraordinary resolution of budget disputes, 9, 20, 106, 109, 113, 132–33, 217–19. See also ad hoc budget negotiations

Federal Bureau of Investigation (FBI), 166

Federal Communications Commission
  (FCC), 150
Fenno, Richard, 5, 27
filibuster, 2, 11, 20, 108, 142, 143, 199,
  202, 205
fiscal policy, 7, 38, 43, 88. *See also*
  inflation; unemployment
fiscal year moved, 33
Foley, Thomas, 91, 92, 113, 115, 122,
  123, 155
food stamps, 62, 66, 167
Ford, Gerald, 37, 44, 49, 53
"four bill" system, 81
Frenzel, Bill, 115
Frist, Bill, 191, 196

General Accounting Office (GAO), 90,
  92, 98, 99, 101, 103
Gephardt, Richard, 50, 51, 89, 91, 92,
  113, 122, 123, 155, 173, 196
Gephardt rule, 50–52, 196
Giamo, Robert, 41, 43
Gingrich, Newt, 123, 132, 158, 159,
  161, 179, 182
Gorbachev, Mikhail, 91
Gore, Al, 145, 148, 200
government shutdowns, 215–17
Gramm, Phil, 57, 62, 65, 66, 86, 88,
  90, 102, 104, 145, 152
Gramm-Latta I, 60, 63, 75
Gramm-Latta II, 64, 65–67
Gramm-Rudman-Hollings, 3, 51,
  82–104, 111, 117, 126, 129, 151,
  159, 178, 204 , 207, 219; exempted
  programs, 97–98; key opposition
  issues, 88–89; original deficit targets,
  93; revised timetable, 94; vote to
  adopt, 92–93
Gramm-Rudman-Hollings II, 104–6
Grassley, Charles, 186, 189, 197
Gray, William, 84
Green, Joyce Hens, 114
Greenspan, Alan, 74, 141, 147
Greenspan Commission (1981–83),
  114–15, 133, 218

Greider, William, 70
gridlock, 2, 7, 18
Guinier, Lani, 146

Hahm, Sung Deuk, 72
Hance, Kent, 67
Hastert, Dennis, 182, 191, 196, 211
Hollings, Fritz, 86, 90, 102
Holt, Marjorie, 42
Holtz-Eakin, Douglas, 193
homeland security, 191
Hope scholarships, 164
Horton, Willie, 112
House Appropriations Committee, 25,
  26, 27; subcommittee chairs, 28, 30
House Budget Committee, 10, 38,
  61–62, 81, 194; committee ideologi-
  cal makeup, 39, 191
House Democratic Caucus, 30
House Ethics Committee, 211
House Government Operations
  Committee, 102
House Rules Committee, 33, 63; rule
  for 1981 reconciliation bill, 65–66
House Ways and Means Committee, 9,
  11, 25, 26, 31, 50, 65, 68, 116, 128,
  173, 185, 197

Iacocca, Lee, 114
*Immigration and Naturalization Service
  v. Chadha* (1983), 101
impeachment, 179–80
income taxes, 193. *See* tax cuts; tax
  increases
incrementalism, 205
inflation, 7, 38, 43, 70
International Monetary Fund (IMF),
  135
Iran-Contra scandal, 104

Jeffords, James, 186, 188, 190
Jenkins, Ed, 116
Johnson, Lyndon B., 29, 31, 49; tax sur-
  charge proposal (1967), 31
Johnson, Tim, 169

Joint Study Committee on Budget
  Control, 32, 33
Jones, James, 57, 62, 63

Kamlet, Mark S., 72
Kasich, John, 159
Kelly, Sean, 18
Kemp, Jack, 56
Kennedy, John F., 47, 49
Kennedy, Ted, 87
Kerrey, Bob, 145, 148
Kerry, John, 87, 204, 221
Kirkland, Lance, 114
Korean War, 48
Krehbiel, Keith, 16, 204–5
Kuwait, 121

Lammers, William, 70
Landrieu, Mary, 169
Latta, Delbert, 39, 62, 71
Leahy, Patrick, 80
Legislative Reorganization Act (1946),
  26
Legislative Reorganization Act (1970),
  10
Lewis, Drew, 114
line-item veto, 51, 170
"lockbox" legislation, 185, 192, 212
Lott, Trent, 170, 171, 173, 174, 182,
  186, 189, 210

macrobudgeting, 1, 5–7, 24, 37, 52, 77,
  178, 203, 209, 210; defined, 5; table
  comparing macrobudgeting and
  microbudgeting, 7
majoritarian institutions, 203
majority party leadership. See party
  leadership
Margolies-Mezvinsky, Marjorie, 148
"marriage penalty," 184, 187, 190, 193
Marshall, Thurgood, 102
Mathiason, David, 115
Mayhew, David, 12, 18
McCain, John, 190, 196, 210
McCubbins, Mathew D., 4, 11, 14, 204

Medicaid, 30, 62, 71, 97, 138, 150,
  164, 166, 168, 176
Medicare, 30, 71, 84, 98, 116, 118, 135,
  138, 145, 149, 150, 160, 163, 164,
  166, 168, 172, 176, 182, 195, 212
Medicare prescription drug benefit bill,
  211, 212, 213
Meese, Edwin, 57, 84
Metzenbaum, Howard, 145
Mfume, Kweisi, 146
Michel, Robert, 122, 132
microbudgeting, 5, 7, 77, 203, 209;
  defined, 5
Miller, George, 103
Miller, James III, 90, 93
Miller, Zell, 186, 196, 199
Mills, Wilbur, 9
Mitchell, George, 113, 115, 117, 122,
  144, 153
Mondale, Walter, 80, 82, 83
Morgan, Mark A., 25
Moynihan, Daniel Patrick, 74, 92, 118,
  140
Mowery, David C., 72
Muskie, Edmund, 39, 43, 208

National Economic Commission (NEC),
  114–15, 133, 218
National Taxpayers Union, 168
"new institutionalism," 4
Nicaraguan Contras, 107
Nichols, Don, 191, 193
Nixon, Richard, 1, 5, 17, 29, 32, 35,
  44, 48, 49, 127, 135
"no new taxes" pledge, 111, 114, 117,
  121
North American Free Trade Agreement
  (NAFTA), 156
Nussel, Jim, 182, 185

Obey, David, 81
Office of Management and Budget
  (OMB), 25, 33, 58, 63, 87, 90, 96,
  97, 98, 101, 103, 105, 118, 120,
  129, 168, 194

omnibus appropriations, 6, 71, 80, 81, 107, 203; and divided government, 216–17

Omnibus Budget Reconciliation Act of 1981 (OBRA-81), 62, 66–67

Omnibus Budget Reconciliation Act of 1987 (OBRA-87), 107

Omnibus Budget Reconciliation Act of 1990 (OBRA-90), 111–36, 138, 143, 178, 205, 212, 215

Omnibus Budget Reconciliation Act of 1993 (OBRA-93), 137–57, 178, 205, 206, 222

O'Neill, Paul, 183

O'Neill, Thomas P. "Tip," 41, 53, 57, 62, 64, 66, 74, 75, 76, 88, 218

Oppenheimer, Bruce I., 10

Organization of Petroleum Exporting Countries (OPEC), 38

Packwood, Robert, 90, 91

Panetta, Leon, 113, 115

parties; and budgeting, 204–4; responsible parties model, 11–12, 212–14

partisan realignment in South, 12

party leadership, 9, 76–77, 144, 151, 155–57, 158, 184, 202, 219–11

party polarization, 12–13, 76, 77, 19, 155, 158, 170, 179, 180, 212–14

party unity voting, 13, 38, 40, 52, 75–76, 108–9, 132–33, 142, 154–57, 175, 179, 186, 198–99, 206–9

path dependencies, 2

pay-as-you-go (PAYGO) rules, 8, 127–28, 133, 135, 136, 152, 178

Peake, Jeffrey, 18

Penner, Rudolf, 93

Penny, Timothy, 148

Pepper, Claude, 64, 74, 85

Perot, H. Ross, 139

"pivotal politics" theory, 16, 204–5

points of order, 202

Poole, Keith, 13

presidential power, 88, 90

Proposition 13 (1978), 42

public opinion; in 1981, 69; in 1984, 83; in 1985, 109; in 1995–96, 161; in 1997, 177; on balanced budget amendment, 178–69; on deficits, 213

Quayle, Dan, 81

Raines, Franklin, 173

Reagan economic and budget plan (1981), 3, 54–81; outline of plan, 58–59; televised appeals for, 59, 60, 69

Reagan, Ronald, 17, 44, 48, 49, 84, 90, 91, 92, 99, 100, 107, 109, 112, 123, 130, 137, 147, 156, 168, 198, 208, 212, 213, 215, 218, 220

"Reaganomics," 56

Regan, Donald, 56, 84

reconciliation, 2, 8, 34, 37, 78, 95, 183, 187, 201–2, 204; move to beginning of process, 44, 54, 58, 78; using for tax cuts, 187–88

reconciliation bills, 6, 107, 117, 142

Reischauer, Robert, 120

Reiselbach, Leroy, 9

Republican Party, 38, 42, 48, 51, 83, 120, 130, 173, 182, 205–9, 221

rescissions, 160

Rice index of cohesion, 207–8

Rodino, Peter, 90

Rohde, David, 4, 13, 204, 208

Roosevelt, Franklin D., 213

Rosenthal, Howard, 13

Rostenkowski, Dan, 57, 67, 68, 116

"rosy scenario" economic forecasts, 60, 94

Roth, William, 56

Rubin, Robert, 139, 169

Rudman, Warren, 86, 90, 102

Rules. See budget rules

Rules Committee (House), 10

Sabo, Martin Olav, 139

Sasser, James, 113, 115, 119, 152

Schick, Allen, 34

Schickler, Eric, 11
Schweiker, Richard, 64
Second Liberty Loan Act (1917), 46
Senate Appropriations Committee, 26,
    28
Senate Budget Committee, 10, 38, 61,
    99, 141, 187, 191, 194; bipartisan-
    ship 1975–80, 39
Senate Finance Committee, 25, 26, 68,
    128, 145, 186, 197
Senate Government Operations
    Committee, 34
Senate Majority Leader, 11. See also
    party leadership
Senate parliamentarian, 187
seniority system, 9
separation of powers, 99
September 11, 2001 attacks, 190, 201
sequester, 86, 92, 103, 127
Sinclair, Barbara, 8
Smith, Nick, 211
Snowe, Olympia, 196, 210
Social Security, 30, 58, 61, 66, 71, 82,
    84, 90, 118, 121, 128, 140, 147,
    149, 170, 183, 202, 212; move off
    budget, 96; private accounts, 221;
    Reagan 1981 proposal to cut, 64–65;
    1983 bailout, 74–75; 1985 COLA
    freeze, 85
Soviet invasion of Afghanistan, 44
spatial models of legislative process, 4,
    16, 204–5, 210
Specter, Arlen, 186, 188
statutory debt limit, 6, 23, 45–52, 87,
    91, 102, 104, 142–43, 192, 196,
    208; as must-pass legislation, 51–52;
    as vehicle for executive oversight,
    46–47; figures on voting patterns,
    49–50; eliminating House vote,
    50–51; partisanship over, 47–50
Stenholm, Charlie, 134, 185
Steuerle, C. Eugene, 71, 72
Stevens, John Paul 102
stock market crash (1987), 106, 113
Stockman, David, 56, 60, 62, 64, 65,

66, 68, 70, 84, 213; "Dunkirk"
    memo, 56
Strategic Petroleum Reserve, 62
Strauss, Robert, 114
student loans, 150
subcommittee bill of rights, 10
sunshine laws, 10, 30
sunset provisions, 187
Sununu, John, 113, 120, 122
supermajority institutions, 2, 4, 20
supplemental appropriations, 6, 134
supply-side economics, 42, 59, 79, 213
Synar, Mike, 93, 99

tax bills, 6
tax cuts, 54, 160, 163, 164, 172, 175,
    212, 219; Bush 2001 plan, 183–91;
    Bush 2003 plan, 191–99; Reagan
    plan, 59, 67–69
Tax Cut Reconciliation Act (2001), 190
Tax Equity and Fiscal Responsibility Act
    of 1982 (TEFRA), 72–74
tax increases, 120, 125, 140, 149, 164,
    222
tax indexing, 60, 68
Tax Reform Act (1986), 6, 100–101,
    108, 130
tax supermajority amendment, 170–71,
    219
theories of Congress, 4, 16, 204, 210
Thomas, Bill, 197
Torricelli, Robert, 169
Tower, John, 86
Treasury, Department of, 46–47, 84;
    actions to avoid default, 47, 104
"triangulation," 179
Truman, Harry S., 26
Tyson, Laura D'Andrea, 139

unemployment, 7, 38, 43, 70, 72
unified government, 137, 154–57
U.S. Supreme Court, 99, 100

veto, 2, 20, 162, 175, 182
veto bargaining, 2, 20, 70, 182, 200

Voinovich, George, 196
Volden, Craig, 77
voting patterns on major budget pack-
    ages; in 1970s, 40–42; in 1980–85,
    75–77; in 1990, 124; in 1993,
    147–48; in 1997, 175; in 2001,
    189–90; in 2003, 195, 197–98

waivers of budget act, 94, 202
War in Afghanistan, 181, 191, 201
War in Iraq, 181, 191, 195, 201
War in Vietnam, 29, 31
war on terrorism, 191

War Powers Act, 51
Weidenbaum, Murray, 57, 60
Weinberger, Casper, 56, 59, 90
welfare, 66, 164, 166
Wellstone, Paul, 145, 190
White, Joseph, 66, 214
Wildavsky, Aaron, 27, 66, 214
Wilson, Pete, 85
Wilson, Woodrow, 11
White, Justice, 102
Whitten, Jamie, 34
Wright, Gerald C., 13
Wright, Him, 113

PARLIAMENTS AND LEGISLATURES
Janet M. Box-Steffensmeier and David T. Canon, Series Editors

The Power of the People: Congressional Competition, Public Attention, and Voter Retribution
Sean M. Theriault

Doing the Right Thing: Collective Action and Procedural Choice in the New Legislative Process
Lawrence Becker

101 Chambers: Congress, State Legislatures, and the Future of Legislative Studies
Peverill Squire and Keith E. Hamm

Authorizing Policy
Thad Hall

Congress Responds to the Twentieth Century
Edited by Sunil Ahuja and Robert E. Dewhirst

Committees in Post-Communist Democratic Parliaments: Comparative Institutionalization
Edited by David M. Olson and William E. Crowther

U.S. Senate Exceptionalism
Edited by Bruce I. Oppenheimer

Political Consultants in U.S. Congressional Elections
Stephen K. Medvic

Hitching a Ride: Omnibus Legislating in the U.S. Congress
Glen S. Krutz

Reforming Parliamentary Committees: Israel in Comparative Perspective
Reuven Y. Hazan

Comparing Post-Soviet Legislatures: A Theory of Institutional Design and Political Conflict
Joel M. Ostrow

Beyond Westminster and Congress: The Nordic Experience
Edited by Peter Esaiasson and Knut Heidar

Parliamentary Representation: The Case of the Norwegian Storting
Donald R. Matthews and Henry Valen

Party Discipline and Parliamentary Government
Edited by Shaun Bowler, David M. Farrell, and Richard S. Katz

Senates: Bicameralism in the Contemporary World
Edited by Samuel C. Patterson and Anthony Mughan

Citizens as Legislators: Direct Democracy in the United States
Edited by Shaun Bowler, Todd Donovan, and Caroline J. Tolbert

Coalition Government, Subnational Style: Multiparty Politics in Europe's Regional Parliaments
William M. Downs

Creating Parliamentary Government: The Transition to Democracy in Bulgaria
Albert P. Melone

Politics, Parties, and Parliaments: Political Change in Norway
William R. Shaffer

Cheap Seats: The Democratic Party's Advantage in U.S. House Elections
James E. Campbell